GREEK
for
PREACHERS

DATE DUE

Chalice Press books by Robert Kysar:
Stumbling in the Light: New Testament Images for a Changing Church

Chalice Press books by Joseph M. Webb:
Comedy and Preaching
Old Texts, New Sermons: The Quiet Revolution in Biblical Preaching
Preaching and the Challenge of Pluralism

GREEK
for
PREACHERS

Joseph M. Webb
Robert Kysar

CHALICE
PRESS

ST. LOUIS, MISSOURI

© 2002 Joseph M. Webb and Robert Kysar

All Bible quotations, unless otherwise marked, are the author's translation.

All quotations marked NRSV are from the *New Revised Standard Version Bible,* copyright 1989, Division of Christian Education of the National Council of the Churches of Christ in the United States of America. Used by permission. All rights reserved.

Those quotations marked RSV are from the *Revised Standard Version of the Bible,* copyright 1952 [2nd edition, 1971] by the Division of Christian Education of the National Council of the Churches of Christ in the United States of America. Used by permission. All rights reserved.

Cover design: Lynne Condellone
Interior design: Hui-chu Wang
Art direction: Michael Domínguez

This book is printed on acid-free, recycled paper.

Visit Chalice Press on the World Wide Web at
www.chalicepress.com

10 9 8 7 6 5 4 3 2 1   02 03 04 05 06 07

Library of Congress Cataloging–in–Publication Data

Webb, Joseph M., 1942–
    Greek for preachers / Joseph M. Webb, Robert Kysar.
        p.   cm.
    ISBN 0-8272-1244-5 (alk. paper)
    1. Greek language, Biblical—Grammar.   2. Bible. N.T.—Language, style.
I. Kysar, Robert.   II. Title.
    PA817 .W34   2002
    487'.4—dc21

                              2001007433

To Andrea Worley and Linda Northrup,
with whom the project began.

Contents

Preface

One of the most significant developments in preaching as we enter a new century is the revival of concern about the Bible's role in the sermon. This is true across the spectrum of theological traditions, both Protestant and Catholic. It is true particularly in the so-called mainline traditions, where the relationship between the Bible and the sermon has become problematic over the past few decades. Even though the effort to "rediscover" the Bible takes many forms these days, its urgency in both pulpit and pew is growing, as most preachers can readily tell. In short, if preaching is to become a viable, even influential, force within Christianity again, it must somehow become more biblical. That is the conviction of the authors of this book and the primary motivation behind this work.

This book has been several years in the making. As both preachers and teachers, we have both been lifelong students of the Greek language. Both of us have been concerned in different ways about the problem of making the Bible—and the New Testament in particular—more accessible both to preachers and to thoughtful lay Christians. Our paths converged over these matters during a series of conversations that Joseph Webb initiated at the annual meeting of the Academy of Homiletics in 1997.

It should be said at the outset that though we are both committed students of the New Testament, we are not literalists with regard to its texts in Greek or in English. We do not believe there is anything intrinsically magic or even necessarily sacred about the original language of the New Testament, even though we both assert the importance of biblical language for the Christian tradition. We are also convinced that the New Testament stands at the heart of our Christian faith; in other books and publications we have both explored in some detail what we believe its role is and should be in both church and pulpit. Our sincere hope is that however we interpret or theologize its content, we treat the New Testament's language with scrupulous care and honest study so that what we say it says comes reasonably close to what it does, in fact, seem to say. And as preachers we can only move toward that high, if admittedly impossible, ideal by turning to the language in which the New Testament was written.

Over the years, textbooks on Greek for New Testament scholarship have appeared often; new ones are still being published. However, books on the Greek text of the New Testament designed specifically for preachers and preaching have been much rarer. The book that is the "immediate" predecessor to this one—the book, in a sense, that inspired this one—was written by the Greek scholar Kenneth S. Wuest and published by Moody Press in 1946. Titled *The Practical Use of the Greek New Testament,* it was revised in 1982 by Donald L. Wise. But it has long since been out of print. This book sets out to do what that one did: to bring the Greek text of the New Testament within reach of anyone who wishes to explore its riches.

We wish to acknowledge with deepest gratitude our friend and editor at Chalice Press, Dr. Jon L. Berquist. A meticulous scholar in his own right, he prods and cajoles until everything in a complex project of this nature is done correctly. He sets high standards and expects them to be met. This book would never have become a reality without his patience and unending encouragement. The book benefited greatly from the painstaking work of the Chalice Press staff and also the close attention to detail of Marianne Blickenstaff of Vanderbilt University.

Finally, when Webb originated this project almost twenty years ago, it was because of insistent prompting from a few laity concerned about a number of troubling matters of church polity and practice. They insisted on being taught, as they put it, the Bible and not just what the preacher thought about the Bible. They wanted to know for themselves what the Greek said. That led to a long series of small group Sunday afternoon meetings around the kitchen table with interlinear New Testaments and lexicons. From that came Webb's devotion to a project of teaching Greek to both lay and clergy who had never studied Greek. It culminated years later in courses in "Greek for Preachers" at the Claremont School of Theology. Shortly after that, Kysar, the Bandy Professor of Preaching and New Testament at Candler School of Theology, joined Webb in bringing the complex task to fruition in this book.

Even though the project proceeded quietly over the years, special thanks go to Jerry and Lela Adams, two of those around that first kitchen table. They provided significant financial assistance so that time and energy, at several points, could be devoted to the work. Gratitude is also extended to several preaching scholars who read the manuscript at various stages of its development, Rev. Richard Eslinger and Prof. Greg Heille, O.P., in particular.

Joseph M. Webb
Robert Kysar

Introduction

You have been assigned, let us say, to preach a sermon on John 21:15–17, the post-resurrection encounter between Jesus and Peter. It is not a welcome assignment. The text is familiar—all too familiar—but it is one that you have avoided for years. Jesus asks Peter three times if he loves him, and three times Peter says that he does. Still, the story has a bad feel to it, an unhappy ending, and you are not sure why. Something seems to be missing. You have consulted commentaries, some of which suggest a problem with the word "love" in the text, but overall it is still not clear. Now a sermon has to be preached on the text. So you read it again from the *New Revised Standard Version* (NRSV):

> When they had finished breakfast, Jesus said to Simon Peter, "Simon son of John, do you love me more than these?" He said to him, "Yes, Lord; you know that I love you." Jesus said to him, "Feed my lambs." A second time he said to him, "Simon son of John, do you love me?" He said to him, "Yes, Lord; you know that I love you." Jesus said to him, "Tend my sheep." He said to him the third time, "Simon son of John, do you love me?" Peter felt hurt because he said to him the third time, "Do you love me?" And he said to him, "Lord, you know everything; you know that I love you." Jesus said to him, "Feed my sheep."

The puzzle remains. What sense is one to make of the text, a text that has produced thousands of sermons over the years, along with countless theories about its significance? Ironically, the actual meaning of the text is startlingly simple and straightforward. But not in most English translations. Only in the Greek text of the New Testament, the language in which these documents were originally written, do we find some meaning to the passage. To see this, we will look at the same three verses by using what is called a Greek-English interlinear New Testament, which is a kind of running translation of the Greek text into English. We shall, however, only be *looking* at Greek words. In the text that follows, an English translation appears *under* the Greek words. Find the times where the English word "love" appears and note carefully the Greek word that appears over it:

Ὅτε οὖν ἠρίστησαν   λέγει τῷ Σίμωνι
Then, when they ate (breakfast) says   to Simon

Πέτρῳ ὁ Ἰησοῦς· Σίμων Ἰωάννου,   ἀγαπᾷς   με
Peter   - Jesus, Simon, son of John, do you love me

πλέον   τούτων; λέγει αὐτῷ, ναὶ κύριε, σὺ
more than these ones? He says to him, "Yes, Lord, you

οἶδας ὅτι φιλῶ σε. λέγει   αὐτῷ, βόσκε τὰ ἀρνία
know that I love you." He says to him, "Feed the sheep

μου. λέγει αὐτῷ πάλιν δεύτερον·   Σίμων
of me." He says to him again a second time, "Simon

Ἰωάννου, ἀγαπᾷς   μὲ; λέγει αὐτῷ· ναὶ
son of John, do you love me?" He says to him, "Yes,

κύριε, σὺ οἶδας ὅτι φιλῶ σε. λέγει αὐτῷ·
Lord, you know that I love you." He says to him,

ποίμαινε τὰ πρόβατά   μου. λέγιε αὐτῷ
"Shepherd the little sheep of me." He says to him

τὸ τρίτον·   Σίμων Ἰωάννου,   φιλεῖς μὲ;
the third time, "Simon, son of John, do you love me?"

ἐλυπήθη   ὁ Πέτρος ὅτι εἶπεν αὐτῷ τὸ τρίτον·
Was grieved - Peter   that he said to him the third time,

φιλεῖς   με; καὶ λέγει αὐτῷ· κύριε, πάντα
"Do you love me," and he says to him, "Lord,   all things

σὺ οἶδας, σὺ γινώσκεις ὅτι φιλῶ σε. λέγει
you know, you know   that I love you." Says

αὐτῷ (ὁ Ἰησοῦς)· βόσκε τὰ πρόβατά   μου.
to him (- Jesus), "Feed the little sheep of me."

What did you see? If you looked for the English word "love," you discovered, even visually, that the first time Jesus asks Peter his question ("Do you love me?"), he uses the Greek word ἀγαπάω (the verb form of ἀγάπη, pronounced *agape*) with the ending grammatically altered to fit the sentence. When Peter answers, though, "Yes, Lord, you know that I love you," he uses a *different* word—φιλέω, with a slightly altered ending to fit the sentence. Then, a second time Jesus asks him: "Do you love me?"

and uses the same word, ἀγαπάω. Peter answers the second time, "Yes, Lord, you know that I love you," but again with φιλέω. Finally, we are told that Jesus presses Peter a third time, except that this time when Jesus asks Peter the question, Jesus drops the word ἀγαπάω and himself uses the word φιλέω. This time, the text says, Peter was grieved, or hurt, but he replied, "Lord, you know all things; you know that I love you," again the word φιλέω, which is the one Jesus has just used.

What is the significance of all this? It is very straightforward, but much more powerful than an English translation is able to render it. The Greek language has multiple, very different words for love, while in English we have only one. If you look up the nouns ἀγάπη and φιλία (from which the two key words of the John text, ἀγαπάω and φιλέω, are constructed) you will see that ἀγάπη is the word for divine love, for the love that is "of God" or "from God." On the other hand, φιλία is the word for friendship, good friends. It is the source from which the English word *philadelphia,* "brotherly love," is derived. So in the text, Jesus asks Peter if he has that divine love for him, but Peter avoids the question and answers, in effect, "Yes, Lord, you and I are very good friends." But that is not the question Jesus asked! He wants to know if their relationship goes beyond friendship to what might be called a divine level. Peter avoids the question the second time and repeats that he and Jesus are "good friends." Then Jesus turns the table, and the third time asks Peter if they really are "good friends." No wonder Peter is grieved—it is not just because Jesus has asked a "third time"; it is because this time Jesus has questioned their friendship. And all Peter can do that third time is reassert that they are "good friends." Peter never answers, in this text, Jesus' question about ἀγάπη.

Now we see the significance of the text, as profound and moving an encounter as one can possibly imagine. You can only see it, however, by seeing the Greek text itself—and then having some idea of what to look for in the text. Recently one of us was teaching an adult class on the gospel of John and pointed out the difference between these two words, both translated "love." A laywoman was indignant that she had no way of knowing this from the English translation. She felt betrayed by her English Bible. The value of knowing the Greek text was obvious, and for the preacher armed with some Greek, the difference becomes the basis for a sermon on this text.

Look at another important text, this time from an epistle, from 1 Timothy 2:11–12. In the NRSV, it reads like this: "Let a woman learn in silence with full submission. I permit no woman to teach or to have authority over a man; she is to keep silent." Here is how one finds these two verses in a Greek–English interlinear:

Γυνὴ   ἐν ἡσυχίᾳ μανθανέτω ἐν πάσῃ ὑποταγῇ·
(A) woman in silence   let learn   in all   subjection;

διδάσκειν δὲ   γυναικὶ   οὐκ ἐπιτρέπω οὐδὲ
to teach   but (a) woman   I do not allow nor

αὐθεντεῖν   ἀνδρός, ἀλλ᾽ εἶναι
to exercise authority (over a) man,   but to be

ἐν ἡσυχίᾳ.
in silence.

This is a text to which we shall return at several points in this book, so we will focus on only one element of it here. Look for the word ἡσυχία, which appears twice in the space of these two short verses. Each time, it is translated *silence,* both in the NRSV and in the interlinear. But there is a very serious problem. If you look ἡσυχία up in a lexicon, you will find that its primary meaning is not "silence" at all. In fact, if you look up the four other New Testament texts in which ἡσυχία or a variant of it appears, you find that the word only sometimes means "silent" or "silence." Often its sense is "at peace" or "peaceable" or "to be left in peace" or "quiet" (meaning at peace). For instance, in Hellenistic Greek outside the New Testament, writers used it to describe "peace and harmony" among citizens of a city. Ironically, the same Greek word, ἡσυχία, appears only a few verses earlier in 1 Timothy 2:2. Even without knowing Greek, you can see the word in an interlinear text, though its ending is slightly different. In verse 2, the writer urges that prayers and supplications be made for kings and all those in positions of esteem, in order that readers may live "peaceful and quiet" lives. In this verse, the word translated "peaceful" is ἡσύχιον which is the equivalent of ἡσυχία.

The same two words also appear in Acts 22:2, 2 Thessalonians 3:12, and 1 Peter 3:4, and in each case mean "quiet" in the sense of "peace" or "peacefulness." For instance, 1 Peter 3:4 describes the inner spirit as "gentle and quiet." First Timothy 2:11–12 should be read to mean that women are encouraged to learn and to do so "in peace," or to be "left in peace" in order to learn. The word σιγή, means more strictly "silence," and the writer could have used it in 1 Timothy 2 if that was the intended meaning. The "traditional" meaning of the passage, however, has been provided by the translators and not by the writer; and the only way one discovers that is by looking up the words that appear in the text.

The point is that 1 Timothy 2:11–12 *does not* in any way direct women to be silent. They are to be "learners," "disciples," and the implication of the statement is that the women are being harassed while they are trying to learn. So the instruction is striking:"Let a woman learn in peace"—with the "subjection" being that of the good student to one's teacher. There are, to be sure, other elements in this verse that go on from this statement, and we shall come to some of those at various points later in this book. Notice that understanding the use of a word in one passage may entail looking for how it is used elsewhere. However, we should never assume that a word is used in the exact same way in different passages. The context in which a word is used is more important than how another writer in a different document might use the same word (as we will see more clearly later).

Of course, not all of the texts of the New Testament are as dramatically in need of examination as the two examples we have used. But you will be surprised at how many of the so-called "problem texts" become clarified when you look at them in a Greek interlinear Testament. What is most important, however, is that virtually every text in the New Testament holds ideas and secrets, nuances and turns of meaning, that can only be seen and appreciated in the Greek text. These are things that do not necessarily call for entirely new translations, but that add insight and precision that are highly valuable for preaching and teaching.

We have a growing number of English-language New Testaments, but there is still no substitute for the biblical documents in their original language. Meaning, we know, is never easily or neatly transferred from one language to another, no matter how good the translation or the translator. This is true with our English-language New Testaments, yet use them we must, trusting that we are doing "the best we can."

But it has not always been this way. The time was, and not very long ago, when anyone who prepared for a life of preaching and ordained ministry was expected, often even required, to learn the original languages, Greek for the New Testament and Hebrew for the Old. Given the importance of the Bible, there was no way to be a pastor without knowledge of the original biblical languages. In a few places, and in a few Christian traditions, that is still the case, but, remarkably, in *very few* places. In most major seminaries, where the next generation of preachers is being taught, neither Hebrew nor Greek is required. They are options in the curriculum, but in our experience of seminary education, they are not options that are pressed in any significant way on students—especially not on students who are preparing for a preaching ministry. Only those who wish to be "scholars" are required to study the biblical languages. For the rest of us clergy, our English translations are what we work with in our classrooms, in our studies, and, yes, in our pulpits.

However, some who have been in the ordained ministry for a few years or more recognize the problem in a different way. Even when students have studied Greek in their theological preparation, whether by requirement or option, the language is sometimes learned in relative isolation from anything one might actually *do* with the language. This does not mean the student only conjugates, parses, and learns some vocabulary in Greek classes. Learning Greek always entails *reading* from the Greek New Testament as part and parcel of that instruction. One reads the text as a measure of how well one has learned the language. The dilemma is that this, of itself, does not prepare us for working week in and week out with the Greek text in preparation for preaching. As a result, in many cases the preacher who "took Greek" in seminary quickly loses it or puts it away after a number of years in the ordained ministry. The usefulness of Greek as a continuous aspect of a pastor's study and sermon preparation is precisely what is not often taught. So even Greek-taught pastors tend to revert to English translations alone for sermon study and preparation. Sometimes this is because of the pressures of ordained ministry, but other times because of the fact that they were not taught how to put Greek to good use in sermon preparation and teaching.

This book, though, is not a lament over what should be or what might have been in today's theological education. Nor is it one more introductory Greek grammar text (of which there are already a good number) designed to cajole the busy pastor into finally learning, or returning to, the Greek that was available in seminary. Most certainly, what we offer in this book is not designed as an easy way to master Greek. We do not pretend to offer readers the equivalent of a Greek course nor to offer shortcuts to acquire skills that you might gain in an academic study of the language.

This is not, in short, a Greek textbook written by Greek scholars for those who are or would be biblical scholars. It is a book written by teachers of Christian preaching for preachers and those who would be preachers of the biblical gospel. It is written by teachers who believe that Christian preachers can and should be capable handlers of the Greek New Testament—not as scholars, *but as preachers*. It is written in the belief that whether readers have ever studied Greek or not, they can master basic tools and understandings for "rightly handling the words" of the Greek text. This is done primarily by learning to work with an interlinear Greek-English New Testament and a good analytical Greek lexicon. The method we propose and will describe is for the sheer purpose of preparing sermons that grow from, and interact with, the dynamic meanings of the Greek text about which one preaches.

Our purposes, though, are more specific than that. They arise from two issues related to the loss of the Greek text in the pulpit. The first is that English translations of the Greek New Testament invariably contain problems of interpretation and communication, often problems of considerable consequence. These range from translating difficult words in one language into similar words in another language, to problems of syntax that, when not clarified, fuel ambiguity and controversy, to various degrees of bias within translators, leading them to see the language being translated through the filter of their own perspectives. There is no easy cure for these problems. We always tend to translate the original language out of our own theological perspective. However, when we ourselves can work directly with the Greek, we are more likely to move toward some solutions to these textual matters. With only a basic knowledge of the Greek, we can foster better understanding of the text for ourselves and for those to whom we preach.

The second issue raised by the loss of Greek study in seminary is that it removes from both preaching and teaching a level of originality, creativity, and intelligence that today's struggling pulpit seems badly to need. There is joy to be had in the Greek language, often fun that can brighten up a sermon. Taking account of it at appropriate moments in preaching not only adds insight, past and present, but also gives the Bible a new sense of exuberance and freshness. Of course, we must be cautious not to get carried away with our Greek "learning." One may be tempted to "show off" in the pulpit by claiming to "know Greek." It is highly repulsive when someone does that to excess in public, and especially repulsive when one does it to excess *in the pulpit*. But, judiciously and frugally handled, the joys of the Greek language of our New Testament are as bright as newly cut diamonds sitting in a store window waiting for someone to pick them up and share them with others.

In short, this book represents an effort to make the Greek text of the New Testament both *usable* and *exciting* to preachers who have never studied Greek, to those who studied it at some point in the past but who were never pressed (or taught) to connect its use directly to preaching, and also to those who are now studying Greek and who would like to make it an active part of their future preaching ministries. The tools for such work do exist and have for some time. With minimal expenditure of time and energy, they can be adapted and used as part of one's regular pulpit preparation. Literally anyone, including lay leaders and church school teachers, can learn to work with the Greek text in a credible and highly original way. The goal of this book is to demonstrate and illustrate how this can be done, not based on "shortcuts" to learning Greek, but based, instead, on one's mastery of the dynamics of the Greek-English interlinear New Testament and the various tools and understandings that support it.

This book is in three parts. The first part is about those various "tools," beginning with the basic reference books one needs. The discussion then moves to the Greek alphabet, which any student must learn. From there we turn to the basic "reading" of the Greek text, by which we mean a reading not yet for meaning, but for sound and pronunciation. These are foundational elements, but they can be done in the course of a few days.

Part 2 is the heart of the book. It contains ten chapters, which present the ten "rules" or "principles" for working with an interlinear Greek-English text. While these are, in a sense, technical matters related to the Greek language, to grammar, and to syntax, they are presented as working *directives* to be used with every text that you might study as a basis for a sermon or lesson. The emphasis is not on learning particular parts of speech or grammatical configurations; it is on becoming familiar with specific aspects of grammar as a way of opening up a text for clarification and enrichment. Each chapter here is amply illustrated with New Testament texts, including sermonic suggestions and observations interspersed with the grammatical explanations.

Part 3 carries the discussion of these grammatical materials toward the pulpit. One section proposes a process by which a preacher might proceed to read, translate and isolate a meaning for a passage, and then continue with devising a sermon theme or focus. There are ways to use the Greek text in preaching and ways not to use it; here, in the third part of the book, are some cautions that are essential in order that the Greek text may enhance preaching without falling into the various pitfalls of scholasticism or egocentricity. Finally, we each offer a sermon to show how an understanding of Greek might lead to preaching. We try to show how certain principles explained in Part 2 contributed to the preparation of our respective sermons.

These three sections of the book lend themselves to different uses, depending on your past experience with Greek and the Greek New Testament. For example, if you have never studied Greek, you will need to start at the beginning, working through the tools and the principles carefully before you get to sermon preparation. However, if you took a course or courses in Greek at some point in the past, you will need only a cursory review of Part 1, if that much. We would suggest going through the alphabet quickly as a refresher, but then turning to the reading exercises at the end of Part 1. You may find yourself remembering some of your Greek knowledge without much effort.

Then read Part 2, the ten principles. Take some notes along the way, but you will undoubtedly find that much of what you learned in your earlier Greek study will come back to you. Treat Part 2 as a refresher course as well, but with some care. It may take you in some directions that you did not focus on during your study of Greek grammar. Then you will be ready to look closely at Part 3, the process of sermon preparation.

If you are currently studying Greek, you may treat this book as a supplementary textbook. It will not replace the work of your course—which will include not only grammatical detail but also vocabulary learning—but it will enable you to keep the needs of your pulpit work in mind as you go through the various elements of your beginning and advanced Greek courses. The correlations between the various principles and your professor's detailed instruction should not be too difficult to draw.

PART 1

THE PRELIMINARIES

CHAPTER 1

Tools for the Work

Using Greek in preaching and in the preparation for preaching requires that you learn to use two kinds of key books on a regular basis. One is called an interlinear New Testament; the other is an analytical Greek lexicon. Other books are very useful, and they will be explained briefly in this chapter, but they are, by and large, optional. An interlinear New Testament and analytical lexicon are not. This means, in short, that whatever New Testament you are accustomed to using in your sermon preparation will need to be replaced by an interlinear New Testament. But every interlinear New Testament carries on its pages a standard English translation, whether *King James, Revised Standard Version, New Revised Standard Version,* or the *New International Version;* so you can choose the interlinear that matches your English preference. But the interlinear text must become your constant working document.

The difference between the Greek New Testament itself and the interlinear Greek-English New Testament is at the heart of the matter. For those who have never studied Greek, the Greek New Testament means nothing. Even for those who have had a year or two of Greek in seminary, handling the Greek New Testament is a formidable undertaking, and many cannot do it. An interlinear Greek-English New Testament, however, is a different story. It is written with a line from the Greek New Testament and a suggested word-for-word English translation on the line directly under it, just as we saw in the interlinear texts of our Introduction.

The entire New Testament appears in this format. The Greek and English lines are interspersed, hence, the *interlinear* New Testament. This part of the text, in most versions, takes up the right two-thirds or so of the page. On the left one-third of the same page, matching the words of the interlinear, is one of the standard English translations to which we referred above. The point is that when you work with an interlinear New Testament, it is not necessary to have another New Testament nearby to supplement it.

The interlinear New Testament can best be thought of as a "working document." That is, it is not a translation itself, but a *guide* from which a thoughtful, even original translation can be made by anyone interested in learning to work with its raw materials. In a sense, the interlinear provides the basic and comprehensive "note-taking" from which a translation can be developed. The work of translation and the formation of meaning are not actually done by the interlinear, so that all the preacher has to do is to read from the interlinear text. When you read the English under the Greek in an interlinear, you will quickly see that the translation is very literal and clumsy. Beginning points, though, are provided, and once they are followed (in ways that will be discussed and illustrated in this book), even preachers who have never studied Greek can explore the meanings embedded in the Greek New Testament.

Calling the interlinear New Testament a "working document" means that it provides direction, help, backup, even a kind of safety net for your study of a text for use in a sermon. It does not, however, do the work of study for you. You, the preacher, still must do the careful, detailed examination of a text, taking your own notes and making your own judgments about a text's meaning, whether you are looking at individual words or word arrangements. In this book, we shall provide you with a set of tools with which you can undertake this textual work for sermon preparation on a weekly basis. In a real sense, with the materials here, you will be able to use the interlinear text to make original and defensible observations about a New Testament text—*observations that will provide new resources for your sermons.* What you will end up preaching is, in a sense, your *own* understanding of the Greek text, calling attention when useful (or even necessary) to features of the text that other translators have either played down, overlooked, or turned in a way that you may wish to "correct." This means that you will want to compare your own translation with the one that is read in the worship service.

One final point about the interlinear Testaments. You will find a variety of English translations in those that are available. But we suggest that you also look at the particular Greek text that is used in an interlinear. As you know, scholars are constantly revising and updating the Greek

Testament in the light of contemporary research. We suggest that the interlinear you use be based on one of the two most recent Greek texts: Eberhard Nestle, Erwin Nestle, and Kurt Aland, *Novum Testamentum Graece,* 27th ed. (Stuttgart: Deutsche Bibelstiftung, 1993), and the third corrected edition of the *Greek New Testament,* ed. Kurt Aland, Matthew Black, Carol M. Martini, Bruce M. Metzger, and Allen Wikgren (London: United Bible Societies). You will find recently published interlinears using one of these two texts, and you will then be sure that you are working with the best of contemporary textual criticism.

The second important book that must become your constant companion in this undertaking is the analytical Greek lexicon. A lexicon is a dictionary. Two kinds of lexicons are available to the preacher— standard and analytical. A *standard* lexicon is a normal Greek to English dictionary. Like any English dictionary, the standard Greek lexicon contains an untold number of Greek words. One hesitates to say that such a lexicon includes all the words found in the New Testament, since many lexicons clearly do not set out to be that comprehensive. In a lexicon, the Greek words are given their English meaning or meanings. In a complete lexicon these possible meanings are numerous, but pocket-sized Greek-English lexicons are more concise in their listings.

The problem with the standard lexicons, however, is that they assume a reader has a fairly comprehensive understanding of the Greek language. For instance, the words of the standard Greek-English Lexicon are listed by their "root words," as they are in standard English dictionaries. Consequently, readers must know the root word for a Greek term they may be looking up in the lexicon in order to find its meaning. However, the New Testament's Greek text very seldom uses the root word. The words are always syntactically arranged, which means they are always used in a way that changes either the word's *ending* or *beginning* (or both). Occasionally, the structure of the root itself is changed by its usage in a particular sentence. For one who has not studied Greek grammar in some detail and retained it, root words are difficult to decipher from their particular forms in the text. As a result, at least initially, the standard Greek-English lexicon is of little help.

For example, Romans 9:22 says that God ἤνεγκεν ἐν πολλῇ μακροθυμίᾳ, which an interlinear New Testament translates "endured with much longsuffering." But the word ἤνεγκεν is actually a form of the verb, φέρω (one meaning of which is "to endure")! Look at the difference between the two words. How would we ever know that the root word of ἤνεγκεν is φέρω? However, if we look up ἤνεγκεν in an analytical lexicon, we easily discover its root verb.

The analytical Greek lexicon has two features that make it extraordinarily useful for the preacher working with an interlinear New Testament. *First,* it contains *every word* of the Greek New Testament exactly as that word appears in the text. Moreover, an analytical lexicon is not arranged by root words, but alphabetically, by words as they are found in the New Testament text. So one may take any word from the Greek text and look it up in the analytical lexicon to find its root word. Of course, if you wish to do so, you can then look up that root word in the standard lexicon. However, that is not usually necessary, since the analytical lexicon in some cases also includes a brief summary of the meanings of the root words as well.

The *second* thing that an analytical lexicon provides is a concise, but indispensable parsing of every word in the Greek New Testament. To parse a word is to list the various forms it takes when it functions in a sentence. If one undertakes a thorough mastery of Greek, one memorizes how every verb is parsed; only in this way can one actually "read" and understand the Greek text without help. For our purposes, however, the parsing is given to us by our analytical lexicon. You are not only given the root of the word that you look up but also the full range of parsed information about the word. With this information, you may make any number of informed judgments about the word's appearance at its particular place in the text.

For example, if you look up the word βλέπουσι in an analytical lexicon, you see the line "3 pers. pl. present. ind. act." and are told that the root of the word is βλέπω, which means "to possess the faculty of sight," or " to see." Furthermore, from the lexicon's entries, you also know that βλέπουσι is third person plural (3 pers. pl.) and is a present indicative active (pre. ind. act.) form of the verb. If we know what third person plural, present indicative active means, we can go back to the text in which the word appears, analyze the word within the text, and even devise our own translation of the phrase in which the word appears. In the course of this book, we shall discuss in detail the meaning and preaching significance of most of the items of information that one is given in an analytical lexicon about a word like βλέπουσι.

The point is that with only an interlinear New Testament, an analytical Greek lexicon, and a basic working knowledge of Greek—such as this book provides—you can open up in a remarkably creative and insightful way the Greek text of the New Testament, as we shall demonstrate fully in the pages that follow. Other books, though, will prove helpful as one becomes adept at the processes that we shall explain. Despite our explanation of the importance of the analytical lexicon over the standard Greek-English lexicon, you may still want a good, well-rounded standard Greek-English lexicon. Several are available. The standard complete lexicon is William F. Arndt, Walter Bauer, F. Wilbur Gingrich, and Frederick W. Danker, *A Greek-English Lexicon of the New Testament and Other Early Christian Literature,* 3d ed. (Chicago: University of Chicago Press, 2000). The actual definitions and explanations of root words found in most analytical lexicons are limited, primarily because providing such definitions is not considered the primary task of the analytical lexicon. The emphasis there is on "analytical." After you have identified the root word with the help of an analytical lexicon, it often is useful to look the word up in a larger and more detailed standard lexicon. So you should have one handy.

Beyond that, three kinds of books will occasionally be of use in work with the Greek text. The first is a Greek New Testament concordance. Preachers know about concordances, but they are usually for English versions of the Bible. An English concordance contains lists—some fairly complete, others only partial—of words along with the specific biblical texts where those words appear. Not only is the book, chapter, and verse noted for each time the word appears, but usually the word appears in a three- or four-word phrase that lets readers know if they have the particular use for which they are looking. Such concordances are available for the Greek New Testament, some of which include every Greek word in the New Testament. They are set up and function exactly like the English concordances. But they are entirely in Greek without any English in sight. This is not a problem for one who develops the working knowledge of the Greek text that is proposed in this book. One learns to recognize and even become familiar with the meanings of many Greek words, enough so to make easy use of the Greek concordance. The standard and classic Greek concordance is *Concordance to the Greek Testament,* edited by W. F. Moulton, A. S. Geden, and H. K. Moulton, 5th ed. (Edinburgh: T & T Clark, 1978).

A good Greek concordance is important to one who works with the Greek text because there are usually a half dozen or more English words used in various contexts to translate the same Greek term. So we cannot rely on any given English translation to indicate what Greek word it is translating. Often, in fact, what one wants to know when dealing with one or more texts in preparation for preaching is how and why the same Greek word is translated so differently at different points in the text. The best resource we have for tracking down different texts with the same Greek word is the Greek concordance.

Finally, several other varied books are helps for working with the Greek text. Many of these may prove valuable as you move through the processes outlined here. We will mention only one example, though in a good religious bookstore you will find others. We often have occasion to turn to George R. Berry's *A Dictionary of New Testament Greek Synonyms* (Grand Rapids: Zondervan, 1979). It is very helpful, even though it is a small book and by no means exhaustive in the Greek words it contains. In a later section, we shall discuss the fact that in Greek, as in almost every language, there are no pure synonyms. Different words always mean different things, even if the meanings are only slightly different. It is often those slight differences, in fact, that can turn the mood or meaning of a text in one direction rather than in another. Yet many words are so close in meaning as to seem interchangeable when they are not. What Berry has done is take a group of Greek words that appear to be very close in meaning—so close, in fact, that they are often treated as synonyms when they are translated into English—and placed them together, briefly outlining their subtle differences.

Many of these resources that we have cited as books can also be acquired in digital form for use on a personal computer. The Greek New Testament with several English translations, an analytical text (showing the form of each word), concordances or search programs, and analytical as well as regular lexicons are all included in some programs for biblical study. You may want to see what's available (and what's available changes nearly every three months or so) and decide if you would prefer working with these resources on a computer.

What we urge in this book is that preachers, regardless of how long they have preached, become new, committed working students of the Greek New Testament. It is possible, we believe, even within the confines of one's pastoral duties, to work regularly and systematically with the Greek Testament and to bring the rich results of that study to the issues and practicalities of the pulpit. Our study of any text for preaching must always include good commentaries, books of biblical era backgrounds, and other resources necessary to do solid historical critical work. Nothing that we say in this book is meant to detract from those rich materials, and we will discuss them in more detail later.

However, a mistake preachers are often tempted to make is to rush to the commentaries or other helps before they themselves have worked directly with the text itself. That personal and immediate immersion in the text in search of its meaning for today is part of what is needed for a renewal of preaching. Behind what follows here is the idea that the pulpit of today desperately needs such a renewal. Not a renewal concocted out of the blue or out of the pop vagaries of our shallow culture, but one developed from original ideas that can still arise from creative, provocative study of the New Testament in the language in which it was written. It is, in every way, not only an exciting and a challenging task, but one that is well within the reach of every working pastor.

CHAPTER 2

Writing and Reading
the Greek Text

One begins by learning to read the Greek text—"read" in the sense of knowing the letters of the Greek alphabet and being able to structure those letters into spoken words. One learns to pronounce the words of the Greek text aloud. There is no substitute for this, and the operative word here is "aloud." Reading the text audibly is important, not only because the human mind registers material much better when it is spoken, but also because so many Greek words have counterparts in English— something that becomes readily obvious when the sounds of the words are actually heard.

The Alphabet

The Greek alphabet has twenty-four letters, compared with twenty-six in English. The first task is to learn the alphabet. Many letters are similar to those in the English alphabet; many are not, however, and some, in fact, are misleading for an English reader. So care must be taken to become familiar with the Greek alphabet. It is best that you learn to write each Greek letter at the same time that you learn its pronunciation. Learning the letters of the Greek alphabet in their proper order is just as important as it is in English, primarily because Greek lexicons (dictionaries) are arranged alphabetically by Greek letters, just as English dictionaries follow the English alphabet. We need not be concerned at this point with learning Greek capital letters, since they are so seldom used; so we will include only the lowercase letters for memorization.

Here is the Greek alphabet, with the name of each letter and a pronunciation guide:

α	alpha	a	as in father
β	beta	b	as in bath
γ	gamma	g	as in giggle
δ	delta	d	as in dental
ε	epsilon	e	as in enter
ζ	zeta	z	as in zipper
η	eta	a	as in date
θ	theta	th	as in thin
ι	iota	i	as in skip
κ	kappa	k	as in kitten
λ	lambda	l	as in lamp
μ	mu	m	as in make
ν	nu	n	as in none
ξ	xi	x	as in hex
ο	omicron	o	as in hot
π	pi	p	as in pipe
ρ	rho	r	as in road
σ, ς	sigma	s	as in stand

(The σ is used when the letter appears within a word, and ς when it appears as the last letter of a word.)

τ	tau	t	as in trout
υ	upsilon	u	as in upscale
φ	phi	ph	as in philosophy
χ	chi	ch	as in chronic
ψ	psi	ps	as in tipsy
ω	omega	o	as in only

The alphabet must be memorized, though it will not take very long to do it, since so many of the letters, with slight variation, are already familiar. Be aware of the four kinds of letters used in writing Greek: (1) those written between the lines, such as α and ε, (2) those that extend above the top line, such as δ and λ, (3) those that extend below the bottom line, such as γ and ρ, and (4) those that extend both above and below the lines, such as ζ and ξ.

Vowels and Diphthongs

After learning the Greek alphabet, both to say and to write each letter in order, it is important to learn the Greek vowels, since these will be important later when we work on the pronunciation of Greek words. There are seven vowels:

α   ε   η   ι   ο   υ   ω

Eight common diphthongs, or combinations of vowels, also must be learned, since each represents a unique form of pronunciation:

αι	pronounced	i	as in aisle
ει	pronounced	a	as in weight
οι	pronounced	oi	as in coil
υι	pronounced	we	as in queen
			(or sometimes wi as in quick)
αυ	pronounced	ow	as in owl
ευ	pronounced	short e	as in wet
ου	pronounced	ou	as in soup
ηυ	pronounced	ayw	as in wayward

Sometimes the Greek text has a vowel with a small mark beneath it, like this omega ῳ. This mark is called an iota subscript, since it is actually the letter ι, or iota, that appears under the vowel. This letter is sometimes referred to as an improper diphthong. The iota subscript is for the purpose of distinguishing different forms of the word in which it appears, forms that are already visible (most of the time) for one working with a Greek-English interlinear text. The iota subscript, however, does not affect the pronunciation of the word in which the vowel appears.

A few other pronunciation notes are important before we turn to work on specific texts for reading.

First, the consonant γ is always pronounced g as in gun and never g as in germ.

The consonant θ is always pronounced th as in thin, never th as in thine.

The consonant ξ is always pronounced x as in sex and never x as in exact.

The consonant σ or ς is always pronounced s as in success and never s as in rose.

One other set of rules is important in the pronunciation of consonants. Whenever the letter γ is followed by a second γ or by a κ, ζ, or χ, the second letter is preceded by an n sound. That is,

γγ is pronounced as ng as in finger,

γκ is pronounced as nk as in sinker,

γζ is pronounced as nx, as in jinx, and

γχ is pronounced as ng as in ring.

In addition, it should be noted that apart from these simple exceptions, whenever a consonant appears, it has its full pronunciation value. Greek has no silent consonants. Hence, in πν the π (or p) is always pronounced, unlike the English words derived from this Greek, such as pneumonia.

Pronouncing Words

We turn next to the pronunciation of words. Three things primarily affect how words are pronounced: first, the breaking down into syllables; second, the accenting of syllables; and third, what are called the breathing marks, or breath marks, on certain words.

Syllables

First, the number of syllables in any word is almost always determined by the presence of vowels in the word. There are exceptions to this, particularly when one encounters the diphthongs that we just discussed. Generally, though, it is safe to assume that each syllable in a word gets its own vowel (or each vowel represents its own syllable), and one can determine not only the number of syllables in a word but also how the syllables of a word break down for purposes of pronunciation. For example, from John 1 let us take the word ἐγένετο and try to determine the number of its syllables. The word contains four vowels, none of which is a diphthong: ε, ε, ε, ο. This means that even though the word is short, it has four syllables. The word will fall apart, as it were, around the vowels. It may be said as short e—ε, gen—γεν, short e—ε, and tah—το. There is the four syllable word: e-gen-e-tah. The key to the breakdown of syllables is in the number of vowels in the word.

The same is true of other words in the first chapter of John, one of the texts printed for reading at the end of this chapter. Find, for example, the word πρός. It can be sounded out letter by letter as one learns to pronounce it: π-p, ρ-r, o-o, ς-s, prahs. In the same text we find the word λόγος. It has one vowel—o—that occurs twice. That tells us that the word has two syllables, one syllable for each o. The word can easily be sounded out, since we now know the Greek alphabet. The word begins with λ-l, then, o, an omicron, pronounced ah, then gamma, γ-g, followed by another omicron, ah, and finally sigma in the form it takes at the end of a word, ς. The word breaks in the middle, as lo-gos or log-os.

The text of John 1 also contains another interesting word, ἀρχῇ (the root form of which is ἀρχή), sounded out for basic pronunciation as α-a, ρ-r, χ-ch, η -long a (ā). Hence, arch ā. The word has two syllables, since two vowels are present. It is pronounced as ar-chā, with each vowel representing a separate syllable. Saying this word aloud, one becomes aware that this is the word from which the English word "archaeology" is derived. If we look closely at the word "archaeology," we will see that the

Greek word archā is paired with the word we looked at a moment ago—logos. Ἀρχή generally means "beginning" or "beginning things," and λόγος means "word" or "words about." So the English term "archeology," in its most basic form, means "words about beginning things." As you begin to read the Greek New Testament in this most basic way, almost every line will reveal some surprising verbal connection like this between Greek and English words.

Accents

Multisyllable words, though, must have accents so that they can be accurately and easily pronounced. As one might expect, the rules governing accent are complex and far beyond the scope of this book. In reading the New Testament text, however, you will find three different kinds of accents, the acute (´), the grave (`), and the circumflex (ˆ). While we are not concerned about why one accent rather than another appears on a word (many books on grammar are available to answer that question), what you need to know is that most, though not all, words will have one of these accents, and some may have more than one. Most importantly, the presence of the accent, whatever kind it is, says which syllable in a word is to receive the verbal force; in other words, which syllable is to be accented. If more than one accent is present—as sometimes is the case—the acute accent (´) always takes priority.

So, in pronouncing words, one divides the word into its syllables and then observes the presence of the accent mark in saying the word, whether reading it in isolation or as part of a Greek text.

Breathing Marks

The third important element in pronouncing Greek words concerns what are called the breath, or the breathing, marks. These must not be confused with accents. The acute and the grave accents are straight marks, either to the right or to the left (´, `). The circumflex is a curve (ˆ). Breathing marks, on the other hand, are symbols that look like raised apostrophes, again either to the right or the left (' or '). These marks appear at three different places: over a vowel at the beginning of a word, over the second vowel of a diphthong, or, in the case of a uppercase vowel or diphthong, just before the letter (as with the alpha in Ἀρχή). The direction in which the apostrophe is turned (to the right or to the left) determines the nature of the breathing mark brought to the word. If the apostrophe is turned to the right ('), it is called a "smooth breathing" mark, or a "smooth breath" mark. Smooth breath marks make no change whatever in how a word is pronounced. It is as if they were not there. If the "apostrophe" is turned toward the left ('), however, it is called a "rough breathing" mark, or a "rough breath" mark. When this appears over (or just before) a vowel or diphthong at the beginning of a word, it has the effect of placing the letter h in front of the word in its pronunciation. Thus the common word, ὑπώ, with the rough breathing mark over the υ and the accent over the ω is pronounced hu-pō with the h sound appended to the front of the word and the accent on the second syllable. It is also not uncommon for both the accent and the breathing mark to fall over the same vowel, particularly with shorter words. One example would be ἵνα, hi-nah, in John 1:7.

Let us draw a few more words from John 1. Look again at the word ἀρχῆ, this time to see that the accent, a circumflex, is on the second syllable, meaning that one emphasizes the *end* of the word rather than its beginning. We also see a smooth breathing mark over the α, which does not change the pronunciation of the word. The mark is simply ignored. In that same phrase (ὁ λόγος), however, is the word (the article) ὁ ("the"). It is not accented. Its accent falls on the next word. But it does have a rough breathing mark over it. So in reading it, what would otherwise be an ah sound becomes a ha sound, with the h necessitated by the rough breath mark.

In verse 2 one finds the word οὗτος, with both the accent (a circumflex) and a rough breathing mark. Both are over the same letter υ, which is part of a combination of two vowels that produces a diphthong, ου. In pronunciation, the diphthong functions as one, not two, vowels, so the word has two syllables, since technically it has only two vowels. The letters ου make up the first syllable, and τος the second. The accent is on the first syllable, but the rough breathing mark means that when the first syllable is pronounced, it must be said with the letter h preceding the οὑ sound, as in who.

Putting It All Together

We may now work out the pronunciation of a longer word from these opening verses of John, a text that we will shortly read at greater length. In verse 6 is the word ἄνθρωπος, with both the accent and the breathing mark over the α. What kind of a breathing mark is it? Will it affect the pronunciation of the word? How many syllables does the word have? In other words, how many vowels are in it? There are three—do you find them? Now work out the sound of each letter, saying it as you go. As you do so, you should be able to tell how the three syllables fall apart among the consonants. The word is ἀν (an)-θρω (thrō—long) - πος (pos—short o). An-thrō-pos. Smooth breathing mark, accent on first syllable. As you say it, you will have no difficulty connecting it to the English word, anthropology. The word means "human" or "humankind."

In the next verse is the word μαρτυρίαν. There is no breath mark, since the word begins with a consonant and not a vowel. The accent is over the ι. First, determine how many syllables the word has by identifying the vowels. Then, sound the word out letter by letter. This will become second nature as you become thoroughly familiar with the letters. You will be able not only to know the syllable count of unfamiliar words quickly but also to tell how the word divides around its consonants. Here the word is μαρ (mar)-τυ (tu)-ρι (ri)-αν (an). Now you can say it as four syllables, with the accent on the third syllable. In saying this word, you may hear another English word, "martyr." The Greek word actually means witness, but the English noun, "martyr," came to mean more narrowly one who is put to death for his or her witness.

Punctuation

Before turning to our practice texts, we should briefly summarize the punctuation you will find in the Greek text of the New Testament. So far as we can discern, the earliest manuscripts contained no punctuation, at least as we know it. However, the scholars who have constructed the Greek text we use have added four basic punctuation marks. The comma (,) and the period (.) are both written on the line and are the same as the English comma and period. The dot written above the line (·) functions something like our semicolon and colon. The question mark (;) written on the line looks exactly like our semicolon.

Practice Texts

At this point, we are not interested in what words mean, let alone in trying to translate anything. We are only interested in learning letters, words and sounds, and connecting them with each other over the course of "reading" the text. We cannot proceed to even a rudimentary exploration of meaning until we spend time on the sounds of the language itself. What follows are four practice texts, with a pronunciation guide under the first two, but not under the second two. Master the reading of these four texts, and then turn in your own interlinear New Testament to continue the process.

First Text—John 1:1–8

(1) Ἐν ἀρχῇ ἦν ὁ λόγος, καὶ ὁ λόγος ἦν πρὸς
En ar-chē en ho logos ki ho logos en pros,

τὸν θεόν, καὶ θεός ἦν ὁ λόγος. (2) οὗτος ἦν ἐν
ton the-on ki the-os en ho logos. hou-tos en en

ἀρχῇ   πρὸς   τὸν   θεόν. (3) πάντα   δι᾽ αὐτοῦ
ar-chē pros ton the-on.   Pan-ta di au-tou

ἐγένετο,   καὶ χωρὶς αὐτοῦ ἐγένετο,   οὐδε ἓν.   ὃ
e-gen-e-to ki chō-ris au-tou e-gen-e-to, oude hen ho

γέγονεν (4) ἐν αὐτῷ ζωὴ ἦν, καὶ ἡ ζωὴ ἦν τὸ
geg-o-nen. Ev au-tō zō-ē ēn, ki hē zō-ē ēn to

φῶς τῶν ἀνθρώπων. (5) καὶ τὸ φῶς ἐν τῇ σκοτίᾳ
phōs tōn an-thrō-pon. Ki to phōs en tē sko-ti-a

φαίνει, καὶ ἡ   σκοτία αὐτὸ οὐ κατέλαβεν.
phi-ni, ki hē sko-ti-a au-toou ka-te-la-ben.

 (6) Ἐγένετο ἄνθρωπος, ἀπεσταλμένος   παρὰ
E-gen-e-to an-thrō-pos, a-pes-tal-me-nos pa-ra

θεοῦ, ὄνομα   αὐτῷ   Ἰωάννης. (7) οὗτος   ἦλθεν εἰς
the-ou, o-no-ma au-tō I-ō-an-nēs. Hou-tos ēl-then eis

μαρτυρίαν ἵνα   μαρτυρήσῃ περὶ τοῦ φωτός, ἵνα
mar-tu-ri-an hi-na mar-tu-rē-sē pe-ri tou phō-tos hina

πάντες πιστεύσωσιν δι᾽ αὐτοῦ. (8) οὐκ ἦν ἐκεῖνος
pan-tes pis-teu-sō-sin di au-tou   ouk ēn e-kei-nos

τὸ φῶς, ἀλλ᾽ ἵνα   μαρτυρήσῃ   περὶ τοῦ   φωτός
to phōs, all hina mar-tu-rē-sē pe-ri tou phō-tos.

Second Text—John 1:14-18

(14) Καὶ ὁ λόγος σὰρξ ἐγένετο καὶ ἐσκήνωσέν ἐν
     Ki ho log-os sarx e-gen-e-to ki es-kēn-ō-sen en

ἡμῖν,   καὶ ἐθεασάμεθα   τὴν δόξαν αὐτοῦ, δόξαν
hē-min, ki eth-e-a-sa-me-tha tēn dox-an au-tou, dox-an

ὡς μονογενοῦς   παρὰ πατρός, πλήρης χάριτος καὶ
ōs mo-no-ge-nous pa-ra pat-ros plē-rēs char-i-tos ki

ἀληθείας. (15) Ἰωάννης μαρτυρεῖ περὶ αὐτου καὶ
al-thei-as.   I-ō-an-nēs mar-tu-rei pe-ri au-tou ki

κέκραγεν λέγων· οὗτος ἦν ὃν εἶπον· ὁ ὀπίσω
ke-kra-gen leg-ōn, Hou-tos ēn hon ei-pon. Ho o-pis-ō

μου ἐρχόμενος   ἔμπροσθέν μου γέγονεν, ὅτι
mou er-cho-me-nos, em-pros-then mou ge-go-nen, ho-ti

πρῶτός μου ἦν. (16) ὅτι ἐκ τοῦ πληρώματος αὐτοῦ
prō-tos mou hēn.   Ho-ti ek tou plē-ro-ma-tos au-tou

ἡμεῖς πάντες ἐλάβομεν καὶ χάριν ἀντὶ χάριτος·
hē-meis pan-tes e-lab-o-men ki   cha-rin an-ti cha-ris-tos.

(17) ὅτι ὁ νόμος διὰ Μωϋσέως ἐδόθη, ἡ
     Ho-ti ho no-mos di-a Mō/u-se- ōs★ e-do-thē hē

χάρις καὶ ἡ ἀλήθεια διὰ Ἰησοῦ Χριστοῦ ἐγένετο.
cha-ris ki hē al-ē-thei-a di-a I-ē-sou Chris-tou e-gen-e-to.

(18) Θεὸν οὐδεὶς ἑώρακεν πώποτε μονογενὴς
     The-on ou-deis he-ō-ra-ken pō-po-te mo-no-gen-ēs

θεὸς ὁ ὢν εἰς τὸν κόλπον τοῦ πατρὸς ἐκεῖνος
the-os ho ōn eis ton kol-pon tou pat-ros e-kei-nos

ἐξηγήσατο.
ex-ē-gē-sa-to.★★

(★The umlaut mark [¨] over the upsilon is known as a diaeresis [or dieresis], used to separate two consecutive vowels into two syllables—which we have indicated by our slash mark [/]—and is sometimes used over the second vowel in a diphthong when the vowels are to be pronounced separately and not as a diphthong.)

(★★Sound this word out and you will hear a familiar word. This is the Greek word from which we derive "exegesis," or in this case "exegeted." We will be using those words often.)

Third Text—Matthew 6:9–15

(9) Οὕτως οὖν προσεύχεσθε ὑμεῖς· Πάτερ ἡμῶν ὁ ἐν τοῖς οὐρανοῖς· ἁγιασθήτω τὸ ὄνομά σου· (10) ἐλθέτω ἡ βασιλεία σου· γενηθήτω τὸ θέλημά σου· ὡς ἐν οὐρανῷ καὶ ἐπὶ γῆς· (11) τὸν ἄρτον ἡμῶν τὸν ἐπιούσιον δὸς ἡμῖν σήμερον· (12) καὶ ἄφες ἡμῖν τὰ ὀφειλήματα ἡμῶν, ὡς καὶ ἡμεῖς ἀφήκαμεν τοῖς ὀφειλήματα ἡμῶν· (13) καὶ μὴ εἰσενέγκῃς ἡμᾶς εἰς πειρασμόν, ἀλλὰ ῥῦσαι★ ἡμᾶς ἀπὸ πονηροῦ. (14) Ἐὰν γὰρ ἀφῆτε τοῖς ἀνθρώποις τὰ παραπτώματα αὐτῶν, ἀφήσει καὶ ὑμῖν ὁ πατὴρ ὑμῶν ὁ οὐράνιος· (15) ἐὰν δὲ μὴ ἀφῆτε τοῖς ἀνθρώποις, οὐδὲ ὁ πατὴρ ὑμῶν ἀφήσει τὰ παραπτώματα ὑμῶν.

(★When a word begins with ρ [rho], it always carries a rough breathing mark and is pronounced rh.)

Fourth Text—Philippians 4:1–7

(1) Ὥστε, ἀδελφοί μου ἀγαπητοὶ καὶ ἐπιπόθητοι, χαρὰ καὶ στέφανός μου, οὕτως στήκετε ἐν κυρίῳ, ἀγαπητοί. (2) Εὐοδίαν παρακαλῶ καὶ Συντύχην παρακαλῶ τὸ αὐτὸ φρονεῖν ἐν κυρίῳ. (3) ναὶ ἐρωτῶ καὶ σέ, γνήσιε σύζυγε, συλλαμβάνου αὐταῖς, αἵτινες ἐν τῷ εὐαγγελίῳ συνήθλησάν μοι μετὰ καὶ Κλήμεντος καὶ τῶν λοιπῶν συνεργῶν μου, ὧν τὰ ὀνόματα ἐν βίβλῳ ζωῆς. (4) Χαίρετε ἐν κυρίῳ πάντοτε· πάλιν ἐρῶ, χαίρετε. (5) τὸ ἐπιεικὲς ὑμῶν γνωσθήτω πᾶσιν ἀνθρώποις. ὁ κύριος ἐγγύς. (6) μηδὲν μεριμνᾶτε, ἀλλ᾽ ἐν παντὶ τῇ προσευχῇ καὶ τῇ δεήσει μετὰ εὐχαριστίας τὰ αἰτήματα ὑμῶν γνωριζέσθω πρὸς τὸν θεόν. (7) καὶ ἡ εἰρήνη τοῦ θεοῦ ἡ ὑπερέχουσα πάντα νοῦν φρουρήσει τὰς καρδίας ὑμῶν καὶ τὰ νοήματα ὑμῶν ἐν Χριστῷ Ἰησοῦ.

When you have reached this point, you should have a certain comfort level with both the recognition and the pronunciation of the Greek alphabet. You should also be able, albeit still with some difficulty, to sound out and read the texts included here. You may want to take your own interlinear New Testament now, select some other texts, and work your way through them, speaking the words aloud. After that, it will be time to move into Part 2. There you will be introduced to a series of principles, most of them grammatical and all of them carefully selected for what they will contribute directly to your handling of the interlinear Greek text. Make notes as you go. You will quickly develop a sense of what you need to learn in order to maximize the material in your own study. After each numbered principle, take time to reflect on and memorize the notes you have made. Now, let us move to Part 2.

PART 2

TEN PRINCIPLES FOR UNCOVERING GREEK MEANING

PRINCIPLE 1

The Presence or Absence of the Article

The first thing to look for in studying a text in an interlinear New Testament is the presence—or absence—of the article. The articles are the little words that are the English equivalent of "a," "an," and "the." In most cases in English, however, the article is of relatively little consequence in determining what a statement means. It has a certain syntactical value, but it just as often smooths out the flow of a sentence.

In Greek, on the other hand, the article may play a crucial role in determining what a noun, a phrase, or even a sentence means. As H. E. Dana and Julius R. Mantey put it, "Nothing is more indigenous to the Greek language than its use of the article." They hasten to add, though, that even scholars "have not accorded it sufficient attention, nor sought with proper diligence to apprehend the real genius underlying its various uses."[1]

Dana and Mantey go on to point out, however, as we should, that Greek grammarians differ among themselves about the importance of the presence or absence of the article in New Testament texts. Some do not think that, in most cases, articles were used with deliberate intent, and therefore they are of little importance in discerning a text's meaning. They suggest, for instance, that an article may be dropped in a text when it appears

---

[1]H. E. Dana and Julius R. Mantey, *A Manual Grammar of the Greek New Testament* (New York: Macmillan, 1927), 135–36.

before a predicate noun, as is the case in John 1:1 (which we will examine below). Others think the presence or absence of an article may be no more than a matter of word order, the result of the influence of Semitic style, or even the simple arbitrariness of a writer.[2]

Notwithstanding the debate over the role of the article in New Testament Greek, we contend that *often, but not necessarily always,* the presence or absence of the article reveals significance for the construction of the meaning of a text. We insist that preachers need to attend closely to this matter simply because on occasions the presence or the absence of an article may suggest something important.

In English, "a" and "an" are usually called indefinite articles, and "the" a definite article. The indefinite article refers to a class of objects, while the definite article indicates a particular one. The Greek language, though, has no indefinite articles. The presence of the article with a noun or noun phrase tends to *create* definiteness, but definiteness of a particular kind, as we shall see in a moment. More importantly, even the absence of the article where a noun or noun phrase appears tends to *create* definiteness, though of a different kind. Some Greek scholars argue that the handling of the article is never haphazard in the Greek language. They claim that it is a specific and well-defined tool of meaning, both complex and easy to recognize. We think preachers should at least initially assume this to be the case, unless they see something that convinces them otherwise.

Articles in Greek

Like a pronoun, the article, when it appears, ordinarily agrees with its noun in gender, number, and case. Those elements—gender (male, female or neuter), number (singular or plural) and case (nominative, genitive, dative, etc.)—are most often indicated by the endings placed on stems or roots of nouns. There are different endings for each of the numbers and cases. In the discussion of Principle 8, we will consider the characteristics of the noun in detail. Since the article must agree with the noun in gender, number, and case, the article must reflect either directly or indirectly the ending of the noun with which it is associated. Therefore, the article in Greek, while it is usually recognizable, is much more varied than the English articles. Here is a listing of the possible articles one will find in an interlinear Greek text, even though each of these will be translated in an interlinear with "a," "an," or "the." One need only become familiar with

---

[2] For a discussion of this issue, see C. D. F. Moule, *An Idiom Book of New Testament Greek,* 2d ed. (Cambridge: Cambridge University Press, 1959), 111–17.

this list, since in most cases it will not be difficult to recognize the article when one finds it.

Singular			Plural		
Masc.	Fem.	Neuter	Masc.	Fem.	Neuter
ὁ	ἡ	τό	οἱ	αἱ	τά
τοῦ	τῆς	τοῦ	τῶν	τῶν	τῶν
τῷ	τῇ	τῷ	τοῖς	ταῖς	τοῖς
τόν	τήν	τό	τούς	τάς	τά

The basic function of the Greek article is to point out an object, to call attention to it, or to emphasize its presence. In a sense, an article sometimes serves to underline or italicize the noun or noun phrase with which it is associated. It serves to distinguish a particular thing from the class or mass with which it could be identified. Its stress is on individual identity. This is most often the case with the use of the Greek article, and it is what makes the presence of the article in the Greek text unique. A noun that has an article with it is called an "articular" noun, and the grammatical construction is also referred to as "articular." ("Articular" is constructed from the word "article.")

When a noun or noun phrase is present *without* an article associated with it, it is called an "anarthrous" construction. ("Anarthrous" comes from two Greek words, *an*, "without," and *"arthron,"* articulation or joint.) This may mean that the emphasis of the noun is not on identity but on the *qualitative* or *character* aspects of whatever the noun is. In some cases, articles are not omitted because they are not needed or because it does not matter whether one inserts the article or not. Among other reasons, they may be omitted in order to convey a specific meaning arising from the noun or nouns used in the sentence. If an author wants to talk about "what something is like," he or she might use an anarthrous noun construction by dropping the article or articles from the usage. This means that when we examine a Greek text, we are not only looking for the presence of articles, but we are also consciously and deliberately looking for nouns that are used without articles. In fact, in many cases, the absence of the article may prove to be more important to the meaning of a text than its presence.

Reading Articles

Look at the following familiar text to see the articular constructions:

Μακάριοι οἱ πτωχοὶ τῷ πνεύματι, ὅτι αὐτῶν ἐστιν
Blessed   the poor in the spirit, for of them is

ἡ βασιλεία   τῶν   οὐρανῶν. (4) μακάριοι οἱ
the kingdom of the heavens.   Blessed   the

πενθοῦντες,   ὅτι αὐτοὶ παρακληθήσονται.
mourning (ones), for   they   shall be comforted.

(5) μακάριοι οἱ πραεῖς, ὅτι αὐτοὶ
    Blessed   the meek, for they

κληρονομήσουσιν τὴν γῆν.
 shall inherit   the earth.

Of course, these are three of the beatitudes from Matthew 5:3–5.
However, look closely for the *articles* in the text. There is an article before
the word "poor" and another before the word "spirit." In the same verse
there is another article before the word "kingdom" and then before the
word "heavens" (which in the Greek text is plural). Now work through
what the presence of those four articles might say about each line. The
presence of the first article in verse 3 makes clear that the text is *not* speaking
about "poorness" in general or even, it appears, a call for one to take on
the character of poorness. Rather, the reference is specifically to *the*
"poor" who are clearly identified. This does not mean that we know exactly
about whom the speaker is talking, but the articular construction seems
to tell us that specific people are in mind.

In the first of the beatitudes in Matthew, there is also the addition of
the qualifying phrase "in spirit." The word for "spirit" also is articular,
which may tell us that the writer probably has some particular "spirit" in
mind. Whatever we say about the idea of "poor in spirit," it will still have
a certain ambiguity about it, since we cannot tell *in what sense* the idea of
"in spirit" is used. Does the passage intend to refer to the idea of a
spiritual condition, or does it mean one is poor in that which *is* spirit?
The text does not help us through that question. Still, the writer seems
to have had something specific in mind. *The* spirit is being identified,
however that specific spirit may be understood. The reference appears
not to be to some quality of spirit, or spirit-likeness, but to something
that is understood specifically as spirit. (Contrast Mt. 5:3 with Lk. 6:20.)
In Matthew 5:5 and 6, the following are all articular: the words for
"meek," "earth," and "righteousness," as well as the reference to hungering
and thirsting ones. We should think carefully through the implication for
such specific designations of these concepts, keeping in mind that specific
things—concrete references—are possibly behind these lines.

At the outset of examining every New Testament text for preaching, we should identify the articles and evaluate the implications of such specific designations. The articles before terms may be deliberate and intended to provide direction for meaning, however subtle that direction may sometimes be.

Reading Anarthrous Constructions

To see a striking example of an anarthrous construction that follows on the heels of an articular one, look at the following text from Matthew 12:33 and 34:

῍Η   ποιήσατε τὸ δένδρον καλὸν καὶ τὸν καρπὸν
Either make   the tree   good and the fruit

αὐτοῦ καλόν, ἢ ποιήσατε τὸ δένδρον σαπρὸν
of it   good,   or make   the tree   rotten

καὶ τὸν καρπὸν αὐτοῦ σαπρόν· ἐκ γὰρ τοῦ
and the fruit   of it   rotten. By for the

καρποῦ τὸ δένδρον γινώσκεται. (34a) γεννήματα
fruit   the   tree   is known.   (You) Offspring

ἐχιδνῶν, πῶς δύνασθε ἀγαθὰ λαλεῖν πονηροὶ
of vipers, how are you able good   to speak evil

ὄντες;
being?

As you see from verse 33, each phrase is articular: "the tree," "the fruit"; "the tree," "the fruit." But verse 34 changes, and the crucial phrase is anarthrous: πῶς δύνασθε ἀγαθὰ λαλεῖν πονηροὶ ὄντες; ("How are you able to speak good being evil?"). Now the emphasis may fall on the quality and character of one's speech. When one is evil, it is not a matter of saying something good or something evil. That meaning would usually use the article. As this text puts it, when one is evil, one's speech cannot be characterized as good. The quality of one's speech tends toward evil.

This is how we try to massage, or play with, the sense of a text when we find constructions such as these. It is not as simple as saying that the text "means this" or "means that." It is, however, a matter of thinking about the implications of the text's language when we find that the article has been omitted or included, as in Matthew 12:33. These are the ways in which one "thinks through" in order to "construct" a viable, and often very important, distinction in the meaning embodied in the Greek text. However, since the use of the article in the New Testament varies remarkably, we cannot always be certain that its presence or absence is as crucial as is the case in the passages we have examined.

Sometimes, however, a preacher may be able to solve thorny textual problems by taking note of the difference between articular and anarthrous constructions. For example, consider the text that appears in 1 Timothy 3:2 and 3:12 and Titus 1:6, which has to do with the need for bishops and deacons or presbyters (elders) to be the "husband of one wife." Some have used the statement to insist that only men, and not women, could hold these positions of leadership, since women could not be the "husband of one wife." Others have insisted that in order to be a bishop one had to be married, and married for the first time.

But the text takes on another possible meaning when we examine its use of articles. Here is how 1 Timothy 3:12a reads in the Greek: διάκονοι ἔστωσαν μιᾶς γυναικὸς ἄνδρες…(literally, "Deacons, be of one wife husbands"). Look for the articular and anarthrous constructions. There is no article here, so the clause is anarthrous. That may mean it is not intended to identify something specific, whether a particular relationship or situation. Such specific designation would often call for the article. On the other hand, it seems likely that the passage intends to indicate a particular *quality* or *characteristic* of a person's life. So the clause suggests that one who would be a bishop or a deacon should be *like* the "husband of one wife." As we play with this text, it suggests that a leader's life should be characterized by that kind of personal faithfulness, devotion, loyalty, or whatever might be epitomized by a person with one spouse. If you will, the quality is that of "husband of one wife-ness." No particular matrimonial state is specified by the text. What is specified is the *kind* of person (male or female) that such a phrase embodies. The anarthrous construction suggests this kind of interpretation and a rather different translation than the usual one.

Special Forms of Articular and Anarthrous Constructions

There are four special and easy to remember forms of the articular/anarthrous construction that are common in the New Testament. The first has to do with *the use of the Greek term for God* (θεός). Whenever the word θεός is preceded by an article, we need to consider whether the writer intends to speak of the divine personality or persona. When θεός is anarthrous, however, it may signify divine essence or divine attributes or activities. In short, it may mean "like God." This distinction is not consistently sustained in the New Testament, but nonetheless it should be considered whenever we encounter θεός in a text.

Bearing this in mind, the opening lines of the prologue to the gospel of John become intriguing:

Ἐν ἀρχῇ   ἦν ὁ λόγος, καὶ ὁ λόγος ἦν πρὸς
In beginning was the word and the word was with

τὸν θεόν, καὶ θεὸς ἦν ὁ λόγος. οὗτος ἦν ἐν
the God, and God was the word; this one was in

ἀρχῇ   πρὸς τὸν θεόν.
beginning with the God.

Look for the articles, especially ones associated with God—θεός and θεόν. Look particularly at the phrase ὁ λόγος ἦν πρὸς τὸν θεόν, καὶ θεὸς ἦν ὁ λόγος. The first use of the word "God" has the article, and the second does not. Greek scholars point out that a construction such as the second phrase, θεός ἦν ὁ λόγος, should usually be translated as "the word was God." This translation is accurate, since when two nouns (such as "God" and "word") appear in the same clause like this, the one that possesses the article becomes the subject of the clause. Hence, "the word was God."

But we are interested in the nature of the articular nouns as they differ from the anarthrous nouns. In the two clauses above—"the word was with God and the word was God"—the first use of God (θεός) is articular, and the second is not. So we might logically consider that the first use of θεός names or identifies God as divine personality, while its second use indicates something God-like or the qualities of God, whatever they might be. The result is that we can create a fascinating distinction in the meaning of the line that goes something like this: "the word was lodged with God, wherever God was (or is), and the word was, itself, God-like (or divine)." Or, even more accurately, we may translate the line, "the word was with God, and God-like was the word." This feature of John 1:1 has caused a great deal of consternation among interpreters. Is the anarthrous construction intended to indicate a divine quality, or is it less significant? We cannot solve this problem, but we can reflect on the difference and the possibilities of meaning it produces. Theologically, it raises the issue of whether or not the text means that God and the "word" are identical.

The second special form of the articular/anarthrous construction has to do with *the immediate repetition of an article between nouns*. For example, in Matthew 3:2 the phrase translated "kingdom of heaven" is ἡ βασιλεία τῶν οὐρανῶν ("the kingdom of the heavens"). Frequently, such a construction not only clarifies but also accents what is embodied in the second noun. So this phrase may correctly be translated "the kingdom of the heavens." However, a translation that emphasizes the use of articles before each noun might render the phrase, "the kingdom, *the one in the heavens.*"

Another example of this special form of articular construction is found in John 10:11, where Jesus identifies himself as "the good shepherd"—ὁ ποιμὴν ὁ καλός, "the shepherd, the good." "The good shepherd" is a fair translation, but the construction may place a much stronger emphasis on the second articular noun than the usual English rendering suggests. To better reflect the Greek, a more appropriate translation might be, "the shepherd, the *good* shepherd." Such constructions are fairly common in the New Testament, particularly in the gospels, and a clear understanding of the role of the article sometimes helps us grasp the special significance of these phrases.

The third special use of the articular/anarthrous construction has to do with *the article's appearance or absence before what are clearly abstract nouns,* of which the New Testament has plenty. Words such as "truth," "grace," "mercy," or "justice" are abstract nouns. When these words are used *without* an article (in an anarthrous construction), they may refer to a very general or abstract idea. However, when they are used *with* an article, we need to ask whether they represent something specific to the text. In other words, they may carry the special sense of a divine activity that the text itself may attempt to convey.

For example, when Pilate confronts Jesus in John 18:38, Pilate asks, Τί ἐστιν ἀλήθεια; ("What is truth?"). His question is anarthrous; there is no article before the noun translated "truth." John may be saying that Pilate asks about truth *in general.* But in the New Testament context, when the word ἀλήθεια (truth) is used with an article, it often refers to divine truth, the truth of the gospel, and specific truth. Granted, one cannot always say what that truth actually is, since the text itself often leaves the notion vague. Nor can we say that there is never an exception to this. What we can say is that when an article is used with the word truth, or some other "technical" theological term, the writer may have something specific in mind, and not simply a general notion. Pilate asks about truth in general, while the one before him is himself "*the* truth" (Jn. 14:6).

Another interesting occurrence of the presence or absence of the article with abstract nouns is found in John 15:26:

῞Οταν ἔλθῃ ὁ παράκλητος ὃν ἐγὼ πέμψω
When comes the comforter whom I will send

ὑμῖν παρὰ τοῦ πατρός, τὸ πνεῦμα τῆς ἀληθείας
to you from the father, the spirit of the truth

ὃ παρὰ τοῦ πατρὸς ἐκπορεύεται…
which from the father proceeds…

Notice the use of the article with the words "comforter," "spirit," and "truth." This echoes the construction we noted a short time ago where two articles appear with two connected nouns.

One other special case of the articular/anarthrous constructions should be kept in mind. It has to do with *the use of the article with multiple nouns connected by the word "and"* (in Greek, καί). When this construction occurs, usually everything that the article, or the absense of the article, means for the first noun, is also meant for the one connected to the first with καί. We find this construction in a striking phrase in Titus 2:13:

προσδεχόμενοι τὴν μακαρίαν ἐλπίδα καὶ
expecting the blessed hope and

ἐπιφάνειαν τῆς δόξης τοῦ μεγάλου θεοῦ καὶ
appearance of the glory of the great God and

σωτῆρος ἡμῶν Ἰησοῦ Χριστοῦ,…
savior of us Jesus Christ,…

An interlinear translates this verse to mean, "expecting (or awaiting) the blessed hope and appearance of the glory of the great God and Savior of us Jesus Christ." But look very closely at this rather complicated phrase. First find the articles. The first one is τήν, and it precedes "blessed hope" (μακαρίαν ἐλπίδα). Then comes the word καί ("and") followed by the word for "appearance," ἐπιφάνειαν. So the article before "blessed hope" also applies with equal force to the word "appearance" and may then suggest the definiteness of each of the nouns.

Look again at the rest of the line to see if you find a recurrence of the very same principle. Look for both words this time—the article and the καί, but skip the article τῆς and go to τοῦ, which is associated with the phrase "great God" as well as with "Savior of us Jesus Christ." The author connects two phrases with καί. If the first of the phrases is articular, we are to regard the next as articular as well. If the first of the two terms or phrases is anarthrous, then so is the second. Consequently, in Titus 2:13

"blessed hope" and "appearance" of "glory" are both articular. Both seem to refer to specific things—whatever they might be. The same is true of the second pair, "great God" and "our Savior Jesus Christ." Both are articular, and, again, the writer may be relating the two and designating two specific and defined entities.

Using Articular and Anarthrous Constructions

Constant awareness of the articular and anarthrous constructions in the Greek text will oftentimes have an impact on how we devise our understanding of a text. However, the student of the text should always be aware that working with the presence or absence of the article may at best be a "pointer" to possible meaning. It may cause us to *ask the right questions about a text,* even though it will not always give us a clearly defined meaning of the text itself. We may gain insights into the meanings on the page, but we must still labor over how those meanings might have been, or even are, intended to play out in our understanding of the text.

This point is crucial, so let us illustrate how the culminating element of the principle of the article might affect a reading of a text. We will do so with a text from Luke 12:51–53:

δοκεῖτε   ὅτι   εἰρήνην παρεγενόμην δοῦναι ἐν τῇ
Do you think that peace   I came   to give in the

γῆ;   οὐχί,   λέγω ὑμῖν, ἀλλ᾽ ἢ   διαμερισμόν.
earth? No,   I tell you, but rather division.

(52) ἔσονται   γὰρ ἀπὸ τοῦ νῦν πέντε ἐν ἑνὶ
       There will be for   from -   now five   in one

οἴκῳ διαμεμερισμένοι, τρεῖς ἐπὶ δυσὶν καὶ δύο
house having been divided, three against two and two

ἐπὶ τρισίν, (53) διαμερισθήσονται πατὴρ ἐπὶ
against three,   will be divided   father against

υἱῷ καὶ υἱὸς ἐπὶ πατρί, μήτηρ ἐπὶ τὴν
son and son against father, mother against the

θυγατέρα καὶ θυγάτηρ ἐπὶ τὴν μητέρα.
daughter and daughter against the mother,

πενθερὰ ἐπὶ τὴν νύμφην   αὐτῆς καὶ
mother-in-law against the daughter-in-law of her and

νύμφη　ἐπὶ　τὴν πενθεράν.
daughter-in-law against the　mother-in-law.

First, locate all the articles in the text, preferably by underlining or otherwise noting where they are. The puzzle of this text is why the articles appear where they do and if their absence or presence means anything. Again, we will initially assume that there is no haphazardness or arbitrariness in their use or placement, and yet both their presence and absence are haunting. Verse 52 has no articles, and in verse 53, these phrases are anarthrous: "Father against son" and "son against father." Yet in the same verse, four phrases include articles: "mother against *the* daughter," "daughter against *the* mother," "mother-in-law against *the* daughter-in-law," and "daughter-in-law against *the* mother-in-law." Notice that after the father-son opposition in verse 52, each ἐπί is followed by an articular noun. The one from whom the subject is being divided is *the* daughter, mother, and so forth.

If the distinction between articular and anarthrous constructions is really important, what does it mean in this passage? Do the constructions imply something about the nature of the various relationships cited? The puzzle is a fascinating one, made all the more puzzling because Luke 12:53 is a loose citation of the Greek version of Micah 7:6. Luke contains three constructions with parallels in Micah. As in Luke, in Micah the father-son opposition is anarthrous, but the rebellion of the daughter is against *the* mother and that of the daughter-in-law is against *the* mother-in-law. Moreover, in Micah the opposition is between young and the old but in Luke it is mutual. There is some manuscript evidence that scribes tried to resolve the issue of the articular and anarthrous nouns—so it is not a new problem. (See also Mt. 10:34–36.)

There may not be an answer to the use of articular and anarthrous nouns in Luke 12:51–53, but the point is that by focusing on the articular and anarthrous dimensions of the text and its phrases, some interesting shades of meaning may be uncovered. Asking the question of any particular text stimulates our thought. Should you ever preach on Luke 12:51–53, exploring the presence and absence of articles may occasion the conception of an idea for the sermon.

PRINCIPLE 2

The Faces of the Verb

Few dimensions of a language are more important than its verbs, those words that designate the nature of action. However, the conjugation of verbs often provides the biggest barrier to even conscientious Greek students who would like to work regularly with the original language in sermon preparation. The question is whether there is a way to simplify the handling of verbs and yet come out with helpful information about the nature of a text's action. Is there an easier way to gain information from verbs that can, on many occasions, illumine one's preaching and teaching? The answer is yes. An understanding of Greek verbs can be simplified, if one allows an analytical lexicon to serve as the companion to an interlinear text.

In many respects, working with Greek verbs is not significantly different from working with English verbs. With a few important exceptions, what we might call the "faces" of the English verb are the same as those of the Greek verb. There are five such "faces," or dimensions, of every verb in the Greek text, and we must remember these five dimensions. They are *tense, voice, mood, person,* and *number.* We can come at these in any order. However, if we have these elements fixed in mind when we look up a verb in an analytical lexicon, we can collect a great deal of information that in turn may be very significant for the understanding of a text.

The Tense of the Verb

We begin with a verb's tense, largely because this is where we find the most significant difference between English and Greek. Tense in

45

Greek is not so much a way to designate time as it is to indicate the *progress of time,* the movement and stoppage of *action,* or the effects of action over time. When we are dealing with a Greek verb, the single most common and important distinction in tense is *the difference between a present tense verb and what is called an aorist tense verb.* (The word "aorist" comes from a Greek term that means "definable" or "limit" and is pronounced AIR-ist.) What is most significant is that there is no true English meaning equivalent to the Greek aorist tense. For some Greek scholars, the aorist tense is the most consequential in the Greek language.

The *present tense* refers to what is usually described as continuous action, sometimes called linear or ongoing action. It is action that began at some point in the undefined past and has not ended. It is "present" in the sense that it continues into the present. The picture that the present tense provides is of something occurring now. It designates action that is right now continuing as it began. The New Testament is filled with present tense verbs, often with rich, movement-oriented imagery. It is intriguing, for instance, that often in the gospels Jesus' statements are introduced with λέγει, the present tense of λέγω, found, for instance, in Mark 14:27.

To examine the present tense, a look at the parable of the ten maidens (Mt. 25:1–13) is instructive. It tells how these ten take their lamps and go to meet the bridegroom. Five take extra oil, and five do not. When the bridegroom is detained, those with extra oil are ready, while those without extra oil are not. In verse 8 the five without oil say to those with plenty:

Δότε   ἡμῖν   ἐκ τοῦ   ἐλαίου   ὑμῶν,   ὅτι   αἱ
Give   us   of the oil   of you, because the

λαμπάδες   ἡμῶν   σβέννυνται.
lamps   of us   are being quenched

The verb, σβέννυνται ("are being quenched"), is in the present tense. Therefore, it indicates that the action of the lamps (their dying down) has been and is still an ongoing action. The lamps are not yet out, but they are gradually dying. The action of a verb in the present tense is always clear and always dynamic with its emphasis on a continuous process.

The *aorist verb,* on the other hand, designates action that is completed. The action occurred, and it is over. The closest parallel to the Greek aorist tense that we have in English is what we call "past" tense. While the aorist is most often translated as a past action, the emphasis falls not so much on its occurrence *in the past* as it does on its being *a past act that has concluded.* There is no sense of the duration of that past action. For this reason, many scholars designate aorist action as representing a "point" of action in the past—what some call punctiliar action. If a line represents the continuous action of the present tense, a dot or a small circle (a point in the past) most often represents the aorist tense.

With this understood, it should be noted that when the aorist tense is translated into English, it is most often rendered as a past tense verb. For instance, all these are examples of aorist verbs translated with an English verb in the past tense: "his leprosy *was cleansed*" (Mt. 8:3b); "the temple *was built* in forty-six years" (Jn. 2:20); and "for your sakes *he became* poor" (2 Cor. 8:9). However, in each of these cases (along with countless others in the New Testament), when we encounter a verb identified in an analytical lexicon as aorist, we should not only read it simply in the past tense, which is the natural thing to do. We should also reflect carefully on what we might call the "aorist nature" of the verb and where it appears. That is, we should think carefully about the "completed" nature of the action being described. More often than one might guess, the use of the aorist verb will throw a particular light and emphasis on the phrase or sentence in which it appears.

A third tense to be learned is the *perfect*. It can be described as a combination of the present and the aorist. When the perfect tense appears in a text, it is always a significant occurrence. A perfect verb may be described as aorist, in the sense that its action was completed at a point in the past. But it is also present tense in the sense that the *effects of the completed action in the past continue into and through the present*. The action was "perfected," or finished, but the results of the action are ongoing. This is a powerful Greek tense, and often very telling and distinctive, particularly in the theological language of the New Testament.

Acts 5:28 is a remarkable example of the perfect tense verb. There the writer has the high priest say, πεπληρώκατε τὴν Ἰερουσαλὴμ τῆς διδαχῆς ὑμῶν, meaning "you have filled Jerusalem with your teachings." The first word is the verb, and, when we look it up in an analytical lexicon, we find it is in the perfect tense. The high priest says, "you have completed your teachings," "you have taught," or even, "you did teach" or "you taught all over Jerusalem." In any case, the action of the teaching is now completed. Still, *the results of the teaching* are going on and on; they are continuous into the present. It is a powerful idea, and one that only a perfect tense verb can convey. Preachers recognize, of course, that the historical beginnings of Christianity are completed in the past but that their results influence the present. Whenever we encounter a perfect tense verb, we should "play with" the full meaning of the perfect, reading the text as fully in light of the perfect tense idea as possible.

Two other verb tenses are important in Greek. One is a modification of the perfect, called *the imperfect tense*. If the perfect tense represents completed action in past time with its effect continuing into the present, the imperfect tense represents actions that are not completed, but are ongoing in "past time." The imperfect implies no ending of the action or no continuation of the effects of the action into the present. However, it is an important tense because, among other reasons, it tends to set up "scenes" in which present or aorist action will then take place.

An example of the use of the imperfect in storytelling is found in Acts 21:20, which reads, Οἱ δὲ ἀκούσαντες ἐδόξαζον τὸν θεὸν εἶπόν τε αὐτῷ ("and those having heard were glorifying God, and they said to him"). The word ἐδόξαζον is the imperfect of δοξάζω, "to praise" or "glorify." "Were glorifying" describes a past action for which there is no specified ending. In this case, the glorifying sets the stage for the aorist verb, εἶπον, "they said." If we read an imperfect verb that way, it is often possible to make significant observations about "what happened" in the past that the text is talking about.

The other noteworthy verb tense for New Testament texts is *the future tense*. It is fairly easy to grasp, since it very closely mirrors the English understanding of future tense. With the future tense, time is very pronounced, though most often indefinite. When a verb is in the future tense, it refers to *no particular time,* but only a time that is ahead. It is the anticipatory tense, but the significance of that anticipation is virtually always a function of the context in which the future tense verb appears. Something "will be," or it "shall be," or it "will come to pass." These are the meanings the future tense most often conjures up in the reader.

These five do not by any means exhaust the tenses in Greek. In particular, scholars will note that we have not discussed the pluperfect. But these five are the tenses most useful to the preacher working with the Greek text. There are also numerous subdivisions or refinements that Greek scholars make within each of these tenses. For example, there are the "constative," the "culminative," and the "gnomic" aorists. Such distinctions are undoubtedly important to the Greek scholar, but they are of less value to the preacher concerned with charting the kinds of meanings that contribute in a fairly direct way to the preparation of sermons.

The Voice of the Verb

Voice is the term used to indicate the relationship between the subject of a sentence and the nature of the verb's action. There are three different verbal voices in the Greek language, two of which are fairly common and easily understood in making the move from English to Greek. When a verb is in the *active voice,* the subject of the sentence or phrase is *doing* the acting. When a verb is in the *passive voice,* the subject of the sentence is *being acted upon.* In this case, the subject is not the one doing the acting, but instead is the recipient of the action, and the action comes from some other source or motivation. The distinction between active and passive voice is common to both English and Greek, and for that reason is easy to understand.

However, the third Greek voice is distinctive and has no direct equivalent in English, so we need to look at it carefully. It is the *middle voice.* Simply put, the middle voice of a verb indicates that the subject of the action acts in such a way as to *participate* in the results of the action. At one level, the middle voice is like the active voice, in that the subject is the one who does the acting. But unlike the active voice, its emphasis is not on the subject's acting itself, but on the subject's being implicated in the full ramifications of the action. You might think of the present tense in terms of an arrow from the subject pointing away from itself and of the middle tense as an arrow pointed back toward the subject.

In no New Testament text can this be more forcefully seen than in the story of Judas in Matthew 27:5. The writer says that after Judas returned and threw down the silver pieces he had received for betraying Jesus, ἀπελθὼν ἀπήγξατο, or "going out" (or "going away"), "he hanged himself." The verb, ἀπήγξατο, is the middle voice of the (aorist) verb, ἀπάγχομαι. Judas was the actor, but he participated fully in, and suffered the full consequences of, his action. That is what the middle voice indicates. The middle voice verb has a pronounced intensity since in a strong manner it represents a peculiar relationship between the action or actions and a subject that takes the actions. It indicates the reciprocal effects of that action on the one who acts or has acted. When preachers see the middle voice, they should stop and savor the power of that voice, shaping the meaning and emphasis of a text. (Sometimes the middle and passive forms of certain verbs are spelled the same. In those cases, we must decide which voice they are by their contexts. However, it is well to try both on and see which provides the better fit. Furthermore, there may be times when it will be hard to understand just how an act impacts the subject of the verb.)

The Mood of the Verb

The third "face" of the Greek verb is its "mood." Mood is a grammatical designation that is often very valuable in throwing light on the subtle but important meaning of a text. In grammar it is usually defined as the relationship between "reality" or "what is" and the action that the verb indicates. Put another way, there are statements of "action" that are called the "indicative" mood, and then there are the statements of "what if" action—that is, actions that are not yet "real" or taken, but that "could be" or "might be." Mood, in other words, is sometimes about the "what if's" of a verb. It distinguishes actual things from those that are not actual, but are possible.

When we encounter a verb in the *indicative mood,* we can take it at its face value. It is a statement of action that occurs in reality. But there are three other moods that you should learn. They all produce the sense of "if" or "what if." The three are the subjunctive mood, the optative mood, and the imperative mood. Of the three, *the imperative* is best known and (one might argue) clearly the most important. The imperative mood expresses the idea that something "will happen if" a particular action is carried out, and that action is most often ordered or mandated in some way. The imperative is then the mood of command. Do this, so that such and such will happen. Or, more implicitly, but still true to the idea: If you do this, that will happen.

The New Testament is filled with verbs in the imperative mood. In the command, "Love your enemies," ἀγαπᾶτε τοὺς ἐχθροὺς ὑμῶν (Mt. 5:44), the verb ἀγαπᾶτε is in the imperative mood. The words that surround the imperative verb indicate what kinds of things will follow *if* the command is carried out. In this case, 5:45 says, "So that you may be children of your Father in heaven." In John 6:20, Ἐγώ εἰμι· μὴ φοβεῖσθε ("It is I, do not be afraid"), φοβεῖσθε is in the imperative mood. The surrounding text (in this case 6:21) suggests what the outcomes will be *if* the imperative is followed. It is this "if" quality of the behavior more than the command itself that is emphasized when the verb is in the imperative mood. Sometimes, however, the outcome is only implied or taken for granted, as is the case in Romans 16:3, "Greet Prisca and Aquila."

The other two moods, the *subjunctive* and the *optative,* are also used in "if" statements. These two can be distinguished by remembering a relatively simple rule. When a verb is subjunctive, it has conditions on it: Such and such will happen *if* the conditions stated in the surrounding text are met. The idea of contingency is present in the subjunctive mood. On the other hand, the optative mood indicates that something *may* happen, but no conditions are specified. It is far more indefinite than the subjunctive. The subjunctive mood is more prevalent in the New Testament than the optative (which is used only thirty-eight times).

An example of the subjunctive is found in John 15:7:"If you remain in me." Here the verb translated "remain" (μείνητε) is subjunctive. In Mary's response to the angel's announcement of Jesus' birth in Luke 1:38, she declares, γένοιτο ("may it be done"), using the optative mood of the verb γίνομαι. When either of these two moods appear, we should frame the verbs and the statements in which they appear to emphasize and take advantage of the "if" quality of what is said.

The Person of the Verb

The fourth "face" of the verb is its person, a term that refers to the subject who is doing the verb's action. *Who* is it? Again, as in English, there are first, second, and third person verbs, both plural and singular. Every verb can be any one of these. First person refers to "I" doing the acting, for example,"I went,""I am going," and "I will go." Second person refers to a "you" acting, for example,"you are going,""you fell down," or "you were the one who said that." Third person refers to "he," "she," or "it" as the actor or the acting agent. What is different in Greek is that "person" is often incorporated into a particular form or ending of the verb itself. Consequently the pronouns, "I,""you,""he,""she," or "it" are often missing. To know what person is contained within a certain verb, it will usually be necessary to look up the verb in your analytical lexicon.

When the personal pronoun itself is used along with a verb that already indicates person, it emphasizes the identity of the actor. For instance, John the Baptist denies that he is the Christ in John 1:20, which says, Ἐγὼ οὐκ εἰμὶ ὁ Χριστός ("*I* am not the Christ!").The pronoun "I" is actually already implicit in the verb, εἰμί, so the explicit addition of ἐγὼ (meaning "I") creates an emphatic statement.

Also related to person is whether the verb is singular or plural—the "number" of the verb. As in English, singular refers to one person acting (or being acted upon), and plural refers to more than one. So when we discover the person of a verb, we also find its number at the same time. For example, a verb will be first person singular or first person plural— "I (or we) did this"—or second person singular or plural—"you did this"— or third person singular or plural–"he, she, or they did that." Again, even though the interpretation is fairly straightforward, the "number" of the verb is often implicit in the verb form in Greek, so apart from memorizing those forms, one must rely on an analytical lexicon for the verb's basic parameters. In what follows, we look more closely at the number of verbs.

When the Greek text is translated into English, though, both person and number can sometimes play crucial roles in how we read a text. An example is 1 Timothy 3, a text that has its counterpart in Titus 2. In 1 Timothy 3 is a list of qualifications required of someone who would be a bishop (ἐπίσκοπος) in the church. Over the years, most English translations of the chapter have rendered its verbs using the word "he," third person singular, with the verb carrying the pronoun within it. The RSV translates verse 1, "If any one aspires to the office of bishop, *he* desires a noble task."

Later, in verse 4, the RSV translation reads, "He must manage his own household well, keeping his children submissive." If a person cannot do this, verse 5 asks, "how can he care for God's church?" It is a simple reading of a very important text as far as the history of the church has been concerned. It is important because for generations the use of "he" in these verses has been taken, at least in part, as a mandate that only men, and not women, can fill the office of bishop. (The NRSV renders verse 1 without reference to the gender of the bishop but in verses 4 and 5 reverts to "he" and "his.")

When we look up the verbs of this text, we find that they are all third person singular. The fact that they are third person singular verbs also tells us that the text could just as accurately be translated with the pronoun "she" as with "he." Third person singular refers to "he," "she," or, in some cases, "it," and does not specify the differences among these three pronouns. The pronouns for the third person singular verb are interchangeable unless otherwise specified—which, in this text, they are not. Grammatically, the text ought to read that if "anyone, either a man or a woman, desires the office of bishop, *he or she* desires a noble task." Verse 5 ought to be translated, "If anyone, male or female, does not know how to manage his or her own house well, how will he or she know how to care for God's church?" The person of the verb does not designate gender.

One other thing should be noted about this passage in 1 Timothy that also bears on the third person singular reading of "he or she." If the writer had intended to designate the masculine "he" throughout the listing of "qualifications," that could have been clearly indicated with the insertion of the word for "male," man (ἀνήρ). Instead, the author of the text inserts a word designed to ensure that the text be read *not as either* exclusively male or female, but *as both* male and female. This is further accomplished in verse 1 with the Greek word τίς, which unmistakably means "anyone." The word τίς appears in both 1 Timothy 3:1 and Titus 1:6, and it is repeated in 1 Timothy 3:5, where the translation is clear: "but if *anyone* (τίς) does not know how to rule his or her household well, then how will he or she care for the church of God?" (See Principle 9 for a discussion of pronouns such as τίς.) The point is that without some other indication, the person and number of the verb alone does not specify the gender of the actor.

The Number of the Verb

The last "face" of the verb is its number—whether it is singular or plural, as we have already noted. Usually, this is a fairly straightforward matter. Either one subject is doing the acting, or is being acted upon, or more than one.

There is, however, one distinction between English and Greek worth mentioning briefly. As you know, English lacks a difference between the plural and singular second person. We use "you" for both an individual and a group. The Greek, however, has specific forms for each. Nonetheless, translators must use the ambiguous English "you" for both. Preachers who can distinguish the difference between the Greek singular and plural second person pronouns have a marvelous advantage. So, for instance, in John 4:46–47 the royal official comes alone to Jesus and asks Jesus to heal his son. Jesus responds in verse 48, "Unless you see signs and wonders you will not believe," but both verbs in Greek are second person *plural* aorist subjunctive verbs: ἴδητε (you see) and πιστεύσητε (you believe). Here Jesus is speaking more to readers than to the father of the ailing son.

What is often crucial for us is that if a verb is plural in Greek, it must refer to something (that is, to an antecedent) that is also plural, just as it must in English. Likewise, if the verb is singular, its antecedent must also be singular. This is the grammatical principle of "concord," "reference," or simply "agreement." Sometimes it is difficult to know to what the verb, or the pronoun contained within the verb, refers. Sentences can get long and convoluted. Often the only help one gets in connecting a verb and its pronoun to an antecedent is by matching it with a preceding noun of the same number. (See Principle 8 for a discussion of nouns and their number.)

Identifying a verb's antecedent is frequently a problem for both translation and meaning. It can result in preachers' having to think deeply about some hidden reason for how a particular verb is used. A good example is 1 Timothy 2:15, the chapter that immediately precedes the one we have just been discussing. No matter how one unravels the Greek text, this is a puzzling section of writing, since (beginning at v. 13) the reference to Adam and Eve and then to childbearing is profoundly elusive to us.

However, verse 15 provides one of those particularly challenging shifts in a verb's number. Most English translations have it read something like the RSV: "Yet *woman* will be saved through bearing children, if *she* continues in faith and love and holiness, with modesty." If you look closely at the verse, however, you see that the verb that comes after the word "if" (μείνωσιν) is not singular, but *plural*. The first verb in the verse (σωθήσεται, translated "woman will be saved") is singular, and seems to refer back to "the woman" (the noun, γυνή, also singular) in verse 14. Yet in verse 15 the second verb is plural (μείνωσιν, "they remain"). The RSV seems to assume that there is a problem with the Greek, and in order to "fix it" translates the verb μείνωσιν as if it were singular. That repair job makes the verse read better in English. Otherwise, a literal but exact translation, similar to that adopted in the NRSV, would be "woman will be saved through bearing children, if *they remain faithful*," because the second verb is clearly plural.

So who are the "they?" Where does one go in the text to find an antecedent that is plural and to which the "they" in verse 15 can refer? It is not a question for which there is an easy answer, if there is an answer at all. Yet it is something that anyone who studies this text carefully must ponder, since it makes an already difficult text even more difficult. It is an example, though, that cautions students of the Bible not to take any verb for granted. We need to look up every verb in order that its person and number become clear to us. Sometimes one is thrown a curve by the unexpected, but often those curves open more fascinating doors for reflection on the nuances of a text and even for preaching those texts.

PRINCIPLE 3

The Precision of the Participle

Even though we have already looked at articles and verbs and how important they are, some Greek scholars place the participle at the heart of New Testament Greek. For example, in his classic introduction to *New Testament Greek for Beginners,* J. Gresham Machen writes that, "experience shows that in learning to read New Testament Greek, the participle is almost the crux of the whole matter."[1] Another author calls the Greek participle "the most versatile of the Greek verb forms and one of the distinctives of the language."[2]

What these two say is understandable. Participles appear on average as every twenty-first word in the New Testament and often at crucial points in virtually every text. More than that, they add a remarkable precision to a Greek text, and often a precision that goes beyond what even a good English translation is able to express. The precision locked up within the participle opens exceptional doors for the preacher in explaining what a text meant when it was written.

What Is a Participle?

In English grammar, we were all taught to recognize a participle as a verb with an "-ing" ending. For example, with the verb "show," the

---

[1] J. Gresham Machen, *New Testament Greek for Beginners* (Toronto: Macmillan, 1923), ix.
[2] William G. MacDonald, *Greek Enchiridion: A Concise Handbook of Grammar for Translation and Exegesis* (Peabody, Mass.: Hendrickson Publishers, 1986), 55.

participle would be "showing," or with the verb "teach," the participle would be the word "teaching." The same is largely true in Greek. A participle is a verb form, which means that it is an "action" word, but it has a greater flexibility than a normal verb. The Greek participle can function as a noun, an adverb, or (as it often does) as an adjective. This is why it is sometimes referred to as a "verbal adjective." It contains within it both description and action in various blends, as we shall see. Ironically, the participle is much more highly developed in Greek than it is in English. This is why, for the student of the Greek New Testament, the participle functions with considerable precision in the formation of a sentence's meaning.

What does the preacher need to know about the Greek participle? Greek scholars have devised many different ways of sorting out the various uses of participles in the New Testament, and we shall not try to rehearse all of those. We think, however, that *the major uses of the participle can be summarized under four roles: Substantive, adverbial, adjectival, and verbal.* Any preacher can work with considerable insight into the Greek New Testament by learning these four uses of the participle in the New Testament. This involves three steps. The first is to learn the difference between "attributive" participles and "circumstantial" ones. The second is to learn how to recognize and handle participles that are usually called "substantive." The final step is to grasp the idea of the "temporal" participle, that is, the way in which the idea of time works in the use of the participle. In covering these three steps, we will survey the most important roles of the participle for preachers.

Attributive and Circumstantial Participles

We begin with perhaps the most important distinction among participles, namely, the influential difference between attributive and circumstantial participles. Ironically, the distinction is tied up with the presence or absence of the article and reinforces the importance of the article we saw in Principle 1. Here is the rule you must keep in mind:

When an article precedes the participle (that is, when it is an articular participle), it is *attributive.*

When the participle appears without a preceding article (that is, when it is anarthrous), it is a *circumstantial* participle.

We can illustrate this crucial distinction with a simple phrase, ὁ ἀπόστολος ὁ λέγων ταῦτα βλέπει τὸν κύριον ("the apostle saying these things sees the Lord"). Now let's write the same sentence a second way:

ὁ ἀπόστολος λέγων ταῦτα βλέπει τὸν κύριον. When you look it up in an analytical lexicon, you learn that λέγων ("saying") is a participle formed from the Greek word λέγω, which means "I say." Just as a participle is often translated into English, it may be expressed with an "-ing" ending, "saying." (Notice that the verb, λέγω, has a family resemblance to the noun, λόγος.)

Having found the participle, we now note in particular the difference between the two sentences we just wrote in Greek. It is so small a difference that one must look closely for it. In the second sentence, there is nothing between the words ἀπόστολος and λέγων. However, in the first sentence, you see the article ὁ between the two of them. Writing either of these sentences in English, we are inclined to clean them up somewhat by adding commas, but Greek has no commas as such. Our commas would make the translation read, "The apostle, saying these things, sees the Lord."

Ironically, however, even with the commas, this English sentence is a fair translation of *either* of the two Greek sentences—the one with the article as well as the one without. There is a significant problem in determining the meaning of the sentence even in the English translation. The problem is that it is difficult to know whether the phrase "saying these things" modifies the noun ("the apostle") that precedes it or the verbal phrase ("sees the Lord") that follows it. In other words, how do we answer this question: Is it the apostle who is "saying these things," or is it that the apostle, as a result of "saying these things," "sees the Lord?" The problem seems simple, and yet the meaning of the sentence rests on what the participle λέγων modifies or with what it goes.

In Greek, however, the problem is solved very easily with the rule governing attribution and circumstance. *Attribution* in this case means the participle attributes something to the noun, and hence modifies it. The participle functions as an adjective—"the seeing apostle." It indicates that the noun is "doing" something. The first rule is:

A Greek participle is always attributive *when an article precedes it.*

An article before a participle equals attribution. So when the participle is attributive, it identifies the apostle as "the one who says these things."

By the same token, the second rule is:

When the participle appears without a preceding article, it goes with the verb or verb phrase instead of the noun.

A participle without an article equals circumstance. In this case, "circumstantial" (or "stands in the circumstantial position") means the participle identifies the verb's action or indicates what sort of action is expressed in the verb. It sets up the "circumstances" of the action. Hence, the circumstantial participle, "saying these things," means that it is connected with and informs us about what takes place in the verbal action, "sees the Lord." The presence or absence of the article points the arrow from the participle to the word or words with which it is to be associated. With an article—participle points to the noun. Without an article—participle points to the verb.

Now look again at the two sentences. The first Greek sentence has the articular participle, ὁ λέγων, that is, it is in the attributive position. The participle is preceded by the article ὁ, so it refers to (or points toward) the noun that precedes it (ἀπόστολος). It refers, that is, to the one who is talking. That is the emphasis of the attributive participle. The best way to translate this Greek sentence is to say that "the apostle, *the one who is saying these things,* sees the Lord." The articular participle in effect answers the question, Which apostle is seeing the Lord? And the answer is, "The one who is saying these things is the one who is seeing the Lord."

When the participle is anarthrous, however—when it appears without the article—it is circumstantial. This is the case with the second Greek sentence: ὁ ἀπόστολος λέγων ταῦτα βλέπει τὸν κύριον. Here the participle goes with the verb, which sets up the "circumstances" of the action. We must work out an English reading of the sentence, however, since the English language does not provide a ready equivalency for what emerges. It will be something like this: "The apostle, in saying these things, is seeing the Lord." With that translation, we can then proceed to interpret the sentence with considerable accuracy: The apostle sees the Lord in the act of saying these things (whatever these things are). Or the apostle is able to see the Lord in the act, or the process, of saying these things. The emphasis, in other words, must relate the participle phrase, "saying these things" with the verbal phrase, "sees the Lord."

One caution is important here. Often in Greek constructions, the participle and its article may not be together, but may instead be separated from each other by another word. Most often that word is a conjunction meaning "for" or "but" or "since," or some such word as that. When conjunctions precede a participle, we should either consider them invisible or move them from their place between an article and its participle to another position. For purposes of deciding whether a participle has a preceding article, conjunctions must not be allowed to interfere. Thus, a construction such as οἱ δὲ ἀποκριθέντες εἶπαν ("And they, the ones answering, said") is articular. Ἀποκριθέντες is the participle, οἱ the article, and δὲ a conjunction (translated "and"). Even though the conjunction separates the article from the participle, it is in effect overlooked in determining the function of the participle and, when translated, moved to a position preceding the article. In Principle 5 we shall consider the importance of conjunctions.

With this distinction between attributive and circumstantial participles in mind, go hunting in an interlinear New Testament for examples of participles. Look especially for their articular and anarthrous constructions. You can pick almost any text in the gospels or the epistles and begin looking. Just as with the word λέγων, the most common ending that identifies a singular participle in the New Testament is -ων. Another common ending is -οντες, used with some plural participles. Of course these are not the only endings with which participles appear, but you should learn that either of these two endings on a verb signals a participle.

Turn, for example, to Matthew 9:31, where you find: οἱ δὲ ἐξελθόντες διεφήμισαν αὐτὸν ἐν ὅλῃ τῇ γῇ ἐκείνῃ ("They but going out spread about him all—land that"). Of course, these words must be reconfigured into decent English, and most interlinears will help you do that. Soon, however, you will do this quite easily on your own. So the sentence in Matthew 9:31 may be translated, "But they, going out, spread about him (spread information or good things about him, as preceding verses suggest) in all that land (or region)." In this sentence find the participle ἐξελθόντες. Notice the participle ending of a plural word, -όντες. Is it an attributive or a circumstantial participle? To answer the question, you must drop or reposition the conjunction δὲ ("but"). Before δὲ is the article οἱ, and it goes with the participle. It is an attributive participle, and it provides the emphasis of the sentence, namely, that "the ones going out" spread the news about him in all of that land.

If you continue reading, you find another participle, this time, however, an anarthrous one. At verse 35 of Matthew 9, we encounter a long and very interesting sentence with three parallel participles:

Καὶ περιῆγεν ὁ Ἰησοῦς τὰς πόλεις πάσας καὶ τὰς
And went about - Jesus the cities all and the

κώμας διδάσκων ἐν ταῖς συναγωγαῖς αὐτῶν καὶ
villages, teaching in the synagogues of them and

κηρύσσων τὸ εὐαγγέλιον τῆς βασιλείας καὶ
preaching the gospel of the kingdom and

θεραπεύων πᾶσαν νόσον καὶ πᾶσαν μαλακίαν.
healing   every disease and every illness.

Here there is a main sentence, "And Jesus went about all the cities and all the villages." One could put a period there and stop the sentence. But what follows is a complex and beautiful series of participial phrases. You can look up the words and find them, but you already recognize the –ων endings that give away some of the singular participles in Greek. Find the participles: διδάσκων ("teaching"), κηρύσσων ("preaching"), θεραπεύων ("healing"). Note that these are participles without articles (anarthrous), so all three are circumstantial. What do they modify, or, perhaps better, emphasize? They do not emphasize the one doing the acting (that is, ὁ Ἰησοῦς). Instead they modify the action of the main verb in the sentence, which is the word for "going about" (περιῆγεν). This is what Jesus was "going about" *doing* in all the cities and villages. It is not so much that it was Jesus who was doing these things as it is *what* Jesus was doing. That is the interpretive accent that anarthrous, or circumstantial, participles provide. In such cases as this, students of the New Testament texts can discern the precise meanings that participles create.

Before proceeding, we should point out that the attributive use of the participle is its *adjectival form,* in which it does the work of an adjective. On the other hand, the circumstantial use of the participle is one of its *adverbial functions.* Instead of modifying a noun, it makes the verb more exact.

Substantive Participles

The "substantive" use of the participle is closely related to the articular form that we have just examined. When a participle is used as a substantive, rather than modifying a noun or a noun phrase, as an adjective does, it functions as a noun itself.

Adjectives offer a good parallel to how the participle works in this case. Adjectives generally modify a noun, and in that sense they are attributive because they assign some characteristic to the noun. (See Principle 9.) However, on occasion adjectives function as nouns. An example is ἀγαθός ("good"). The Greek phrase might use the adjective to identify a person as good, for example, ὁ ἀγαθὸς ἄνθρωπος ("the good person," as in Luke 6:45). However, ὁ ἀγαθός can of itself mean "the good person" with a noun implied in the adjective, or it can serve as a noun by itself, meaning "the good" (see Rom. 7:13).

In a similar way, an articular participle can work as a noun does, that is, substantively. The example we used earlier, ὁ λέγων, is a substantive participle, since it works as a noun ("the saying one"). Unlike the attributive participle, however, *when a participle serves as a noun (i.e., substantively), it can be either with or without an article.*

The substantive participle is virtually always understood as "the one who," which is similar, of course, to the attributive form. However, here the emphasis falls on the "one who," since no other noun in this "substantive" mode is designated. In other words, the participle does not modify another noun but stands by itself as a noun (that is, functions as a noun).

Take this phrase as an example: ὁ πιστεύων εἰς τὸν ἐγείροντα. Two participles appear, πιστεύων, (from πιστεύω, the verb "to believe") and ἐγείροντα (from ἐγείρω, to "arouse" or "raise"), and each is preceded by an article, ὁ or τὸν. This phrase makes for very interesting thought. It is literally translated, "the one who is believing in the one who is raising." The presence of the articles places the full weight of emphasis on the persons who in this case are doing the acting, that is, the believing and the raising. When it stands alone, the word πιστεύων means believing, but when an article is added before it and it is substantive, it becomes "the one who is believing." Note that in this phrase, one substantive participle is the subject (πιστεύων) and the other the object of the action (ἐγείροντα). This suggests the versatility of the substantive participle in Greek. The phrase can be translated, "the one who believes in the one who is rising."

Sometimes, depending on the context, when the participle's gender is masculine, the translation might express gender. Occasionally the article ὁ suggests that the participle should be translated, "he" or "the man," but more often it means simply "the" or the "one who." In Greek, gender is not usually a designation of "sex," but of language itself. Only the context will indicate whether the participle is actually referring to men, women, or things.

Temporal Participles

The fourth dimension of the participle you need to learn is not directly related to any of the three that we have discussed so far. While participles function as adjectives or even as nouns, the temporal ones relate specifically to the time dimension of the action in a sentence. Like the other two, it is often crucial not just to establish meaning, but to give a remarkable precision to that meaning.

In English, we have only two basic temporal or time-related forms of the participle, and they tend to be fairly weak in their emphases. We have present participles, which usually end in -ing, and past participles, which usually end in -ed, -d, -t, or -en. The latter are usually written as past tense words, such as "looked," "slept," or "spoken." By and large, they are words that can be taken as simple past tense verbs because they appear exactly as the past tense verbs appear. Only the context in which they are found can distinguish them specifically as participles. In Greek, however, according to some scholars, the participle has as many as ten distinctive forms—present, future, aorist, perfect active, present and perfect middle or passive, future and aorist middle, and future and aorist passive. This reflects both a fine-tuning of the participle within the language and a sense of a special force or power accorded to it.

For our purposes, we will be concerned with only three of the participle forms—the present, the aorist, and the future. However, this must be clearly understood: *In terms of its temporal character, the participle is always an adjunct to the main verb (or verbs) of a sentence.* J. Gresham Machen (whom we quoted at the beginning of this discussion) says it very well: "The tense of the participle is relative to the time of the leading verb."[3] In other words, the statement of time in a sentence is always contained within the main verb. Therefore, in every case, the idea of present tense, aorist tense, or future tense contained within the participle is *in relation to* the time or action of the main verb of the clause or sentence.

To put this as simply as possible:

If a participle is in the *present tense*, it is viewed as containing action that takes place *simultaneously* with the main verb of the sentence.

If the participle is in the *aorist tense*, it is understood that the action of the participle took place, and was completed, *before* the action of the main verb in the sentence took, or is taking, place.

If the participle is in the *future tense*, it is understood that it will take place at some point *after* the action of the main verb is completed.

Often a participle in the future tense conveys a sense of a goal to be reached as a result of the action contained within the main verb of the sentence. This is true whether the main verb of the sentence is present, aorist, or future. No matter when the action of the main verb is set, the action of the participle is always *in relation to* that verb.

Translating Temporal Participles

How then do we translate the action of various participles? All participles can be spoken of as ongoing action, however awkward it may

---

[3]Machen, 105.

sometimes be. The use of the -ing ending in English can be worked into speaking so that one remains clear about the nature of the participle. Often, however, an English phrase can be used to indicate this particular "time" dimension of the participle in its relation to a main verb. *With a present participle* (one in which the participle's action is concurrent with that of the main verb), the phrase, "while one does this," is useful. Or the phrase "as one goes about this" is another way to say the same thing. The phrase itself suggests the concurrent actions. For instance, John 6:59 reads, Ταῦτα εἶπεν ἐν συναγωγῇ διδάσκων ἐν Καφαρναύμ ("He said these things in a synagogue while teaching in Capernaum"). The main verb is aorist (εἶπεν), and the participle is present (διδάσκων). The present participle describes an action that took place in that period during which Jesus "said these things."

When a participle is aorist, a phrase can be used that makes clear that the action is prior to that of the main verb. Most common here are phrases such as "after one has done this, then" followed by the action of the main verb; or even "when one had done that, then," and the main verb's action follows. A variation on our earlier example will illustrate this point: ὁ ἀπόστολος εἰπὼν ταῦτα βλέπει τὸν κύριον. The main verb (βλέπει) is present tense, but the participle, εἰπὼν, is the aorist participial form of λέγω and describes an action completed in a past time. Hence, the apostles said these things and then "saw the Lord." We might translate the sentence, "After the apostle had said these things," (or "when the apostle had said these things") "she or he saw the Lord." There are other variations, and you can work with English in order to clarify the nature of the participle's time in any particular text.

This temporal quality of the participle is evident in one of the more interesting texts in the New Testament, namely, Matthew 28:19–20, what the church has historically called the great commission of Jesus. The precision of the temporal qualities of the participles in these verses shows what preachers can learn from a study of them in the Greek. The saying is set up with verse 18, but then 19 and 20 read like this in an interlinear:

πορευθέντες οὖν   μαθητεύσατε πάντα τὰ
Going   therefore disciple   all the

ἔθνη, βαπτίζοντες αὐτοὺς εἰς τὸ ὄνομα τοῦ
nations, baptizing   them into the name of the

πατρὸς καὶ τοῦ υἱοῦ καὶ τοῦ ἁγίου πνεύματος,
father and the son and the holy   spirit,

διδάσκοντες αὐτοὺς τηρεῖν   πάντα ὅσα
teaching   them to observe all   whatsoever

ἐνετειλάμην ὑμῖν·
I command   to you.

This well-known text has a precision to it that is often not appreciated, and that the preacher might very well choose to explore. In most translations, this sentence begins with an imperative: "Go, therefore, into all the world and make disciples of all nations." But let's look more closely at the language of the sentence, particularly at its main verb and its participles.

Four words here should be looked up in an analytical lexicon. The four in the order in which they appear in the passage are: πορευθέντες, μαθητεύσατε, βαπτίζοντες, and διδάσκοντες. Three of the four are participles, but the second of the four is not. Rather, it is a second person plural, aorist, imperative, active form of μαθητεύω. This is the main verb, and it supplies the imperative in the sentence. Since this is an *aorist* imperative, however, it means that it was a command given in the past. (This may be related to the fact that the text is presented as a quotation of what Jesus said at some point in the past.) This means that the primary sense of the sentence is in reference to an action already completed. The root verb (μαθητεύω) means to help people understand. It does not mean "to teach" *per se,* but puts more direct emphasis on the "learner" than does the word "teach" (διδάσκω). Μαθητεύω means to "disciple" others, assisting them in becoming practicing disciples, and doing everything necessary to help them grasp and put into practice what they learn.

The imperative is not the first word of verse 19, πορευθέντες, as is implied when it is translated as the imperative, "Go." The imperative of the verse is that one "disciple" others and "help people learn." What we see is that the other three words in our list above are all participles: πορευθέντες, βαπτίζοντες, and διδάσκοντες. When you look them up and note the parameters given for each by an analytical lexicon, one thing is particularly striking. The first of the three (πορευθέντες) is an aorist participle, and the remaining two (βαπτίζοντες, and διδάσκοντες) are present participles. Πορευθέντες is the aorist participial form of its root verb, πορεύομαι, and means to move from place to place, to move about.

What are we to make of the meaning of these three participles as they relate to the action commanded by the main verb's imperative? Since the main verb (μαθητεύσατε) is aorist, it means that it is a command from the past, a completed action: "You are to make of people true learners!"

But the aorist participle that begins the sentence gives the idea of "going" before it mentions the command to "make learners." Those who are addressed in this passage are *already going*. They are already in the process of "having gone," even before the aorist "command" was, or has been, given. One is already "moving about," going here and there. It is in that "going here and there" that the disciples are now faced with a new directive: to make learners.

The other two participles, however, baptizing (βαπτίζοντες) and teaching (διδάσκοντες) are both *present* participles. Their action is simultaneous with the making of the learners. As one goes about making learners, one is also to be about the work of baptizing and teaching. A possible translation that would better capture the sense of this sentence is, "Therefore, going about, make disciples of (or 'disciple') all people, while you are baptizing them...and teaching them." What are the theological and practical implications of this understanding of the so-called "great commission"?

The point of this analysis is that there is a striking precision of language and intent created by careful attention to Greek participles. Those who wrote knew how to use the participles to say what they wanted to say with some exactness. Finding that exactness by one's own attention to the participles throws a light on almost any New Testament text, just as it does on the "great commission." This fact not only invites students of the New Testament to careful study but also offers valuable insights for the preaching to those who seek to break open and analyze the text.

PRINCIPLE 4

The Play of the Prepositions

In Greek, prepositions function essentially as they do in English, and it is as difficult to write a Greek sentence without one as it is an English sentence. Most scholars believe that prepositions started out as adverbs, since their primary function is to mark the direction and position of the action designated by the verb. As a result, prepositions make verbs more precise and often add new dimensions and emphases to verbal action. Specifically, *prepositions define the relationship of a verb's action with regard to nouns (or substantives).* To work efficiently with the Greek text of the New Testament, it is necessary to learn the prepositions.

The list of Greek prepositions, though, is fairly long, and in this chapter we can provide only a digest of a selected number of them. But the list is not as daunting as it sounds at first, since many, if not most, of the Greek prepositions are quite recognizable from their English counterparts. However, we advise you to make a list of your own and keep it at hand for study, at least until you know them on sight.

Prepositions are found in two forms in the Greek text. First, they often *stand alone,* virtually always modifying the action of a verb or verbal form in relation to a noun. As we shall see, they are small but very important words. Second, prepositions are sometimes *prefixes of words,* two and three letter additions attached to the front of a word. These, too, are profoundly important uses of the preposition. They are usually prefixed to add clarity of direction carried by the word, usually a verb but sometimes a noun. Even more important than clarity, a prefix adds a conscious, powerful statement of emphasis of direction to the word with which it is associated. It is important to note how a prefix changes the meaning of the verb to which it is attached and learn to read and interpret those words with the full weight of the prepositional prefix. However, be warned that in a few cases where a preposition is prefixed to a verb there is no clear explanation for why or how a resultant meaning emerges. For instance, how the addition of the preposition ἀπό to the verb ἀλγέω creates a word that means "to cease to feel" is unclear (Eph. 4:19).

In addition to modifying, clarifying, and emphasizing the action or location of verbs, prepositions also have objects, which are the nouns that usually follow them and to which they point. A sentence such as "He went to the store" makes this clear. He went where? In this case, "store" is the object of the preposition. The verb is "went," and the preposition "to" clarifies the verb. It makes clear the action of "going." Going "to" the store distinguishes this going from, say, going "through" the store. In simple sentences that have their clear counterparts in the Greek text, one becomes aware of the crucial role that prepositions play in opening up the meaning of a New Testament sentence.

For our purpose the question is: How should we work with the meaning of prepositions? Most Greek grammar books take pains to emphasize that any given preposition can have a wide variety of meanings, depending on the case of its object, among other things. (For more on case, see Principle 8 on nouns and adjectives.) You can, of course, learn all these variations, but we suggest that you work with certain "primary meanings" whenever they work well. You may want to build or acquire a chart of the variations of prepositions in terms of case. A few grammars include such a chart.[1] However, for the preacher, knowing the primary meaning of the preposition works very well, and an analytical lexicon will tell you if the general meaning of a preposition happens to be different in a given text. We do want you to learn to "play" with a preposition's primary meaning within any given phrase or sentence. Ironically, "playing" with a preposition can often yield new and highly usable insights into a text, and throughout this chapter we shall try to illustrate this.

Following is a listing, with some brief explanation, of the most important prepositions. Admittedly, the definitions are in many cases oversimplifications, but they give you a general sense of each word's meaning.

---

[1]See, for instance, H. E. Dana and Julius R. Mantey, *A Manual Grammar of the Greek New Testament*, 2d ed. (Cambridge: Cambridge University Press, 1959), 114.

διά—**Through**

Sometimes (as when used with the accusative) διά can carry the idea of "because of," but the notion of "going through" or "acting through" should be the first sense one uses to discern the meaning of this preposition when it occurs with a noun in the genitive case. "Going through" tends to refer to a place toward which the action of the verb points. On the other hand, "acting through" refers to a medium of some kind through which the action is mediated. Those are the major uses of διά.

In Matthew 7:13, Εἰσέλθατε διὰ τῆς στενῆς πύλης means, "Enter through the narrow gate." And in 2 Corinthians 5:7, διὰ πίστεως γὰρ περιπατοῦμεν translates, "for we are walking through faith." Notice that in the first case, "through" means a passage through a period of time, and in the second case, it is a means by which one lives. There are times when the direct idea of "through" will seem a bit awkward. However, even with that awkwardness, the idea of "through" can throw new light on even the most familiar texts.

The preposition διά can also be seen used as a prefix in a word such as διαμένεις, which we find, among other places, in Hebrews 1:11. If you look this word up in an analytical lexicon, it will tell you that διαμένεις is made up of two words: the preposition διά, and the verb μένω. When you look up that verb, you learn that it means to dwell, or to lodge, or to stay in a place (see Principle 10). Yet the usual translation of διαμένεις is simply "remain." What difference, then, does the prefix διά make? The whole of the first half of Hebrews 1:11 reads, αὐτοὶ ἀπολοῦνται, σὺ δὲ διαμένεις, which we can translate, "they will perish, but you are remaining." When you think about διαμένεις in this context, the simple translation "remaining" takes on additional dimensions and becomes rich and full. "You are *remaining through.*" Here the compound verb suggests, "you are sticking it out *through* whatever comes. You are absolutely steadfast through whatever you are facing. You are living, lodging, dwelling where you are. You are facing it all and not perishing."

That is how one can "work through" a word with a prepositional prefix, translating the word, but adding to it the full weight of the preposition that it carries. It may not be that every word with a prefix proves to be as rich as διαμένεις, and occasionally it may be hard to see how the preposition changes the meaning of the word in any significant way. However, the results of taking a prepositional prefix seriously are always worth the research and reflection.

ἀπό—Off or Away From

This common preposition tends to convey the idea of separating from, or moving "off of the edge" of something, and of "getting back away from" the edge. Those distinctive meanings of the word can be very important and should be learned. A simple use of ἀπό is found in Matthew 8:11, in which Jesus promises πολλοὶ ἀπὸ ἀνατολῶν καὶ δυσμῶν ἥξουσιν ("many will come *from* east and west"). We will shortly distinguish ἀπο from the next preposition, ἐκ, which carries the idea of "out of" or "away from."

Ἀπό is also one of the most common prefixes, from which countless verbs are made. When a word is constructed with ἀπό, sometimes the third letter (o) will change. This is an example of a grammatical rule concerning the first letter of the word to which a prefix is attached. If the prefix word ends in a vowel and the word to which it is attached begins with a vowel, then most often the concluding vowel of the prefix is dropped. For example, ἀπέχω is the verb ἔχω ("to have") with ἀπό attached. Since adding the prefix puts two vowels together, the omicron of ἀπό is dropped. Often one can still recognize it as a prefix, but sometimes it is necessary to look up the compound word in order to discover the presence of the preposition. When ἀπό is a prefix, it may add a significant dimension of both meaning and force to the word with which it appears. So for instance, ἀπέχω usually means "to receive," "be distant," "keep away," or "abstain."

Another example of a compound verb is in Hebrews 11:26, where the word ἀποβλέπω is clearly a construction of ἀπό and βλέπω, a verb that means "to see," to "have sight." Βλέπω usually carries the weight of "gazing upon" something. So when the verb appears with ἀπό attached, the new word suggests "gazing away from other things," or diverting one's gaze or sight from other things and, by implication, toward something specific. It is to look earnestly away from things that are calling for one's gaze. Prefixing the preposition ἀπό onto βλέπω gives that verb a new meaning and creates a powerful and significant idea.

ἐκ—Out of or From Within

This is the preposition that appears to be similar in meaning to ἀπό, but which denotes a somewhat different sense. Grammarians, however, are far from agreement concerning the precise distinction between the two. In some ways, it is considered a stronger word than ἀπό, and implies a coming out from deep within something. In the story of Philip and the Ethiopian in Acts 8:39, there is the phrase ὅτε δὲ ἀνέβησαν ἐκ τοῦ ὕδατος, "and when they came up out of the water." In this case, ἐκ is "out of" the water, and in a sense suggests from deep "within the water." In

Ephesians 4:29, reference is made to every corrupt word that proceeds out of one's mouth, and the phrase is ἐκ τοῦ στόματος ὑμῶν. In this setting, ἐκ implies the notion that what comes out of one's mouth does so from "deep within" one's being.

Ἐκ is also a prominent prefix to which one should stay attuned. The verb ἐκβάλλω, for instance, is common in the New Testament. Obviously, it is a compound verb comprising the preposition ἐκ and the verb βάλλω. By itself the verb is already a strong word and means to "throw" or "place." But when a writer adds the prefix ἐκ to it, the word becomes even more vigorous and takes on the meaning "to throw out," "to cast out," or "to reject." In Acts 27:38, for example, the ship on which Paul was sailing had to be lightened because of the storm, so all excess food was ἐκβαλλόμενοι——"being thrown out" into the sea. The word is also used in other contexts, but with the full force of the ἐκ in place. Interestingly, Mark 1:12 uses the verb ἐκβάλλω to speak of how the Spirit "threw Jesus out" into the wilderness to be tempted.

One should be aware, though, that when ἐκ appears as a prefix with some words, the κ changes to ξ and appears as ἐξ. So you may encounter the word ἐξελέηοντο, which the lexicon will tell you is constructed of ἐκ plus λέγω. We know ἐκ (with the κ here turned into ξ) means out, and λέγω means to say or to speak. So the resulting verb (ἐκλέγω) means to "speak out" with force. Actually it also may mean to speak out from deep within oneself. But it goes further. The idea is that when people choose to speak, their speaking aligns them with certain things and against other things. It is a strong, rich concept, created from a word for speaking and the preposition ἐκ.

This important preposition is sometimes also used to identify from where one comes, where one originates, or where one's roots are. In 1 John 2:19, the author speaks of people who have separated themselves from the congregation and say they are ἐξ ἡμῶν, "not of us" or "not out of us." Later, in 2:29 the same author states that "everyone who does right is born *of him*" (ἐξ αὐτοῦ γεγέννηται, that is, "born of God" or "born out of God"). Their origin is from God.

ἐν and εἰς—In and Into

These prepositions are so closely related, and so common in the Greek New Testament, that we may consider them in tandem. They are distinctly different, however; and it is that difference that one must learn and use. Ἐν is the preposition of place, or even rest or repose (that is, "in"). It is where something "is." In some settings, ἐν can mean "with" or "by means of." But learn it as place, and let that guide what you find within almost every clause or sentence where ἐν appears.

Εἰς, on the other hand, is the preposition of movement, of motion. It means "into," as in the expression, "to go into." In fact, it is one of the most common words in the entire New Testament. Regardless of the clause or sentence in which it appears, you will do well to "play with" the idea of "going into," no matter whether that seems immediately to fit naturally or not. It will, invariably, suggest the nature of the text's meaning. For instance, what might it mean for an author to write of believing εἰς rather than believing ἐν Jesus? (Compare John 3:36 and 3:15.)

Εἰς is a prefix to about ten words used in the New Testament. An example is the verb εἰσακούω where it is linked with the verb ἀκούω, which means "to hear." One of the meanings of εἰσακούω, however, is "to obey." Obeying suggests a hearing that penetrates the will and produces action.

(Be careful not to confuse the prepositions εἰς and ἐν with εἷς and ἕν, which are forms of the number "one" or "someone." Notice the latter pair have rough breathing marks.)

ἐπί—Upon

This preposition does not so much mean "above" as "upon" or "on top of" and (with the dative case) "at." In Luke 2:14, for example, when the angels sing, "Peace upon earth," the phrase uses the word ἐπί: ἐπὶ γῆς εἰρήνη. There is a force to the preposition that we can add to the English phrase as we translate it. In some cases the preposition ἐπί does not simply designate a location. Its force sometimes carries into attitude. However, the grammarians say that the precise meaning of this preposition is so fluid as to be nearly impossible to pin down with certainty.[2] That frees us to think creatively about the variations of "upon" in terms of its meaning in any particular passage.

As an example, look at Matthew 18:13. There Jesus is talking about the lost sheep, and he says that when the sheep is found, the shepherd "rejoices over it," more than "over the ninety and nine." The word translated "over" in each case is ἐπί. Here we are invited to "play with" the preposition in that particular construction. It is not a throwaway word, but may have been carefully chosen and used. One rejoices "all over" that found lamb. With a different construction, the author could have said

---

[2]C. F. D. Moule, *An Idiom Book of New Testament Greek* (Cambridge: Cambridge University Press, 1959), 49.

the lamb's discovery was a cause for rejoicing without the use of the preposition. But the writer wanted to use the preposition ἐπί. Therefore, we should attend carefully to its impact on the meaning of the verse.

As with other prepositions, there are certain constructions with ἐπί in which the idea of "upon" seems remote and strange. On those occasions, let an interlinear's translation assist you. For instance, in Jesus' tiny parable in Luke 14:31–32, the text speaks of a king's seeing a mighty army marching toward his own meager forces. Verse 31 suggests that he would ask this question: εἰ δυνατός ἐστιν ἐν δέκα χιλιάσιν ὑπαντῆσαι τῷ μετὰ εἴκοσι χιλιάδων ἐρχομένῳ ἐπʼ αὐτόν; ("if he is able with ten thousand to oppose the one who comes *against* him with twenty thousand?"). In this case, ἐπὶ is properly translated "against." But what if we thought about the preposition in terms of its general meaning "upon"? The enemy comes against the king, and the opposing troops come "upon" him.

κατά—Down

Κατά usually means "down" or "down from," but not "under." This is an active-oriented preposition. It suggests *movement* more than location or position and should be read that way. Again, this is a very common preposition and a very important prefix. We find words that begin with κατά throughout the New Testament, and an analytical lexicon will always indicate the component parts of the resulting words. For example, καταισχύνω comprises the preposition κατά and the verb αἰσχύνω, which means to "shame" or "dishonor" or "disgrace." In 1 Corinthians 1:27, Paul says God chose the foolish things of the world in order that God "might shame the wise men" (καταισχύνῃ τοὺς σοφούς). (Notice that in this compounding of the verb, the last alpha of κατά and the first one of αἰσχύνω are merged.) Because of the prepositional prefix, the word for shame becomes a complex idea, conveying not just shame but the added notion of "bringing down" into shame. It is well worth our trouble to think through the notion of καταισχύνῃ, which Paul seems deliberately to have chosen.

It is not uncommon to find κατά used in the sense of "against." Still other times, it seems to convey the idea of trying to bring another down. In Acts 24:1, for example, charges were brought κατὰ τοῦ Παύλου, "against Paul." Still, the idea of "down" may be a part of this sense of the word. However, note too that κατά sometimes (usually with the accusative case, which we will discuss later) means, "according to," and the titles attached to the four gospels read, for example, ΚΑΤΑ ΛΟΥΚΑΝ, "According to Luke."

Depending on the words that follow them, many prepositions appear in what seem to be an abbreviated form. This is the case with κατά, which will be spelled κατ᾽ or καθ᾽ whenever it precedes a word that begins with a vowel. For example, γνωστὸν δὲ ἐγένετο καθ᾽ ὅλης τῆς Ἰόππης, "and it became known throughout all Joppa" (Acts 9:42).

ἀνά—Up

This is the counterpart to κατά and means "up." It appears as a prefix of verbs, and also stands by itself, but is sometimes spelled ἀν᾽. It does not refer primarily to a location or position, but to upward motion, and we should read it in a text with that notion.

The same is true when ἀνά appears as a prefix. The best-known word that takes ἀνά as a prefix is ἀνάστασις. An analytical lexicon may explain the combination ἀνάστασις as ἀνά plus the verb ἵστημι, which means "to stand" or "to stand up erectly." When the preposition ἀνά is added to the verb, however, it becomes "to rise up," with the emphasis on the word "up." See Luke 2:34, where Simeon says to Mary that her child "is destined for the fall and the rising (ἀνάστασιν) of many in Israel." In the New Testament, ἀνάστασις (or some variant of it) is most often translated "resurrection." Significantly, the presence of the preposition as a prefix gives the actual force to the word when it is used to talk about "resurrection."

An easy contrast between the use of κατά and ἀνά as prefixes are in the combinations ἀναβαίνω ("to ascend") and καταβαίνω ("to descend") found in John 3:13: καὶ οὐδεὶς ἀναβέβηκεν εἰς τὸν οὐρανὸν εἰ μὴ ὁ ἐκ τοῦ οὐρανοῦ καταβάς, ὁ υἱὸς τοῦ ἀνθρώπου, which translates, "No one has ascended into heaven except the one who descended from heaven, the Son of Man." The two words are also used more mundanely for "going up" and "going down" geographically (see Lk. 2:4 and 19:5).

μετά—Together With

This is a word that often conveys the idea of "holding together with." It is a preposition that suggests doing things to, for, or with someone else. The root meaning may be "in the midst of," but it is most often translated simply "with." (However, when used with the accusative case, as we will discuss below it means "after.")

When μετά appears as a prefix with another word, we can explore how this notion of "together with" can be merged with the attached word, and that exploration often yields interesting, significant insights. For example, a word such as that in Luke 3:11, μεταδότω (from the verb, μεταδίδωμι) is worth examining. Μετά is attached to the verb δίδωμι, which means "to give," "to hand over," or "entrust." Luke reports that John the Baptist says, "Whoever has two coats must share [μεταδότω—an aorist imperative of μεταδίδωμι] with anyone who has none." However, the saying is about more than giving a coat to another. "Giving with" may suggest that it is also the act of establishing a relationship with the person to whom the coat is given—or at least the idea is worth thinking about. The μετά as a prefix provides a striking dimension to the word and to the text itself.

Among its other most impressive uses as a prefix are the μετά-words that suggest change. See μετά in the New Testament word μετανοέω. In this case, μετά is combined with the word for "mind" (νοῦς) to produce the verb "change of mind." This is the word most often translated "repentance," but that means a transformation of the whole person.

πρό—Before

This preposition is the source of the prefix "pro," found in many English words, such as "proactive." In addition to its positional meaning and emphasis, πρό can also often have an important temporal meaning, depending on the phrase in which it appears. Standing alone in a text, this word can have fascinating overtones. This is the case in Galatians 1:17, where Paul is talking about his early life. He says that he did not go up to Jerusalem τοὺς πρὸ ἐμοῦ ἀποστόλους, "to the apostles before me." In other words, he denies going to see those who were established apostles. Paul is concerned to say that he was also designated an apostle, or came to understand himself as one, but did not depend on the others. He was an apostle as they were, except that they came πρό ("before") him in time. In other cases, however, the word has a simple positional meaning. In Acts 12:6, for example, the guards are πρὸ τῆς θύρας ("before" or "in front of the door") of the cell in which Peter is imprisoned.

As even a casual reading of an interlinear text will demonstrate, πρό is also a common prefix. When you have discovered the root word in the lexicon and understand its meaning, you can begin to work with πρό as both a qualifier of meaning and a provider of emphasis. For instance, when is the temporal sense of πρό emphasized, and when is it not?

In the word προλαμβάνω, πρό has been added as a prefix to λαμβάνω, which is a verb that means "to receive" or "take." Προλαμβάνω can mean "to do something beforehand" (for instance, Mk. 14:8), and there the temporal sense of πρό is still evident. However, when is the temporal sense of πρό in προλαμβάνω emphasized, and when is it not? The compound verb can also mean to "overtake or surprise" a person (for example, Galatians 6:1), and in this case the prefix has a conceptual rather than a temporal force. With the help of our tools, we have the opportunity to play with both possibilities.

πρός—Facing, Near

Πρός is obviously related to πρό. Both as a stand-alone word and as a prefix, πρός may denote either position or motion (nearly always with the accusative case). When it indicates motion, πρός suggests motion toward something or someone (see Mt. 3:13), but we will encounter it most often in its sense of position—"at," "near," and so forth. A more complicated use of the preposition entails its meaning "concerning" and "in view of." Still, a general sense of near or facing is a helpful way to approach any use of πρός.

Sometimes it is essential that we reflect on a complex preposition such as this one in order to allow it to throw light on a text. A good example is Ephesians 3:4, where the author is talking about the reader's having "heard about" his stewardship of God's grace and of the mystery he tried to make known to them "as he had previously written." But there was apparently some skepticism among the readers, and so he is writing about it again. Then verse 4 adds, πρὸς ὅ δύνασθε ἀναγινώσκοντες νοῆσαι. This is a difficult phrase, and interlinear texts as well as commentators have trouble with it. Some translate the phrase, "as to what you are able by reading to understand." But in order to get a sense of the meaning of πρός in this phrase, we should begin with the idea of "near" or "toward." The author seems to suggest that readers will understand him much better *after* they receive and finally read what he is now writing. In this case, it appears that πρός has some sense of "in accordance with." Readers can make their judgments "in accordance with" what they can read, that is, when the letter is "near." The preposition πρός is very helpful, but also complex. It may help to start with its major meaning and work with it as part of a larger context.

παρά—Beside

This is most often a position or location preposition, from which many Greek (and some) English words are constructed. Some scholars suggest that this is a preposition that can have about as many meanings as it has uses, but all of them will be variations of "beside" or "alongside" or "an alignment of things." Sometimes it refers to location alongside another person or thing, and other times movement toward coming beside another. A common usage is found in John 1:39, where the disciples went to see where Jesus was staying, καὶ παρ᾽ αὐτῷ ἔμειναν τὴν ἡμέραν ἐκείνην, "and they stayed with (or beside) him that day."

However, παρά particularly adds its special emphasis when it serves as a prefix for another word. For example, the common New Testament word παρκαλέω is a combination of the preposition παρά and the verb καλέω. This prefix enhances the significance of καλέω many times over. The verb means "I call," and—when prefixed with παρά—it is a strong calling, a pleading or a beseeching. Literally, however, that meaning is created by the idea of "I am calling to my side." So the word sometimes means to "invite" or "call on another for aid." That is the idea conveyed by the addition of the prepositional prefix.

περί—Around or About

As one should have been able to tell by now, many Greek prepositions have close English counterparts and are not difficult to learn. Περί is a particularly good example. Many English words have "peri-" prefixes, such as perimeter. At one level, περί refers to circumference, to the border or the distance around something. But like so many of these prepositions, at another level, it is sometimes used metaphorically.

In its metaphorical use, περί has the sense of what we might call "coming full circle," or being completely finished. One finds that meaning at several points in the New Testament, for example, in reference to the removal of sin. Our sins are "completely" taken away. For instance, in Matthew 26:28, it has the sense of "for the sake of": τὸ αἷμά μου τῆς διαθήκης τὸ περὶ πολλῶν ἐκχυννόμενον ("my blood of the covenant which is poured out *for* [or *for the sake of*] many"). Here it appears περί is used almost synonymously with ὑπέρ, since the parallels to this passage in Mark 14:24, Luke 22:20, and 1 Corinthians 11:24 use ὑπέρ instead of περί. You can sometimes use the word "surrounding" as a way to explore περί in various texts. To do so opens some most interesting doors of meaning. The word is also used to mean "with regard to" and "before," among others.

ὑπέρ and ὑπό—Over and Under

These are common prepositions and are easy to remember. We can understand both as locational or positional, but also at times as having a metaphorical meaning as well. Actually, however, the New Testament never uses ὑπέρ in a simple spatial sense of "over." That role is reserved for ἐπί (see for instance, Jas. 5:14, where "over" in the expression "pray over" translates ἐπί.) One exception is Hebrews 9:5, where ὑπέρ appears as a prefix in ὑπεάνω to say the cherubim were "above" the altar. However, New Testament writers almost always use ὑπέρ to express superiority or rank. So for instance, God places Jesus "over" (ὑπέρ) all things in the church

(Eph. 1:22). For this sense, it is sometimes used as a prefix to suggest "extreme." This is the case when the Philippian hymn prefixes the verb ὑψόω ("to exalt") with ὑπέρ in order to declare that God "highly exalted (ὑπερύψωσεν)" Christ (Phil. 2:9).

Used metaphorically (and with the genitive case), ὑπέρ means "on behalf of" or "concerning." Jesus' words at the Last Supper in Mark 14:24, Luke 22:20, and 1 Corinthians 11:24 use ὑπέρ in the sense of "on behalf of." Second Thessalonians 2:1 is an example of the use of ὑπέρ to mean "concerning" or "about." The chapter begins with ὑπὲρ τῆς παρουσίας τοῦ κυρίου...which translates "concerning (or with regard to) the coming of the Lord."

Ὑπό, however, can be used to designate both a spatial sense of under and a metaphorical sense of those who are "under" authority of another. In Matthew 8:8–9 we see both of these uses in the words of the centurion who asks Jesus to heal his ailing servant: Κύριε, οὐκ εἰμὶ ἱκανὸς ἵνα μου ὑπὸ τὴν στέγην εἰσέλθῃς,...καὶ γὰρ ἐγὼ ἄνθρωπός εἰμι ὑπὸ ἐξουσίαν, ἔχων ὑπ᾽ ἐμαυτὸν στρατιώτας...("Lord, I am not worthy to have you come *under* my roof...for I am a man *under* authority with soldiers *under* me"). The first use of ὑπό means under in the spatial sense, while the next two refer to rank and station.

When used with the genitive case, ὑπό can also suggest what is called "agency," or the means by which something is done, but that usage too follows from the notion of "under." Note the use of ὑπό in the phrase from Matthew 1:22...τὸ ῥηθὲν ὑπὸ κυρίου διὰ τοῦ προφήτου λέγοντος,...("the things spoken *by* the Lord through the prophets, saying"). With ὑπό, it is possible to understand the phrase as "spoken *under* the aegis of the Lord," or "*unde*r one's identity as Lord."

As with all prepositions, use of ὑπέρ and ὑπό can sometimes intensify the meaning contained in the phrases or sentences, but that can be detected only within the context of particular occurrences of the preposition.

σύν—Together With

Since it forms a part of so many very important New Testament words, this is an influential preposition. (When it appears as a prefix of some words, the ν sometimes changes to an μ, so that the word is spelled συμ-.) This is a "unifying" preposition, an emphatic expression of togetherness. As a prefix, it emphasizes togetherness no matter what the root word happens to be. Therefore, preachers need to watch for this significant little three-letter word.

Σύν is the preposition from which the Greek word συναγωγή is constructed. Pronounce that word out loud, and you immediately become aware that it is "synagogue." It means the assembly, the gathering, and the coming together of the family of God. The root verb is ἄγω, which means to "lead" or "bring." But with σύν as its prefix, it becomes "bring together" or "lead together." It is a gathering together with, a binding together of people. The addition of σύν to ἄγω creates not only a new word but a whole new concept as well.

ἀντί—Against, Instead of, or Face-to-Face

This remarkable preposition is less common in the New Testament, but when it appears, it carries dramatic force. It is the most oppositional of all the prepositions, and, in effect, the counterpart of σύν. Ἀντί indicates the replacement of one thing by another. Sometimes it identifies a simple matter of exchange (as, for example, in Jn. 1:16). Often, however, it indicates some struggle or conflict involved in the replacement .You find ἀντί standing alone as a preposition, for example, in Matthew 2:22, ἀκούσας δὲ ὅτι Ἀρχέλαος βασιλεύει τῆς Ἰουδαίας ἀντὶ τοῦ πατρὸς αὐτοῦ Ἡρῴδου ἐφοβήθη ἐκεῖ ἀπελθεῖν ("But hearing that Archelaus reigned over Judea instead of his father Herod, he feared to go there"). Here ἀντί is a replacement word (that is, Herod replaced by Archelaus), but in this context it conveys overtones of fear and even violence.

However, most of the time when we find ἀντί, it is a prefix on another word. As a prefix, it often carries this same strong sense of conflict. We find an example in John 19:12. There, Pilate is seeking to release Jesus. However, the religious leaders insist that to release him would make Pilate no friend of Caesar: πᾶς ὁ βασιλέα ἑαυτὸν ποιῶν ἀντιλέγει τῷ Καίσαρι ("everyone making himself a king is speaking against Caesar"). In this case, ἀντί combines with λέγει (third person, singular, present, indicative active of λέγω, "I speak") to produce ἀντιλέγω, which means to "speak against." It is an ominous word in this context, but made even more so by the use of ἀντί in the verb. This is nearly always a powerful preposition wherever one finds it in the Greek text.

Conclusion

Those are the major prepositions that appear throughout the Greek New Testament, both by themselves and as hearty additions to other words. They always add an important dimension to what a text means—and you need to learn them well. Once you do, you will be surprised at how much you are able to glean from the subtleties of a text.

PRINCIPLE 5

Connecting with the Conjunctions

As they are in English, conjunctions in Greek are connecting words. They tie together words, phrases, clauses, sentences, and sometimes even paragraphs. But most conjunctions do more than that. They also play a key role in how a phrase, a clause, a sentence, or even a paragraph is to be understood. This is the case because, while connecting parts, conjunctions also suggest the relationship between or among the parts. What a text means can sometimes turn on the use of a conjunction. In English, for instance, if we read, "he went to the store and came back," we learn one thing. However, the sentence, "he went to the store but came back," suggests something rather different. The disparity between "but" and "and" is very important. In short, students of the New Testament must learn to focus on and grasp the importance of this part of speech.

In this chapter, we shall divide the major Greek conjunctions into three kinds: those that introduce *explanatory* materials, those that indicate the *purpose* or the goal of something, and those that *shift the direction* of the sentence or the paragraph's action. In a real sense, besides their connecting function, conjunctions provide particular kinds and degrees of emphasis on things that are said in the text. The nature of a conjunction's emphasis is of special concern to students of the Greek New Testament. What we will call the *explanatory conjunctions* provide a distinct but relatively low level of emphasis on the materials that they introduce. The *purposive conjunctions,* however, furnish a noticeably higher level of emphasis on what follows them, since the purpose for which something is said is often as crucial as what is said. The *shifting conjunctions* offer the most intense emphasis for what follows them, since they are the conjunctions that change the direction of a discussion.

καί, a Simple Connector

Before we turn to these three kinds of conjunctions, however, we must take account of the most common conjunction of all. It does not fit well in any of the three categories we have just mentioned, because it is purely a connector and does not set out to provide any special emphasis or hint at any particular relationship between the parts. This conjunction is καί. It is the Greek equivalent of and most often translated with the English word "and." It connects equal pieces, in a sense, of whatever kind. Consider, for instance, Acts 6:7: Καὶ ὁ λόγος τοῦ θεοῦ ηὔξανεν καὶ ἐπληθύνετο ὁ ἀριθμὸς τῶν μαθητῶν ἐν Ἰερουσαλὴμ σφόδρα, ("And the word of God grew, and the number of the disciples in Jerusalem was multiplied greatly"). The word καί appears twice in the sentence and serves its normal and simple "connecting" function. The use of καί is not unusual, particularly in narratives, and often appears five and six times in the course of a single complex sentence.

However, καί is a remarkably versatile word. If a writer seeks to convey a certain nuance of connection, καί can sometimes mean "also," or even "indeed." But one can virtually always tell from an interlinear Greek text what καί means in a particular passage. In Hebrews 2:14, καί again appears twice, once with the text calling for the translation "and," while the other is best understood as "also": ἐπεὶ οὖν τὰ παιδία κεκοινώνηκεν αἵματος καὶ σαρκός, καὶ αὐτὸς παραπλησίως μετέσχεν τῶν αὐτῶν ("Since, therefore, the children have partaken of blood and of flesh, also he himself in like manner shared in same things.")

Having said this about καί, we now turn to the three classes of conjunctions. As with prepositions, there is no suitable substitute for making a list of key conjunctions (including the ones that we shall note here) and keeping the list nearby. With enough work in Greek, you will come to know the list and be able to spot and work with a range of the conjunctions. In almost all cases, if we concentrate on a key conjunction when it appears, the texture of what we find in the text will be greatly enhanced.

Explanatory Conjunctions

Explanatory conjunctions indicate either that what follows will explain what has gone before, or that what follows is a condition for understanding what has gone before. Although this certainly does not exhaust the list of these conjunctions, four of them are particularly important and are ones preachers should come to recognize.

Γάρ—*For*

Γάρ usually means "for" or "now" and is a common word in the Greek text. We can readily see the way in which saying "for" or "now" opens a path to some kind of clarification of what has just been said. For example, in Matthew 1:21, the verse begins, "And you will call his name Jesus," and continues αὐτὸς γὰρ σώσει τὸν λαὸν αὐτοῦ ἀπὸ τῶν ἁμαρτιῶν αὐτῶν ("for he shall save his people from their sins"). The explanatory nature of the γάρ clause is obvious both here and in most places in which it appears. Note that the conjunction γάρ appears as the second word in a sentence or clause, not the first.

As many conjunctions do, γάρ places stress on what follows it. It is like a flashing light that signals an important explanation. With the particular conjunctions that follow, the degree of this kind of emphasis will become stronger and stronger.

It should be noted, too, that a fairly common construction in the Greek text is the pairing of the words καί and γάρ to produce the expression, καὶ γάρ. When these two conjunctions appear together, we should assume a particularly strong emphasis on what surrounds them. For example, in Acts 19:40, the text reads: καὶ γὰρ κινδυνεύομεν ἐγκαλεῖσθαι στάσεως, which may be translated, "For indeed we are in danger of being charged with insurrection." The use of καὶ γάρ accents the text in such a way as to make the grammar match the force of the text's content. "Indeed" may seem a weak English equivalent, but it is about the best we can do to capture the concern of the Greek. The dual conjunctions καὶ γάρ add to the intensity of the statement.

ὅτι—*That (or Because)*

This is a common explanatory conjunction that stresses what follows it. See, for example, Mark 2:16: καὶ οἱ γραμματεῖς τῶν Φαρισαίων ἰδόντες ὅτι ἐσθίει μετὰ τῶν ἁμαρτωλῶν καὶ τελωνῶν ἔλεγον τοῖς μαθηταῖς αὐτοῦ· ὅτι μετὰ τῶν τελωνῶν καὶ ἁμαρτωλῶν ἐσθίει; The NRSV translates the verse this way: "When the scribes of the Pharisees saw *that* he was eating with sinners and tax collectors, they said to his disciples, 'Why does he eat with tax collectors and sinners?'" (Note the ; which is the Greek equivalent of our question mark.) In this case, ὅτι tells us what the scribes saw but also explains why the scribes ask their question of the disciples. The ὅτι is most often a direct statement of explanation, but often with a bit of a punch for what follows. In Mark 2:16 the punch is the fact that Jesus offends the scribes with his behavior and begins to alienate himself from the religious leaders. The second ὅτι in this passage represents the way in which this conjunction is used to introduce direct discourse.

Interestingly, some of the early Christian creeds in the New Testament use ὅτι to connect each affirmation with the others, suggesting the accentuation the conjunction provides. See 1 Corinthians 15:3–5 for an example. When ὅτι provides a reason for what precedes it, it may be translated "because." An example is found in Mark 1:34, where the narrator tells us that Jesus healed and cast out demons, "and he would not permit the demons to speak, because (ὅτι) they knew him."

ἄρα—*Therefore*

This is probably the most common of the several Greek conjunctions that have the sense of our English word "therefore." (An interlinear New Testament will inform you of some of the others.) Sometimes ἄρα may be translated as "then" (in the sense of "therefore"), "consequently," "so," or "as a result." But "therefore" is a simple translation with which to begin. Again, ἄρα tends to emphasize what follows it, which usually is a kind of conclusion drawn from the preceding clause or clauses. Moreover, when ἄρα appears with another conjunction, as it sometimes does, the emphatic nature of what is being said is all the more important.

A good example of the use of ἄρα with another conjunction is found in Galatians 3:7. Γινώσκετε ἄρα ὅτι οἱ ἐκ πίστεως, οὗτοι υἱοί εἰσιν Ἀβραάμ. Many of the interlinear Greek Testaments translate this sentence, "Know, therefore, that they that are of faith, these are the sons of Abraham." Notice that the conjunction ἄρα is set alongside ὅτι. This alignment of the two conjunctions is Paul's way of beginning a new topic in his discussion, and he does so by unmistakably stressing that Christian believers are Abraham's descendants even as the Jews are.

διό—*Therefore (strongest)*

This is an explanatory conjunction that is stronger than ὅτι, even though both are sometimes translated "therefore." One of the most interesting uses of διό is found in 2 Corinthians 4:13. Paul quotes Ἐπίστευσα, διὸ ἐλάλησα from Psalm 115:1 as it is found in the Septuagint, but then makes use of the quotation for his own purpose: κατὰ τὸ γεγραμμένον, Ἐπίστευσα, διὸ ἐλάλησα, καὶ ἡμεῖς πιστεύομεν, διὸ καὶ λαλοῦμεν. We might translate this, "according to (or subsumed under) the thing having been written, 'I believed, and therefore I spoke,' and we believe, and therefore we speak." Paul uses the conjunction διό twice in the parallel constructions. The psalmist believes *and for that reason speaks,* and likewise Paul and his companions "believe and *therefore* speak." The strength of διό underlines the fact that speaking arises from faith. In a similar manner elsewhere, διό strengthens the statement of which it is a part.

Purposive Conjunctions

These conjunctions indicate "why" something has been done or said in the preceding sentence or sentences. The attention is on "why" one is doing, or has done, something; or, in some cases, why one *should do* a particular thing. Keep in mind that this is a major role of purposive conjunctions. They are the "in order that" conjunctions and virtually always mean "in order that" with varying degrees of force. There may be a difference in the force of the three we will discuss here, though that is not always the case in the New Testament. Nonetheless, we will start with what might be the weakest of the purposive conjunctions and move to those that may intend a stronger sense of purpose. All may be translated "in order that."

ὅπως

῞Οπως is common in the New Testament, as for example in Matthew 22:15: Τότε πορευθέντες οἱ Φαρισαῖοι συμβούλιον ἔλαβον ὅπως αὐτὸν παγιδεύσωσιν ἐν λόγῳ ("Then going, the Pharisees took counsel in order that they might ensnare him in a word"). Why did the Pharisees take counsel? In order to determine how they might trap Jesus. There is importance in the "why" of this sentence, as one can readily tell by what it says; but the emphasis is heightened by the presence of ὅπως.

ὥστε

At first, this appears similar to the preceding conjunction, and in some ways it is. But ὥστε may suggest that the purpose is even more intent than when a writer uses ὅπως. One finds ὥστε, for instance, in Luke 4:29. This passage follows Jesus' rejection at the synagogue in Nazareth, and the angry leaders intend to kill Jesus: καὶ ἤγαγον αὐτὸν ἕως ὀφρύος τοῦ ὄρους ἐφ᾽ οὗ ἡ πόλις ᾠκοδόμητο αὐτῶν ὥστε κατακρημνίσαι αὐτόν. The NRSV translates this sentence, "and they led him to the brow of the hill on which their town was built, *so that* they might hurl him off the cliff." The conjunction ὥστε links the leaders' action with their intended purpose.

ἵνα

This is far and away the most important of the "in order that," or purposive, conjunctions, and, without question, must be learned. (The word ἵνα is pronounced "hi-na.") As do the first two purposive conjunctions we examined, ἵνα carries a rough breathing mark over the first vowel. This conjunction appears at a number of strategic places throughout the Greek New Testament and is nearly always a key word. In what might be the strongest possible way, it answers the question "why" of what precedes it, sometimes with unexpected results. However, often it is translated simply as "that," "so that," or even "when" (see Jn. 16:32). Still, we are safe in supposing that in most cases, "in order that" is a good point at which to begin considering the meaning of a particular use of ἵνα.

Watch for ἵνα in the controversial passage about marriage in the light of the church found in Ephesians 5:33: πλὴν καὶ ὑμεῖς οἱ καθ᾽ ἕνα, ἕκαστος τὴν ἑαυτοῦ γυναῖκα οὕτως ἀγαπάτω ὡς ἑαυτόν, ἡ δὲ γυνὴ ἵνα φοβῆται τὸν ἄνδρα. The RSV renders this passage, "However, let each one of you love his wife as himself, and let the wife see that she respects her husband." The NRSV, on the other hand, puts it this way: "Each of you, however, should love his wife as himself, and a wife should respect her husband." The ἵνα phrase is the key and a controversial part of this sentence. The first part of the sentence is an imperative—a command. Sometimes ἵνα introduces an imperative (especially when it is expressed in the subjunctive), and some commentators think that is the case in Ephesians 5:33. Others, however, read this ἵνα clause as more of a wish— a desired consequence.

We contend that the latter view is more likely. In this passage, the husband is directed to love the wife as himself. However, as some of the interlinear versions indicate, the ἵνα clause should probably be translated "*in order that* the wife may respect her husband." As in virtually all places where it appears, ἵνα expresses in this case a strong purpose. The wife is not directed to respect her husband, as the husband is directed to love his wife. Instead, the husband's love for his wife is "in order that" she might respect him. (The verb, φοβῆται, is subjunctive.) Without that love, it is suggested, no respect is, or even should be, forthcoming. (The issue of how to translate φοβῆται is still another matter, but we think "respect" is more likely the meaning than "fear.")

The controversy over Ephesians 5:33 aside, wherever the word ἵνα appears, it directs attention to and puts stress on what follows it. Sometimes even interlinear translations will use only the single word "that" or even some other term, such as "lest," to translate ἵνα. In searching for our own translation, we preachers should first, however, turn what follows ἵνα into an "in order that" phrase. In doing so, we will then be able to appreciate fully the significance of the sentence. Not all the uses of ἵνα are as dramatic as the one in the text from Ephesians, but in all of them the conjunction plays a crucial role of setting up, and even clarifying, the emphasis of the sentence.

Take another example—this time Colossians 1:18: καὶ αὐτός ἐστιν ἡ κεφαλὴ τοῦ σώματος τῆς ἐκκλησίας· ὅς ἐστιν ἀρχή, πρωτότοκος ἐκ τῶν νεκρῶν, ἵνα γένηται ἐν πᾶσιν αὐτὸς πρωτεύων. In literal English, it might read this way: "And he (Christ) is the head of the body, of the church, who is the beginning, firstborn from the dead *in order that* he may be holding first place in all things." The purpose of Christ's leadership in the church and of his resurrection is to give him supremacy over all. The ἵνα clause states Christ's purpose in lucid terms.

"Shifting" Conjunctions

The last group of conjunctions is different from the others. Those in this group indicate a shift or pivot in the direction of the statement underway. Sometimes these are called adversative or adversarial conjunctions. The three most important shifting conjunctions may indicate degrees of opposition in the transition they introduce. The shift may be modest, as when the word δέ is used. Or the turn may be somewhat more emphatic, as when ἀλλά or οὖν appears. Or still again, the shift may be both bold and decisive, as when πλήν is used. But like the other conjunctions, these connecting words are always important, and one does well to take note of them every time they appear. We will look at each of these "shifting" conjunctions briefly.

δέ—*But*

This is a very common conjunction, almost as common in the New Testament as καί. However, unlike καί, which serves as a fairly simple connector, δέ indicates a turn of meaning. It connects, but in a way that actually breaks, however slightly, the flow of the sentence. In a sense, δέ is one way an author might qualify a statement several times. A writer might start on a thought, and then adjust it with δέ, and adjust it again, and then again, and so on. Such a pattern is a relatively common, but very important, form of discourse.

In a text such as 1 Corinthians 1:10b, we see the shift that takes place with δέ: ἵνα τὸ αὐτὸ λέγητε πάντες καὶ μὴ ᾖ ἐν ὑμῖν σχίσματα, ἦτε δὲ κατηρτισμένοι ἐν τῷ αὐτῷ νοῒ καὶ ἐν τῇ αὐτῇ γνώμῃ. In English this reads, roughly, "in order that you all say the same thing, and not be among you divisions; but (δέ) you may having been joined together in the same mind and in the same opinion." Paul's purpose is that there be no divisions among the readers, *but* that they be of the same mind. From division to unity—in this case, that is the kind of shift signaled by δέ. It is not drastic, but it fine-tunes an idea as it unfolds in a text. We need to pay careful attention to the fine-tuning that results from δέ.

Look, for example, at a complex verse in which δέ plays a key role, specifically, Galatians 2:20. We are interested in the first half of the verse and will quote it with our own interlinear translations so that you can note the use of δέ:

ζῶ δὲ   οὐκέτι ἐγώ,   ζῇ   δὲ ἐν ἐμοὶ Χριστός· ὃ
live but no longer I,   lives but in me   Christ.   What

δὲ νῦν   ζῶ ἐν σαρκί, ἐν πίστει   ζῶ   τῇ τοῦ
but now I live in flesh   (by) in faith   I live   of the

υἱοῦ τοῦ θεοῦ...
son   of   God...

Read in literal Greek, this familiar text requires some work to make any sense in English. Notice δὲ appears three times. For one thing, this indicates that the thought is complex and that the writer is working through it carefully as he goes. In the preceding verse, he says he has been "co-crucified" (συνεσταύρωμαι—a word with a συν prefix) with Christ. Then verse 20 begins, "*but* I no longer live, *but* Christ lives in me; *but* what I live now in flesh—I live by faith in the son of God." The conjunction δέ actually molds the thought of this passage. We ourselves can become a part of that molding process when we focus on how δέ works in the text.

ἀλλά—*But (emphatic)*

Ἀλλά, like δέ, is a common conjunction in the New Testament. It too means "but," however, nearly always with a more discernible intensity of shift than is the case with δέ. Sometimes ἀλλά is translated "however" to capture its emphatic adversative (or oppositional) tone. Other times, when the English needs to be even more emphatic, translators render it "certainly." These may seem like small distinctions, but they may prove important ones. If we compare closely the difference in the occurrences of δέ and those of ἀλλά, we find that sometimes the tone of what is said will be different, depending on which conjunction the author uses.

For an example, we may select a text, such as 1 Corinthians 2:6–7a, in which both words appear.

Σοφίαν δὲ λαλοῦμεν ἐν τοῖς τελείοις,
Wisdom but we speak in (among) the perfect ones,

σοφίαν δὲ οὐ τοῦ αἰῶνος τούτου οὐδὲ τῶν
wisdom but not of the age this one neither of the

ἀρχόντων τοῦ αἰῶνος τούτου τῶν
rulers of the age this one the

καταργουμένων· ἀλλὰ λαλοῦμεν θεοῦ
ones being brought to nothing. But we speak of God's

σοφίαν ἐν μυστηρίῳ,...
wisdom in mystery,...

This is a simple but very dynamic text. Twice δέ appears before the text switches to ἀλλά. The switch appears to be deliberate and designed to add not just to the texture but also to the meaning of the sentence itself. Each of the two occurrences of δέ makes an adjustment in the statement. Verse 5 speaks of "human wisdom," and the first δέ in verse 6 turns the subject from "human wisdom" to another kind of wisdom. The second δέ paves the way to say that speaking wisdom among those who are being perfected is different from the previously mentioned human wisdom. Paul says the wisdom we speak is not the *wisdom of this age,* nor of *the leaders of this age,* who are in the process of being demoted. The ἀλλά then introduces the contrast between speaking with the wisdom of this age and speaking God's wisdom in mystery. Ἀλλά sets apart the final source of the wisdom Paul claims to be speaking. It provides a stronger disconnection, the stronger shift, in the movement of thought.

When ἀλλά is followed by a word that begins with a vowel, its final α is dropped, and the word becomes ἀλλ᾽. If you look at 1 Corinthians 3:1, you will find ἀλλ᾽ used in place of ἀλλά. In this chapter, too, Paul continues to employ a fine distinction between δέ and ἀλλά. In verse two, he says, "I fed you with milk, not solid food, for you were not ready for solid food." He then continues, ἀλλ᾽ οὐδὲ ἔτι νῦν δύνασθε, "but neither are you able now." In this sentence, ἀλλά again places the emphasis on this phrase and contrasts it with the earlier part of the verse. The NRSV tries to capture the radical sense of ἀλλά here by translating it "even now."

In the well-known line of 1 Corinthians 3:6, Paul writes, "I planted, Apollos watered, but God gave the growth" (or "made to grow")—ἐγὼ ἐφύτευσα, Ἀπολλῶς ἐπότισεν, ἀλλὰ ὁ θεὸς ηὔξανεν. Once again Paul uses ἀλλά to stress the shift of thought or the contrast of the subjects— human planting and God's causing growth.

πλήν—*Nevertheless*

This is probably the strongest of the disconnecting conjunctions, stronger even than ἀλλά. It often represents a full halt or an interruption of a process of thought in order to shift directions. It's like a runner who comes to a complete stop, turns around, and then starts running again. As the classic lexicon of Bauer, Arndt, Gingrich, and Danker puts it, πλήν represents the "breaking off of a discussion and emphasizing what is important."[1] It always comes at the beginning of a sentence or a clause, separating whatever precedes it from what follows it. The best English translation to capture this sudden break and change of direction remains "nevertheless."

Two texts, in particular, will help illustrate the importance of πλήν. The first is Ephesians 5:33. This is the text concerning the mystery of the church and of marriage to which we referred earlier. To place πλήν in its context in this verse, we need to read both verses 32 and 33:

τὸ μυστήριον   τοῦτο   μέγα ἐστίν· ἐγὼ δὲ λέγω εἰς
The mystery this one   great   is.   I   but   say   into

Χριστὸν   καὶ   εἰς   τὴν ἐκκλησίαν.
(as to) Christ   and   into (as to) the   church.

(33) πλὴν   καὶ ὑμεῖς οἱ καθ᾽ ἕνα, ἕκαστος
Nevertheless also   you   one by one,   each

τὴν ἑαυτοῦ γυναῖκα οὕτως ἀγαπάτω ὡς ἑαυτόν...
- his own   wife   so   let love   as himself...

As you can see for yourself, in this statement πλήν is significant in that it signals a major shift in direction. "I am speaking about Christ and the church," the writer says. "Nevertheless, I am talking about husbands loving their wives as themselves." The conjunction πλήν is important in signaling an abrupt shift. It provides a break and a change of course back to what seems to have been a marriage metaphor for the church.

Another text in which πλήν also has significant implications is 1 Corinthians 11:11, even though the surrounding verses are necessary

---

[1]William F. Arndt et al., *A Greek-English Lexicon of the New Testament and Other Early Christian Literature,* 2d edition (Chicago: The University of Chicago Press, 1979), 669.

to get the first word of verse 11 in perspective. The passage beginning with verse 2 is controversial, and its meaning is not easy to figure out. The verses immediately preceding 11 are about the relationship between men and women under Jewish law. This culminates in verses 8 and 9 in what amounts to a restatement of what is found in the Torah (see Genesis 2:22–23), "For man was not made from woman, but woman from man. Neither was man created from woman, but woman from man." Verse 10 then begins with διά ("therefore" or "for") and goes on to say, "a woman ought to have a symbol of authority (ἐξουσία) on her head, because of the angels" (NRSV). We know the Jewish source of the logic reflected in verses 8 and 9, and we know that Paul probably repeats that logic virtually as he and his fellow Jews learned it. However, we do not know the source from which the reference to the angels comes.

Nonetheless, at the very beginning of verse 11, there is the word πλήν "nevertheless." If we take that conjunction seriously, it calls for a halt to what has been said in verses 8–10. It signals a shift in argument, as Bauer puts it, and breaks off discussion in order to emphasize something more important. Verses 11 and 12 read:

πλὴν   οὔτε   γυνὴ   χωρὶς ἀνδρὸς οὔτε ἀνὴρ
Nevertheless, neither woman without man   nor man

χωρὶς γυναικὸς ἐν   κυρίῳ· (12) ὥσπερ γὰρ ἡ
without woman   in (the) Lord.   For as the

γυνὴ   ἐκ τοῦ ἀνδρός, οὕτως καὶ ἀνὴρ διὰ
woman (out) of the man   so also man through

τῆς γυναικός· τὰ δὲ   πάντα   ἐκ   τοῦ
the woman.   But all things (are) (out) of the

θεοῦ.
God.

Compare the lines following "nevertheless" (πλήν) with the lines that precede it. They are almost mirror opposites of each other. In verses 8–10 women are described as in some sense under the authority of men. Then, with "all things being of God," verses 11 and 12 assert the absolute equality of men and women. After πλήν, the key phrase is ἐν κυρίῳ— "in the Lord." What Paul says here is nearly identical in substance to his famous words in Galatians 3:28: "there is no longer male and female; for all of you are one in Christ Jesus." (See the next principle.) "In Christ" there is neither woman without man, nor man without woman. Woman originally came from man, but from that time on, men have come from, or through, women. The key position of πλήν plays the role of announcing such an abrupt shift in thought.

We have not exhausted the list of Greek conjunctions, but it was not our intention to do so. Instead, we have singled out some of the most important ones, grouping them into categories that you can readily learn. The substance of this discussion should be committed to memory for regular use in your study of the Greek New Testament. Whatever other conjunctions you come across you can look up in an analytical lexicon. The point of this discussion has been to suggest that we preachers should treat all conjunctions as important in adding nuances of meaning in any given text.

Piecing Together the Particles

The word "particle" is from a Latin term that means "small part." In a way, as H. E. Dana and Julius R. Mantey point out, they are the little words that are not easy to classify—the "odds and ends" of grammar. These "odds and ends" can become confusing and frustrating to beginning readers of the Greek text. For some grammarians, any small word in a Greek text qualifies as a particle, including prepositions, conjunctions, and even, in some cases, adverbs. Nevertheless, the Greek language treasures its particles; and when they appear in the New Testament, special attention must be paid to them.

As Dana and Mantey put it:

> The fact that they are seldom used makes their use all the more significant, for it is evident that each occurrence of a particle was necessary to help express the writer's ideas. In them lurk hidden meanings and delicate shades of thought that intensify and clarify the thought of the sentence. Unless one learns to understand and appreciate their significance, he [or she] will miss getting the author's full thought, and fail to realize the benefit of the niceties of Greek.[1]

In this chapter, we shall briefly discuss some of the most important particles under two headings: the *emphatic* or *intensive* particles, and the

---

[1]H. E. Dana and Julius R. Mantey, *A Manual Grammar of the New Testament* (New York: Macmillan, 1927), 258.

negative ones. One will find others from time to time, and an analytical lexicon will identify them. The choices we make here, though, are designed not just to indicate some of the key words that the student of the text should learn but also to alert you to the importance of devoting attention to these "little words."

Intensive Particles

ἄν *and* ἐάν *(No English Equivalent)*

Ἄν is an indefinite particle, with emphasis or intensity given to the word "indefinite." The problem is that it has virtually no clear English equivalent. It forcefully implies vagueness or uncertainty. The closest we get to ἄν in English is the word "ever," as in "Will that ever take place?" Or, "I don't think I will ever see him again." "Ever" suggests the particular vagueness or uncertainty the word conveys. The point is that whenever ἄν appears in the Greek text, we should focus on the uncertainty, vagueness, or even open-endedness of the statement.

Ἄν can stand alone in texts and be easily recognizable. That is the case, for example, in Mark 6:56. Often when this happens, it is accompanied by another particle, indicating a general person, a vague time, or even a generic place. The Mark text says, in part, καὶ ὅπου ἂν εἰσεπορεύετο εἰς κώμας ἢ εἰς πόλεις ἢ εἰς ἀγρούς...In this passage, ἄν follows another particle, ὅπου, a word that suggests place. So the text may be understood to say, "And wherever he (Jesus) entered into villages or into cities or into country." The word "wherever" is chosen to render ὅπου (where) and ἄν (ever).

Sometimes the presence of the "other" particle with ἄν must be inferred, although that is not usually difficult to do. Matthew 25:27, for instance, reads, ἔδει σε οὖν βαλεῖν τὰ ἀργύριά μου τοῖς τραπεζίταις, καὶ ἐλθὼν ἐγὼ ἐκομισάμην ἂν τὸ ἐμὸν σὺν τόκῳ. ("It was incumbent on you therefore to put my silver pieces to the bankers, and, coming, I would have received whatever was mine with interest.") The word ἄν stands alone to emphasize the uncertainty of amount, and the word "whatever" appropriately picks up that vagueness.

What is particularly significant about ἄν, however, is that it is often subsumed (usually as a suffix) within another word. Because its two letters are so simple, a reader can often take them as part of the word itself rather than understanding that they are creating and emphasizing the uncertain "ever" dimension of the word of which ἄν is a part. The merger of ἄν and another word creates what appears to be a "new word." The most common of these is ἐάν, which some scholars take to be merely a variant spelling for ἄν. Ἐάν functions as a synonym for ἄν, and sometimes appears alone. This is the case, for instance, in Acts 8:19: δότε κἀμοὶ τὴν ἐξουσίαν ταύτην ἵνα ᾧ ἐὰν ἐπιθῶ τὰς χεῖρας λαμβάνῃ πνεῦμα ἅγιον. ("Give me also this authority in order that whomever I lay my hands on that person may receive the Holy Spirit.") Ἐάν (translated "whomever") stands alone but gives the entire sentence its peculiar accent. The Spirit can come to anyone. Just as ἄν does in the Markan passage cited above, ἐάν often stands alongside another particle.

Because of the emphatic uncertainty provided by ἄν and ἐάν, it often occurs with the subjunctive or optative moods of the verb, which we discussed in Principle 2. These moods are the "if" verbs that are conditional, sometimes with an uncertainty about their outcome. Thus, both ἄν and ἐάν can sometimes be translated with an "if" phrase, as, for example, "if ever I should see you again," or "I do not know if that will happen ever again." These are important emphases of New Testament text when they appear. (Acts 9:2 is an example of ἐάν used in a conditional clause with εὕρῃ, a subjunctive verb form of εὑρίσκω.)

γέ—*Indeed*

This too is an emphatic or intensive particle, but it very specifically intensifies the word with which it is associated. In English that intensification is often found in our word "indeed," as in "he is *indeed* the one who went in." Other words can sometimes be used to translate γέ, such as "in fact," "even," and "at least." Sometimes, too, γέ will appear along with other particles. When that happens, γέ usually increases the emphasis on a word or concept. In Ephesians 3:2, for example, εἴ γε ἠκούσατε τὴν οἰκονομίαν τῆς χάριτος τοῦ θεοῦ τῆς δοθείσης μοι εἰς ὑμᾶς ("if, indeed, you heard the stewardship of the grace of God given to me for [or from within] you"). The RSV translates the γέ phrase (εἴ γε ἠκούσατε) "assuming that you have heard." That translation is correct, but one could argue that it does not precisely convey the full intensity γέ gives to the phrase. A still weak English translation that at least moves us in the right direction is "assuming that you *really* heard." The NRSV is perhaps the best: "for surely you have already heard." When we understand the emphasis γέ gives the verb "you heard" (ἠκούσατε), we have found something quite unique in the text and something the writer seems to have felt very deeply.

Exactly the same emphasis comes a few verses later in a clause in Ephesians 4:21, εἴ γε αὐτὸν ἠκούσατε καὶ ἐν αὐτῷ ἐδιδάχθητε ("if, indeed, you heard about him and were taught in him"). Again the RSV uses the word "assuming" to catch the flavor of γέ, but it is probably better

said as, "If, as you say, you heard"; or even, "If, knowing that you heard."
In this case, γέ may convey a kind of questioning or skepticism both of
the "if" and the notion that they indeed did hear. The NRSV, in this case,
captures some of that questioning by rendering the clause, "For surely you
have heard about him."

ἤ—*What?*

This is a complicated particle, but well worth our closest attention
when it appears. First, it is complicated because of its similar appearance
to a number of other words. Notice that the single letter η can sometimes
appear unaccented (ἡ), and then it is treated as an article. The word, ἦ, is
an adverb that means "truly." But with an acute accent (´) and smooth
breathing mark (᾿), ἤ becomes a particle; and often a very distinctive
one.

One of the most distinctive uses of ἤ arises because it is what we call
a "disjunctive" particle and denotes separation. Often the separation is a
form of contrast, a way of setting things in opposition to each other. In
English this opposition is sometimes stated as "not this, but that." So for
instance, ἤ...ἤ is often translated "either...or." The particle frequently
introduces rhetorical questions, as it does in Romans 3:29: ἤ Ἰουδαίων
ὁ θεὸς μόνον; ("Or is God the God of Jews only?") Notice that Paul uses
the particle to make a disjunctive comparison with what has come before
but also to emphasize the contrast. The contrast is between people being
justified by faith apart from works (stated in v. 28) and the ridiculous
possibility that God is the God only of Jews.

Frequently, therefore, ἤ carries an emotional wallop. It is useful to think
of it as reflecting an emphatic response to something. That something is
usually revealed in the context. To capture that emphatic response in ἤ,
some scholars and translators have landed on the "What?" with an
exclamation point. (For example, "What! Is God the God of Jews only?")
When we encounter ἤ, at the very least we should examine its meaning
carefully and consult Bauer or one of the other good Greek lexicons (see
chap. 1).

Two examples of how ἤ is often used are found in 1 Corinthians. In
the Lord's Supper passage of 11:21–22a, Paul writes, ἕκαστος γὰρ τὸ ἴδιον
δεῖπνον προλαμβάνει ἐν τῷ φαγεῖν, καὶ ὃς μὲν πεινᾷ ὃς δὲ μεθύει.
(22) μὴ γὰρ οἰκίας οὐκ ἔχετε εἰς τὸ ἐσθίειν καὶ πίνειν; ἢ τῆς ἐκκλησίας
τοῦ θεοῦ καταφρονεῖτε,...In this case, ἤ appears in a rather odd place,
midway through the clauses of verse 22. The RSV translation, however,
moves it to the first word of verse 22, where it most likely belongs when

the Greek becomes English. In that position it interprets another participle, μή (see below). The translation of verse 22 in some editions of the RSV and in the NRSV reads, "What! Do you not have homes [houses in RSV] to eat and drink in?" Note that again ἤ introduces a rhetorical question: "Of course, you have homes to eat and drink in." This is, to be sure, a strong use of ἤ, but it is not the only place where it seems to have such force.

We also find ἤ in the controversial passage in 1 Corinthians 14:34–36. The issue here is whether women should be silent in the churches to which Paul is writing. Starting with verse 34 are what, on their surface, appear to be directions that women *should* be silent in the churches and not be permitted to speak. Instead, Paul says, ὑποτασσέσθωσαν, καθὼς καὶ ὁ νόμος λέγει, "let them be submissive (or subject), as the law says" (verse 34b). Then he goes on, ἐν οἴκῳ τοὺς ἰδίους ἄνδρας ἐπερωτάτωσαν, "let them question their own husbands at home." Then, the particle ἤ appears at the beginning of verse 36. The RSV captures its force with "What?" The NRSV, however, renders it mildly with "Or." However, here the particle seems to express a more emphatic form of disjunction than what is conveyed in a simple "or." Significantly, what follows are some biting questions that remind us of those that surround the ἤ in the text of 1 Corinthians 11:21–22. In this case, the rhetorical questions are: "Did the word of God go forth (or originate) from you? Did the word of God reach only to you?"

The ἤ plays the same role here as it did in 1 Corinthians 11. Paul appears first in verses 34 and 35 to reiterate what he understands the teaching and practice to be in the church, or churches, to which he is writing. The church, or churches, are teaching that women are to be silent, that it is shameful for women to speak, and that if women wish to know anything about church matters, they should talk with their husbands at home. But then Paul writes ἤ ("What!"). And the questions that follow have the force of "How could you do that? How could you teach those things? Do you think that in saying such things you are speaking for God?"

The problem is whether the questions in verse 36 are directed toward the women who are unruly in church or toward those who have forced the women to be silent. Some interpreters, of course, understand Paul to be asking these questions of the women of the church. Are they so confident that they can violate traditional practices? However, in our judgment, here the particle ἤ likely provides a transition that contrasts what the churches have been teaching with what Paul now has to say about those teachings. What are often viewed as Paul's statements about women may not be his at all, but may reflect his rhetorical handling of the statements of others. But the interpretation of the passage must depend on larger issues and contexts.

Granted, not all the appearances of ἤ in the New Testament have this kind of importance. But the particle can have, depending on the context in which it appears. It is interesting that the RSV and NRSV differ in the ways they handle the ἤ in the 1 Corinthian passages. This suggests that translators are not always sure how this little particle functions in its context. The point, however, is that sometimes ἤ is a very emphatic or intensive particle and that its use often intends to separate one idea from another with considerable opposition or contrast. Whenever we come upon this little word, it behooves us to give careful attention to what it conveys and what surrounds it. To do so will often yield fruitful insights and ideas. Moreover, those insights may sometimes be ones that are downplayed, or even missed, in some standard English translations of the New Testament.

The Negative Particles

There are two basic negative particles, and both of them are simply ways of saying "no." However, they both appear in various combinations and forms in the Greek text. You can learn to recognize them fairly easily. One of the two negative particles is μή, and the other is οὐ. The two are sometimes combined in οὐ μή, but there may be a difference between them. Of the two, μή may be the weaker negative, and οὐ the stronger. That distinction will prove interesting for us in text after text.

μή—*No, Not (qualified)*

Simply put, μή is often a "light touch" negative. Some scholars suggest that it is the negative of "idea," of a wish, of an intention, or of a thought, as opposed to of a behavior or what actually is. Οὐ, on the other hand, is the negative of action. Consequently, οὐ is used most often with the indicative mood and μή with all the other moods. While there are dozens of good examples of μή in the Greek text, we can see its nature and most common purpose in Luke 4:42b: καὶ οἱ ὄχλοι ἐπεζήτουν αὐτὸν καὶ ἦλθον ἕως αὐτοῦ καὶ κατεῖχον αὐτὸν τοῦ μὴ πορεύεσθαι ἀπ᾽ αὐτῶν, "and the crowds sought him, and came up to him and detained him not to go from them." There is the negative wish or intent expressed in this occurrence of μή. The crowds do not so much *prevent* Jesus' leaving them as they *wish* he would not.

Three additional examples will indicate how μή is sometimes used in the New Testament. The first is the same passage we discussed above under the use of ἤ, namely, 1 Corinthians 11:21–22a. Verse 22a reads, μὴ γὰρ οἰκίας οὐκ ἔχετε εἰς τὸ ἐσθίειν καὶ πίνειν; ἢ τῆς ἐκκλησίας τοῦ θεοῦ καταφρονεῖτε... ("What? Do you not have houses to eat and drink in?"). The ἤ emphasizes the contrast with what has come before, and μή states the negative. In this case, as we have suggested, the first particle gives μή a stronger tone than it often has.

A different kind of "wish" or "idea" element of this negative can be seen in Galatians 5:26 and is an example of the use of μή in imperatives: μὴ γινώμεθα κενόδοξοι, ἀλλήλους προκαλούμενοι, ἀλλήλοις φθονοῦντες, or "Let us not become conceited, provoking one another, envying one another." Here is a desire that we not become these things. It is not a statement that we are not conceited or that we are not provoking and envying others. Rather, it expresses what Paul does not want us to be and do.

Still another example is in 2 Corinthians 11:16: Πάλιν λέγω, μή τίς με δόξῃ ἄφρονα εἶναι· In English, "Again I say, may not anyone think me foolish." You may see a pattern emerging here. Μή often appears as a very personal use of the negative, and indicates the negation of an idea. However, it is nearly always used with participles, no matter whether it is a denial of a wish or a fact.

We should also be on the watch for the use of μή as a prefix on other words, and particularly as a prefix on other particles or conjunctions. Here are only a few of the possibilities:

μηδέ combines μή and δε to produce "but not."

μηδείς (or μηδεμία or μηδέν) produces a stronger negative, such as "no, not all," "nobody," or "nothing."

μήγε combines μή and γέ ("indeed"), resulting in "indeed not."

μήτι joins μή and τί (a pronoun used in asking questions) to produce a word used in questions to which one expects a negative reply.

μήτε unites μή with the connective particle τέ to produce "may not," or in some cases, "neither...nor."

You will become familiar with these uses of μή alone and in combination with other words. It is always worthwhile to think through the implications of the particle for the sentence in which it appears.

οὐ *and* οὐκ—*No, Not (emphatic)*

This is the other designation for the negative and probably the more absolute of the two. Οὐ means "no," and it replaces the "wish" quality of μή with a sense of strong denial, especially of what appears to be reality. However, you should first understand that this negative appears regularly in four forms. In every case, these are the same word.

When it immediately precedes a word that begins with a consonant, it is spelled οὐ.

When it is used before words that begin with a vowel, it is spelled οὐκ.

When the next word begins with a vowel that carries a rough breathing mark, οὐκ becomes οὐχ.

Finally, when it is the final word of a clause or when the author wishes to emphasize it, it is spelled οὔ.

Like μή, οὐ also appears as a prefix on other words. This simply means the negative of the word with which it is combined. The word to which it is attached becomes, in effect, a strong statement of denial. Although many words are prefixed with οὐ, these are a few examples along with the resulting general meaning:

οὐδαμῶς becomes "by no means."

οὐδέ becomes "not even" or "also not."

οὐδείς (or οὐθείς) becomes "no one."

οὐδέποτε becomes "never" or, more accurately, "not even ever."

οὐδέπω becomes "not yet."

οὔτε becomes "neither."

Three texts adequately illustrate the use of both οὐ and μή. The first is 1 Corinthians 2:8–9:

ἦν   οὐδεὶς τῶν ἀρχόντων τοῦ αἰῶνος τούτου
which not one of the rulers   of   age   this

ἔγνωκεν· εἰ γὰρ ἔγνωσαν, οὐκ ἂν   τὸν κύριον
has known, for if they knew not would the lord

τῆς δόξης ἐσταύρωσαν. (9) ἀλλὰ καθὼς
of glory they crucified.   But   as

γέγραπται,   ἃ   ὀφθαλμὸς οὐκ εἶδεν
it has been written, "Things which eye   did not see

καὶ οὓς οὐκ   ἤκουσεν καὶ ἐπὶ   καρδίαν
and ear did not hear   and on(in) heart

ἀνθρώπου οὐκ   ἀνέβη,   ἃ   ἡτοίμασεν ὁ
of humans did not come up, the things prepared

θεὸς τοῖς ἀγαπῶσιν αὐτόν.
God for the ones loving him."

Look for the οὐ negatives in this familiar text and then think about
their importance in the sentence. You see οὐδείς and then οὐκ four
times. "*Not one* of the leaders of this age has known, for, if they had, they
would *not* have executed Jesus. Moreover, eye has *not* seen, ear has *not* heard,
and it has *not* even come upon the heart of humankind what God has
prepared for those who love God." The repetition of the negatives gives
a particular tone to the text, making it a strong and absolute statement
that has been carefully devised.

Many statements in the New Testament include both οὐ and μή, and
it is useful to see how their differences show up in creating a text's
meaning. One such example comes a few verses before the text in
1 Corinthians that we just examined. Verses 4 and 5 of chapter 2 read:

καὶ ὁ λόγος μου καὶ τὸ   κήρυγμά μου   οὐκ ἐν
And the speech of me and the proclamation of me not in

πειθοῖς   σοφίας [λόγοις] ἀλλ᾽ ἐν ἀποδείξει
persuasive of wisdom words, but in demonstration

πνεύματος καὶ δυνάμεως, (5) ἵνα ἡ
of spirit   and of power   in order that (the)

πίστις ὑμῶν   μὴ   ᾖ ἐν σοφίᾳ ἀνθρώπων
faith   of you may not be in wisdom of humans

ἀλλ᾽ ἐν δυνάμει θεοῦ.
but in   power of God.

The difference between οὐ (or οὐκ) and μή is clear in this sentence.
Paul says that his proclamation was emphatically not in persuasive words
of wisdom, but in the spirit and power of God so that "your" faith may
not (hopefully not) be in human wisdom but in the power of God.

The third text that provides a useful illustration of οὐ (or οὐκ) is found
in a familiar passage, Galatians 3:28, which reads:

οὐκ ἔνι Ἰουδαῖος οὐδὲ Ἕλλην, οὐκ ἔνι
There is not Jew   nor Greek; there is not

δοῦλος οὐδὲ ἐλεύθερος, οὐκ ἔνι ἄρσεν καὶ
slave nor free;   there is not male and

θῆλυ· πάντες γὰρ ὑνεῖς εἷς ἐστε ἐν Χριστῷ Ἰησοῦ.
female. All   for you one are in Christ Jesus.

Because of the importance of this verse, it is worth a close look. As we have indicated, a literal translation of οὐκ ἔνι is "there is no." Ἔνι is always used with οὐκ in the New Testament, and many scholars believe the two words intend an emphatic denial. (See also 1 Cor. 6:5 and Col. 3:11.) However, some have claimed that these two are combined to produce a prohibition rather than a statement. Some interlinear texts also put it, "there cannot be" Jew nor Greek; "there cannot be" slave nor free; "there cannot be..." It is a strong negative.

However, our point is another matter. Look at the clause about "male and female." Instead of the negative between them (οὐδέ), there is καί. In the first two couplets, the two groups are contrasts or opposites, and the words are separated by a negative: Jew as opposed to Gentile, slave as opposed to free. However, when Paul comes to the relationship between the genders, they are not opposed to each other, but represented as a pair: male *and* female. What does that mean? The text provides no clear answer. However, once preachers have found that wording, the question of its meaning is worth our best thought. This is a good example of trying to determine if a certain occurrence has special meaning or if it is simply a stylistic slip on the part of the author.

Sometimes both of the negatives that we have discussed appear side by side. That is usually taken as the strongest possible negative available to a New Testament writer. One finds this, for example, in Matthew 5:20: λέγω γὰρ ὑμῖν ὅτι ἐὰν μὴ περισσεύσῃ ὑμῶν ἡ δικαιοσύνη πλεῖον τῶν γραμματέων καὶ Φαρισαίων, οὐ μὴ εἰσέλθητε εἰς τὴν βασιλείαν τῶν οὐρανῶν. ("For I tell you that if your righteousness does not exceed that of the scribes and Pharisees, by no means shall you enter into the kingdom of the heavens.") In the first phrase, "if your righteousness does not exceed," we find μή used as a qualified negative. Then only a few words later is the double negative, οὐ μή. The sense seems to be, "by no means whatsoever will you enter the kingdom." It is a forceful negative, for which English translations seem to come up short of the Greek.

In closing this section, we should point out that in Greek, unlike English, a double negative is not bad grammar. On the contrary, the more negatives that are used, the more emphatic they become!

PRINCIPLE 7

The Infinitive's Finishing Action

No part of speech occurs as often in the Greek New Testament as the infinitive. In English it is the construction best known for being a verb preceded by "to:" "to run," as in, "He is going to run." The main verb of that sentence is "going," but the infinitive is "to run." Even though the word "to" does not identify the presence of the infinitive in a sentence in Greek as it does in English, the use of the infinitive in Greek is almost identical to its use in English. Moreover, the basic translation of a Greek infinitive into English often uses the word "to." This means that even though an infinitive in Greek can be more complicated than "to run," at its most basic level, the "to" will provide a workable way to read it.

The infinitive is called a verbal noun, which means that it can function as either a verb or a noun. Actually the infinitive can serve as a noun (for example, the object of the main verb—Jn. 4:33), as an adverb (for example, to state purpose—Mk. 3:14), as a complement to the main verb, as a finite verb in indirect discourse, and as other things. While we will take note of the infinitive's substantive (or noun-like) qualities and uses, even they are closely related to its principal function as a verb. The infinitive serves, in effect, as a partner of the main verb. It can also work as the subject or the object of a verb—which is one of its substantive characteristics. It can give added force and direction to the verb. It carries out, or finishes, the action set up by the verb.

Often it sets up "what might happen" if the verb's action is carried out; that is, it can imply the potential action of the verb, or what will or might result when the action of the main verb is done. In weighing the meaning of a sentence or a clause, one must always pay attention to the action of the infinitive and its relation to the action of the main verb.

Although for our purposes it is not the infinitive's most compelling dimension, we will begin by taking note of the use of the infinitive as a noun, or its substantive use. Scholars believe that the Greek infinitive probably began as a noun or a noun form, and it often has the force or the importance of a noun. Still, seeing it as a verb form, or an action word with the power of a noun, is what indicates more than anything else the importance the infinitive has in Greek sentences.

All this becomes much clearer, though, when we look at two of the major forms the infinitive takes in the Greek New Testament. We will consider the "anarthrous infinitive" and the "articular infinitive."

The Anarthrous Infinitive

The words "anarthrous" and "articular" have to do with the absence or presence of an article. In Principle 1, we discussed in detail these concepts. Similarly, we now look at the article's presence or absence with an infinitive. The fact that it is important whether an infinitive has an article with it or not is tied to its "noun" character. In terms of the use of the article, the infinitive is treated like a noun. As we saw in Principle 1, determining whether an infinitive has an article with it or not makes an enormous difference in understanding it. The general principle is this: *If an infinitive is anarthrous (that is, if it has no article with it), it most often functions specifically to complete the action indicated by the main verb of the sentence or clause.*

Anarthrous infinitives are usually called "complementary" infinitives, since they are said to "complement" the main verb. In most cases, with an anarthrous infinitive, the main verb "needs" the infinitive in order to be completed. This means that the main verb is usually one that expresses anticipation of some kind, and that anticipation is "finished" or "fulfilled" by the infinitive that follows it. This includes, though is not limited to, verbs such as "can," "able," "want," "wish," "about to," "going to," "ought to," and others of that nature. These are verbs that cause one, in a sense, to say "can what?" or "able to do what?" or "want to do what?" or "ought to do what?" The verb makes us ask, "what," and then the immediate presence of the anarthrous infinitive supplies the "what" (which is an action of some sort). Generally speaking, the emphasis surrounding the anarthrous infinitive falls on the action of the main verb rather than on the infinitive itself.

For example, Philippians 1:12 has an anarthrous infinitive:
Γινώσκειν δὲ ὑμᾶς βούλομαι, ἀδελφοί, ὅτι τὰ
to know   but you   I want,   brothers,   that the

κατ᾽   ἐμὲ   μᾶλλον εἰς   προκοπὴν   τοῦ
things about me rather toward advancement of the

εὐαγγελίου ἐλήλυθεν,...
gospel   have come...

We might assemble the Greek this way, "But I want you (or wish you) to know, brethren, that the things that have come (to you) about me are, rather, for the advance of the gospel." The first word of the sentence is the infinitive γινώσκειν. It is anarthrous and connected with βούλομαι ("want"), the verb of the clause. "I want you" needs the infinitive "to know" in order to specify what exactly the writer wants. This is the most common anarthrous infinitive construction.

However, two things should be noted. First, -ειν is a common ending on infinitives. That ending, in fact, becomes the easiest way to recognize an infinitive. Not all forms of an infinitive have that ending, of course; but whenever one finds a word that ends in -ειν, it is an infinitive. The basic endings of the infinitive are these:

Active	**Middle and Passive**
-ειν	-σθαι
-ναι	-θηναι
-αι and -σαι	

Second, notice that the infinitive construction very often appears (as it does in Philippians 1:12) with ὅτι, the word usually meaning "that." When it does, it often introduces an indirect quotation. In other words, "I want you...to know...that," and then the material is said as quotation, but without quotation marks. (This is similar to English where "that" serves to introduce a quotation—"she said that we should meet her there.")

We find a different construction with the infinitive in a text such as Romans 3:28:
λογιζόμεθα   γὰρ δικαιοῦσθαι   πίστει ἄνθρωπον
we understand for to be justified by faith (a) person

χωρὶς   ἔργων νόμου.
without works of law.

The text says "we understand," but *what* is it that we understand? We understand a person "to be justified" by faith without works of law. "We understand," λογιζόμεθα, is the main verb, but it is incomplete as it stands. So the anarthrous (and passive) infinitive, δικαιοῦσθαι, completes what it is that "we understand."

Another example, somewhat more complex, is in Acts 1:16. Here, after the people are addressed, the writer uses the verb ἔδει, a form of δέω. It refers to the idea of binding, having to do something, or having to carry something out. "Behooved" is the old word often used to translate it. The incompleteness is obvious. What was necessary? What is being bound; or what is behooved? The answer is found in the anarthrous infinitive, πληρωθῆναι, meaning "to be fulfilled," or "it is necessary for the scripture to be fulfilled."

Ἄνδρες ἀδελφοί, ἔδει   πληρωθῆναι τὴν
Men,   brothers, it was necessary to be fulfilled the

γραφὴν ἣν   προεῖπεν τὸ πνεῦμα τὸ ἅγιον
scripture which spoke before the spirit   the holy one

διὰ   στόματος   Δαυίδ...
through (the) mouth   of David...

The Articular Infinitive

The other use of the infinitive is the articular one, meaning, of course, that the infinitive has an article with it. Characteristically, with articular infinitives the presence of the article *accents* the infinitive's substantive quality (that is, its role as a noun). Most often, when the infinitive is preceded by an article, it indicates a specific emphasis. By using an article with the infinitive, an author may wish "to make the expression specific or general," as Dana and Mantey put it.[1] However, like the use of the article in general, this view is not held by all Greek grammarians.

The articular infinitive plays many roles. Just as the anarthrous infinitive "finishes" the verb to which it is attached, *the articular infinitive emphasizes its own action.* Whereas the anarthrous infinitive tilts the stress of the action toward the main verb of the sentence—supplementing it, as we have said—the articular infinitive claims importance for its own action. However, as we will see below, the articular infinitive is a most versatile construction.

---

[1] H. E. Dana and Julius R. Mantey, *A Manual Grammar of the Greek New Testament* (New York: Macmillan, 1927), 211.

If you think back to our first principle on the difference between the absence or presence of the article in a noun construction, you will recall that the absence of the article (the anarthrous construction) sometimes (but not always) suggests the general quality of the noun's meaning, while the article's presence (the articular construction) often (but again not always) indicates the specific meaning of "this" particular noun. A noun with an article tends to identify it with this one thing and no other.

With some variation, that kind of distinction holds when we consider the articular infinitive. The articular infinitive often means the *particular action of this infinitive.* That is, in conjunction with the main verb, the articular infinitive places the stress on *the act of doing* what the infinitive suggests. It is often a very significant accent, going beyond what a pure verb can accomplish. The difference may sometimes seem subtle, but in many sentences, the presence of the articular infinitive can be instrumental in grasping significant nuances of meaning.

One other thing should be said. It is very common for an articular infinitive to appear with a preposition. The components of this construction are the infinitive, an article, plus a preposition. These three may be arranged in various ways, but usually they are all easily visible. One should, in fact, watch for this arrangement, since it will most often be valuable as a unit. In these cases, the preposition is treated as a regular preposition and usually indicates, as we saw, the "direction" of the action (see Principle 5). But in conjunction with an articular infinitive, it indicates *the direction of the infinitive's action,* as opposed to the direction of the main verb's action. So this construction emphasizes not only the action of the infinitive but also its direction. Over time you will learn not only to see these articular infinitives with a preposition but also to recognize how they add texture and even bite to what the writer is saying.

The articular infinitive with a preposition often poses an odd arrangement of words in the Greek text, and we have to think through and even decipher that arrangement as we construct our translations. Still, this deciphering often reveals interesting and valuable nuances of meaning. One such passage is Acts 1:3, in which we find this construction:

οἷς   καὶ παρέστησεν ἑαυτὸν ζῶντα μετὰ τὸ
to whom and he presented himself living after the

παθεῖν αὐτὸν ἐν   πολλοῖς τεκμηρίοις, δι᾽
to suffer him in (by) many   proofs,   through

ἡμερῶν τεσσεράκοντα ὀπτανόμενος αὐτοῖς καὶ
days   forty   being seen by them and

λέγων   τὰ   περὶ   τῆς βασιλείας τοῦ θεοῦ·
speaking the things concerning the kingdom   of God.

First, locate the construction comprising an infinitive along with its article and preposition. It is μετὰ τὸ παθεῖν, literally, "after the to suffer." Following the construction is αὐτόν, which adds specific identity to the phrase (that is, it tells us whose suffering we are talking about). However, we are now prepared to ask, what observations might be made about the first half of this sentence from οἷς καί through αὐτόν?

To begin with, we need to make sure we can clarify somewhat the arrangement of the words in order to get a sense of the infinitive's meaning in English. As in some interlinear texts, the easiest way, of course, is to say that he presented himself "after he suffered," or "after his suffering." In this case, the preposition would take a temporal meaning. That seems clear enough. But the very construction invites us to look more carefully at the overall phrasing.

The main verb is παρέστησεν, "he presented himself," or "he made himself visible" "after" he suffered. Since the main verb is followed by an articular infinitive rather than an anarthrous one, it is not that the action of the infinitive complements or completes the main verb's action. This verb would make sense without the infinitive phrase. In this case, the infinitive adds a new dimension of the main verb. Since this infinitive is articular, its emphasis falls on its own action, and the infinitive's action may be understood, at least subtly, as still going on. He "presented himself," but he did so after going through the action of suffering. The infinitive may underscore the act of suffering *as well as* the action of the main verb— "he presented himself." The article with the infinitive along with the preposition invites us to understand the sentence this way.

However, there is also the matter of the preposition, μετά. A simple translation is "after," giving it a directional and temporal action. But it is a preposition worth full consideration. To be sure, μετά can mean "after," and sometimes that is the best way to translate it. At the root of μετά, however, is the idea of "in the midst of," or "fully engaged with," or even "to be surrounded by." In English, as in Greek, there are many words prefixed with "meta-." "Metaphysical," for instance, can mean "with the" physical, but it also suggests to "encompass" and even to "rise above" the physical. It is a complex term, in part because its Greek prepositional prefix, μετά, is complex. Those complexities should be thought through in a text such as this one from Acts 1.

So we might pose questions like these in reflecting on the meaning of the preposition μετά in the infinitive phrase of Acts 1:3: Did he present himself *after* he suffered? Or did he present himself *in the midst of* his sufferings? Or might we say, *in the process of rising above* his sufferings he presented himself? Of course, there are no clear answers to these questions. In fact, ruminations like these about a preposition used with an articular infinitive indicate ways in which both idea and nuance can be teased from a richly packed phrase in the text. In other words, μετά may not indicate just a time or a sense of sequence—"after she did one thing, she next did another." It may also be a way for the author or interpreter to set thought processes in motion and to express more than what any individual word is able fully to express.

Another example of this form may be seen in Acts 4:2, which reads like this in an interlinear text:

διαπονούμενοι   διὰ   τὸ διδάσκειν
being greatly troubled because of   to teach

αὐτοὺς τὸν λαὸν   καὶ καταγγέλλειν ἐν τῷ
them   the people and   to announce   by (in)

Ἰησοῦ τὴν ἀνάστασιν   τὴν ἐκ νεκρῶν,
Jesus   the resurrection   from the dead,

As becomes clear, the presence of the infinitive causes more disruption in the English "reading" of a text than do most other Greek constructions. So one must work with an interlinear and one's own sense of the text in order to explore both the infinitive's meaning and its unique contribution to the whole sentence. Verse 2, in this case, is a fragment of the sentence that begins in verse 1. The continuation of the sentence in verse 2 begins here with a participle, but then we have the infinitive construction—the infinitive διδάσκειν, the article τό, and the preposition διά. Furthermore, if we look closely, we see that καί sets up a second and parallel infinitive connecting the second infinitive in the sentence, καταγγέλλειν, with the first, διδάσκειν. This means that we should treat καταγγέλλειν as articular and as prefaced by the preposition διά.

The first verse of chapter 4 says that while the disciples were speaking to the people, the priests, the captain of the temple, and the Sadducees "came to them." They are, verse 2 tells us, "greatly troubled," and then the sentence offers two pieces of information. The first is that the disciples were teaching (διδάσκειν) and preaching (καταγγέλλειν), and the second is that they were talking about Jesus' resurrection from the dead. The verses tell us what the disciples were doing (teaching and preaching) and specify the content of their actions (teaching and preaching Jesus' resurrection). We must take both of these as important in this text. However, what might the author intend by using an article with the two infinitives? Does the construction of the infinitive phrases suggest that *what* the disciples were doing (their preaching and teaching) was of more concern to the Jewish authorities than was the content of what they were saying (Jesus' resurrection from the dead)? It is difficult to say and perhaps may be a small matter. Yet it is worth pondering, especially if we are seeking a nuance in the text worthy of preaching.

Hebrews 2:15 also provides another striking look at this infinitive construction.

καὶ ἀπαλλάξῃ   τούτους, ὅσοι   φόβῳ
and he might release these,   as many as by fear

θανάτου διὰ   παντὸς τοῦ ζῆν   ἔνοχοι
of death through all   (their) living being subjected

ἦσαν δουλείας.
were (to) slavery.

The complexity of the sentence is noteworthy, and unraveling it is not easy. Again, verse 15 completes the long sentence begun in verse 14. It indicates that Jesus partook of flesh and blood, like all humans, in order that he might destroy the power of death. Verse 15 continues by explaining the results of the destruction of death. The common way to read what follows the verb ἀπαλλάξῃ is "as many as through all their lives were subject to slavery," or something very close to that.

The infinitive in the sentence is ζῆν, a form of ζάω, "to live." No exact translation into English is even possible here, so it is necessary to construct the "sense" of the sentence, rather than simply transferring its language into English. The Greek infinitive construction is both articular and prepositional, even though the prepositional phrase is modified by the presence of παντός ("all") between the preposition (διά) and the infinitive (ζῆν). However, that intrusion should not obscure the fact that διά goes with ζῆν. Christ releases "as many as" were ἔνοχοι, which (as an analytical lexicon will tell you) is a form of the noun ἔνοχος, meaning a particular kind of slavery, or literally, "to be bound by things that one holds inside." But the binding, in this case, was the "fear of death" (φόβῳ θανάτου). In that context, the infinitive phrase follows: διὰ παντὸς τοῦ ζῆν. The phrase may be translated "through all of their living," or to use a translation that stresses the substantive sense of the infinitive, "through all of their time to live."

What are the implications of saying it that way? Is that the same as saying "all their lives" (as the NRSV renders it) or "lifelong bondage" (the RSV translation)? Or does it suggest something different? Does the articular infinitive construction place emphasis on the "to live," the process of living, or even the character of living? The emphasis, in other words, could be as much on the "act of living" in a particular way as it is on the fear of death or even the metaphorical slavery.

Another text that indicates the unique power of this infinitive construction is Galatians 3:23:

Πρὸ τοῦ δὲ ἐλθεῖν τὴν πίστιν ὑπὸ νόμον
before - but to come the faith under law

ἐφρουρούμεθα συγκλειόμενοι εἰς τὴν
we were guarded (or kept) being shut up (as) to the

μέλλουσαν πίστιν ἀποκαλυφθῆναι,
being about faith being about to be revealed,

Again, it is necessary to reconstruct a complex sentence carefully from Greek to English. Be aware, first, of the fact that the sentence has two infinitives or infinitive constructions: ἐλθεῖν, "to come," at the beginning of the sentence, and, at the end of the sentence, ἀποκαλυφθῆναι, "to be revealed" (a passive infinitive). The first one, ἐλθεῖν, is the articular construction, with the preposition πρό. The second infinitive (ἀποκαλυφθῆναι) is an anarthrous construction and modifies the second occurrence of the noun, πίστιν, "faith." Look at the two phrases in tandem:

πρὸ τοῦ δὲ ἐλθεῖν τὴν πίστιν

and

πίστιν ἀποκαλυφθῆναι.

When seen this way, they take on new interest, even though we will leave it up to the reader at this point to think through the implications of these particular infinitives. Again, we may ask whether these are small and insignificant things about the text. For some, the answer will be yes. But for those who want to explore as many possibilities for the richness of a text as possible, or for those who seek more keenly a sense of what the writer might have meant, these are not small matters at all. Instead, they are dimensions that anyone who takes the time and effort can open up from verses such as these.

PRINCIPLE 8

The Case of Nouns
and Adjectives

Most grammar books on Greek or any language deal with nouns and adjectives first. In many ways, this is proper, since they represent the most basic use of words. Nouns name things. Adjectives describe or modify nouns. In the phrase "a hot towel," towel is the noun and hot is the adjective that describes the towel. In another form, the sentence "the bike is red" has a noun, bike. It also has a connecting verb, "is," that associates the subject (bike) and the predicate (red). The adjective "red" describes the bike.

These are, in a sense, the large building blocks of the sentences of most languages, certainly both English and Greek. In this discussion we shall call attention to the most important elements of both nouns and adjectives for anyone working with an interlinear Greek New Testament. We treat them together because of their general similarity and the ways in which they invariably reflect each other. That is, both nouns and adjectives have three basic sets of common characteristics: number, gender, and case. In fact, whenever they appear together (as they most often do), they must match in all three of these characteristics. This is one of the easiest ways for the Greek student to know which adjectives go with which nouns— they become sets. In what follows, we shall discuss nouns first and then adjectives; but virtually everything that we say about nouns in terms of number, gender, and case applies equally to adjectives.

We should say, too, that number, gender, and case in Greek are part of the formation of other parts of speech, each of which is related in some way to nouns. By their spelling, pronouns, articles, participles, and numerals, as well as nouns and adjectives, all demonstrate number, gender, and case. You will become more familiar with these as you work with your reference tools.

Nouns

Number in Nouns

In various ways, we have already discussed the noun's number, and since it is a commonplace idea, we will only mention it briefly again here. The number of the noun refers to whether it is singular or plural. Is only one of what is named referred to in the sentence? If so, the noun is singular. Or are more than one referred to in the sentence? If so, the noun is plural. Number in Greek is really no different than number in English, and this bears little discussion. What you should be aware of, however, is that in Greek (as often in English), whether a noun is singular or plural frequently plays an important role. Particularly in a complex sentence the words around the noun (adjectives or other modifying words) may raise the question of which words go with the noun in question. While the answer to that can sometimes be complicated, any word that modifies a noun must agree with it in number. There are occasions, then, when the simple matter of number clarifies which words go with which others.

Gender in Nouns

Nouns are also classified by their gender, even though the meaning of that is often misunderstood. In Greek, as in other languages, every noun is either masculine, feminine, or neuter. The misunderstanding arises when gender in language structure ("grammatical gender," we might say) is taken to be the same as physiology—as sexual designation. The grammatical terms masculine, feminine, and neuter probably did arise in Greek as a way of differentiating human genders, but over time that function changed. Though the reasons to a large extent have been lost over time, certain nouns have come to be designated as masculine, feminine, or neuter, but not because they refer to men or women or things. In dealing with the Greek of the New Testament, interpreters must take care in handling the differences in grammatical gender. Essentially, we need to keep two things clearly in mind.

First, there are places in the New Testament in which the feminine gender is used for females and the masculine for males. For instance, the names of women are still usually in the feminine gender, such as "Chloe" (Χλόη) in 1 Corinthians 1:11. This is important to us because it sometimes helps us discern the identity of persons mentioned in the New Testament and thereby come to a better appreciation of the role of women in the early church. For example, in Romans 16 Paul sends greetings to a series of people. Among them, in verse 12, Τρύφαιναν and Τρυφῶσαν (Tryphaena and Tryphosa) are both females, while Ἰουνιᾶν ("Junia") in verse 7 could be either, since the form is the same for masculine and feminine.

Furthermore, sometimes writers use certain words in the feminine gender to distinguish women from men. Examples include these: ἡ κυρία distinguishes a female mistress from a male master, ὁ κύριος. A female slave may be referred to with δούλη and a male slave with δοῦλος (see Acts 2:18). The word for woman and wife, γυνή, is feminine (see Jn. 2:4).

Second, however, in many cases the grammatical gender distinction has absolutely nothing to do with human gender. Sometimes words that refer to females are feminine, as for example, the word θυγάτηρ, which means "daughter" and is a feminine noun. However, the word for "little girl" (κοράσιον) is neuter (see for example Mt. 9:24), and so is the word παιδάριον (see Mt. 11:9), which means "little boy" or "young slave." Χείρ ("hand"), κεφαλή ("head"), and γαστήρ ("stomach") are all feminine, whether they refer to a man's body or a woman's. The words for foot (πούς) and finger (δάκτυλος) are always masculine, but eye (ὄμμα) and breast (στῆθος) are always neuter. The list of both masculine and feminine Greek words that defy any logical connection to male or female could be extended almost endlessly. The distinctions concerning gender are often arbitrary.

Therefore, the particular importance as far as gender is concerned is limited. One cannot ever conclude that because a particular Greek word in a New Testament text is, for example, masculine, that it must refer to a male. As we noted earlier, there is no reason to take the masculine words used in 1 Timothy 3 to characterize the person who aspires to be a bishop (ἐπίσκοπος) in the church as referring to men alone. Other examples of passages in which the gender of a noun does not identify human gender include those that use the word μαθητής (disciple). In spite of popular views, this masculine noun refers to followers of both genders, as a comparison of Luke 24:6 and 9:22 indicates. The words for prophet (προφήτης) and apostle (ἀπόστολος) are additional examples. The latter is another instance of the flexibility of grammatical gender. While the word ἀπόστολος is masculine, the noun for "apostleship" or "the office of apostle" is feminine—ἀποστολή. (See Acts 1:25 and Gal. 2:8.) By means of their sermons, preachers who can handle the gender of Greek nouns are able to call into question some popular assumptions about the roles of men and women in the New Testament.

However, a noun's gender is always important because it helps us determine what, if any, article goes with it. As we suggested above, sometimes it is not immediately clear which article goes with which noun. Sometimes the answer can be found in the principle that the noun and its article must match, and gender (like number) is one of the key ways in which that match is made. However, you will need to look up most nouns in a lexicon to determine for certain its gender, since some masculine nouns have what may appear to be feminine endings and vice versa.

Finally, we should alert you to the fact that some words are spelled the same in two or more genders. (See below for an example.) In these cases, it may be impossible to know which gender is meant, and it may not matter. However, occasionally it is worth toying with the possibilities of meaning resulting first from taking the word to be of one gender and then from the other.

Case in Nouns

We come to the major dimension to be learned about Greek nouns: the significance of "case." There is some question about the number of cases in Greek, and grammarians have proposed as few as five and as many as ten different cases. Our experience is that if you develop an understanding of the uniqueness of five basic cases, you will be equipped for useful insights into numerous New Testament Greek texts. Of course, these five cases are the same for adjectives as for nouns. Even though a full understanding of cases in the Greek language is beyond the scope of the skill you are developing for this project, each of the five cases suggests its own unique viewpoint, and you should learn those five distinctive viewpoints and bring them to any text in which a particular case appears. We remind you, too, that the first thing you are told when looking up the meaning of a noun or an adjective in an analytical lexicon is its case. We turn now to the five basic cases—the nominative, the genitive, the accusative, the dative, and the vocative.

The Nominative Case (Designation)

The nominative case is *the naming case, the case of designation.* Even though this is certainly not always true, most often the nominative case designates, or identifies, the subject of the verb's sentence. The nominative can also be found as the predicate of the sentence (that is, a noun that is equated with the sentence's subject—see below). Proper names are also often in the nominative case, and the "independent" nominative names an idea rather than an object. (For instance, in both Lk. 21:6 and Mk. 8:2, the word "days"—ἡμέραι—is in the nominative case.) Nevertheless, the most common use of the nominative is to name the subject of a sentence or a clause. The nominative "designates"; it "points to" what a sentence or a particular clause is *about*.

Consider, for example, John 3:35: ὁ πατὴρ ἀγαπᾷ τὸν υἱὸν καὶ πάντα δέδωκεν ἐν τῇ χειρὶ αὐτοῦ, "the father loves the son, and has given all things into his hands." The word "father" is the subject of the sentence and is in the nominative case. It is the father who "loves" and who "has given" all things into the son's hands. The "father" identifies the one whom the sentence is about and (in this case) the one who does the action. Another example is in Luke 9:38: καὶ ἰδοὺ ἀνὴρ ἀπὸ τοῦ ὄχλου ἐβόησεν λέγων, "And, behold, a man from the crowd called aloud, saying." Ἀνήρ, man, is in the nominative case, since the sentence is about him and what he is doing.

Sometimes the nominative is more complicated, as when it appears in the predicate of a sentence. One sees this, for example, in Ephesians 2:14, Αὐτὸς γάρ ἐστιν ἡ εἰρήνη ἡμῶν, "for he is our peace." "Peace" (εἰρήνη) is the predicate and in the nominative case. As such it is equated with the subject of the sentence (αὐτός). Notice, however, that it still designates what the sentence is about.

The Genitive Case (Definition)

The genitive case in English is often called the "possessive" case, but in Greek that is not the best way to think of it. The genitive case in the Greek language is predominantly *the case of definition,* and should always call definition to mind. The genitive always defines something, and what it most often defines is some noun that precedes it. In a phrase such as ἐπιστρέψαι καρδίας, "to turn the hearts" (Lk. 1:17), which hearts are intended? A definition of "the hearts" is needed, so we look at the word that follows this phrase, which is πατέρων, the genitive plural, "of the fathers," or the "fathers' hearts." Hence, the genitive defines or specifies which hearts are turned and immediately follows the noun that it defines.

A couple of dimensions of the genitive case can be seen in Matthew 5:20, a verse we have used to demonstrate the double negative:

λέγω γὰρ ὑμῖν   ὅτι ἐὰν μὴ περισσεύσῃ ὑμῶν
I say for to you that except   exceeds   of you

ἡ δικαιοσύνη   πλεῖον   τῶν γραμματέων καὶ
the righteousness more than of the scribes   and

Φαρισαίων, οὐ μὴ εἰσέλθητε εἰς τὴν
Pharisees   by no means will you enter into the

βασιλείαν τῶν οὐρανῶν.
kingdom of the heavens.

First, note that in this passage a genitive pronoun, ὑμῶν, actually precedes the word that it modifies. "Except the righteousness shall exceed" immediately raises the question, what or whose righteousness? Ὑμῶν answers the question: "Except the righteousness *of you*" or "*your* righteousness." Moreover, the genitive pronoun is plural, meaning "all of you." But what is it your righteousness must exceed, or whose righteousness should yours exceed? Answer: Exceed the righteousness of the scribes and Pharisees. Those nouns and the article that applies to both are genitive plural—τῶν γραμματέων καὶ Φαρισαίων. They define the righteousness that disciples are to exceed. (Note that this implies that the scribes and Pharisees are indeed righteous!)

But there is more in this passage. If your righteousness does not exceed theirs, you shall, by no means, enter into the kingdom. But what kingdom is meant? The kingdom itself must now be defined. Again, it is a genitive noun, along with a genitive article, that does the defining: τὴν βασιλείαν τῶν οὐρανῶν, "the kingdom of the heavens." *That* is the kingdom. But notice, too, that the genitive noun and its article are again in the plural: the kingdom "in the heavens."

There are many genitive forms, but three are of importance for us:

The genitive of *possession*, as when one says "the book of John," or "the book that belongs to John."

The genitive of *relationship*, as in the phrase, "the Son of God," where "of God" is in the genitive case.

The genitive of *place*, as in Acts 19:26, where Paul says, "You also see and hear that not only in Ephesus," and Ephesus is in the genitive—Ἐφέσου.

Scholars construct many other genitive forms, but in various ways their function is in every case to define something or someone.

One important ambiguity sometimes appears in the genitive of possession, namely, the difference that has been called the "subjective" and "objective" genitive. This occurs when it is uncertain whether the genitive *produces the action* of the word it modifies or *receives the action*. For instance, when does "the love of God" mean God's love for us (a subjective genitive) and when does it mean our love of God (an objective genitive)? In the event you find this kind of ambiguity in the genitive, you might "play" with its two possible meanings.

Clearly the work of the genitive case is the act of defining and defining again. Its role of clarification and of the narrowing of meaning is one that the student of the Greek text should not miss.

The Accusative Case (Limiting)

Scholars tell us that this is the most widely used case in the Greek New Testament. The accusative case can be considered the case for *indicating limitation*. If the nominative is the naming case, and the genitive is the defining case, this one is designed to provide the boundaries around the actions of the sentence. If the sentence says, "I am sending you," it may be a complete sentence grammatically, but it has no boundary to it; it provides little sense for grasping what is going on. It is too open-ended because it lacks a limiting factor or a qualification. On the other hand, "I am sending you to the store" or "I am sending you for a loaf of bread" both have a limiting factor within them or added to them. It is the equivalent of saying, "I am not sending you to the post office or to the dry cleaners, but I am sending you to the store." The accusative case adds specificity. It is close to, but not exactly the same as, what in English we call the "direct object."

This accusative, limiting construction is present in a variety of ways on almost every page of the New Testament. In John 8:46b, for example, we find Jesus asking this question: εἰ ἀλήθειαν λέγω, διὰ τί ὑμεῖς οὐ πιστεύετέ μοι; The punctuation clues us to translate this as a question, "If I say truth, why do you not believe me?" The word ἀλήθειαν, "truth," is in the accusative case and limits what it is that Jesus says that should produce faith.

Or take a clause such as this one from 2 Timothy 4:7: τὸν καλὸν ἀγῶνα ἠγώνισμαι, "I have fought the good fight." "I have fought" would be too open-ended. Fought what, we would ask. So "the good fight" (τὸν καλὸν ἀγῶνα) is accusative and limits what has been fought. Or look at John 14:26, where Jesus speaks of what the Counselor (Holy Spirit) will do: ἐκεῖνος ὑμᾶς διδάξει πάντα, "He will teach you all things." What will the Spirit teach you? All things—πάντα. The accusative adds a distinctive limitation to the clause, albeit an expansive one! Again, in John 15:15, Jesus says: οὐκέτι λέγω ὑμᾶς δούλους, "No longer do I call you servants," with "servants" (δούλους) in the accusative case. "No longer do I call you" needs the limitation that the word "servants" provides.

As with the other cases, when one gets a sense of what the presence of a noun in the accusative case does with its limiting quality, most sentences can be read with a clearer grasp of what they hold. You can simply stop and say that a word is accusative; it is limiting. Then ask, what does it limit? Why does it make that limitation? By working with these kinds of questions, new insights often can emerge.

The Dative Case (Personal Interest)

This is the case that is the closest to our English "indirect object." It is a case that we might usefully designate as reflecting "*personal interest.*" The nominative case names, the genitive case defines, the accusative case limits, but the dative case provides the personal element in a sentence's action. It is the case that in English must be said with a "for" or a "to," as in, "I am going to speak privately *to* the apostles." In a Greek sentence such as this, the word "apostles" is in the dative case. What the dative recognizes is the personal dimension, often the personal relationship that underlies the sentence. "I am going to give this pendant to that man." In this case, "man" is in the dative case. It may sometimes be used with objects, rather than persons, but even then the objects tend to be personified.

Some of the best and easiest examples of the role of the dative case are found in the use of pronouns rather than nouns or adjectives. So allow us to cite a few of them as a way of clarifying the function of this case.

In 1 Corinthians 5:9 are these words: Ἔγραψα ὑμῖν ἐν τῇ ἐπιστολῇ μὴ συναναμίγνυσθαι πόρνοις, or, "I wrote to you in the epistle not to associate intimately with fornicators." The little word ὑμῖν is dative, plural. If one leaves it out, the sentence is proper and clear: "I wrote in the epistle not to associate intimately with fornicators." But look at how the whole feel of the sentence changes when the dative case is present: "I wrote *to you* in the epistle." The dative case often contributes a vivid sense of personalness or relationship in what is communicated.

For another example, consider Matthew 13:13: διὰ τοῦτο ἐν παραβολαῖς αὐτοῖς λαλῶ, ὅτι βλέποντες οὐ βλέπουσιν καὶ ἀκούοντες οὐκ ἀκούουσιν οὐδὲ συνίουσιν. It is a long, but very important verse, which may be translated, "Therefore I speak to them in parables, because seeing they see not, and hearing they hear not, neither understand." In this construction, αὐτοῖς is dative, third person, plural. Again, remove it and the sentence is good: "Therefore I speak in parables, because seeing," and so forth. The dative certainly adds specificity: "I speak (not just to anyone, but) *to them* in parables." Moreover, the dative "to them" also adds an undeniable personal element to the entire statement.

To see how a dative noun (in this case combined with a dative pronoun) provides this personal tone to a statement, look at Luke 11:13, which reads, "If you then, who are evil, know how to give good gifts *to your children,* how much more will the heavenly Father give the Holy Spirit to those who ask him!" The recipients of the verb "give" are in the dative, which personalizes that action. In the Greek, "to your children" is τοῖς τέκνοις ὑμῶν. Think of how personal this statement is as a result of that dative phrase.

The Vocative Case (Direct Address)

This last case is the case of direct address, both in Greek and in English. For our purposes, it is worth recognizing, since one encounters it over and over again in the New Testament. The vocative is usually a naming with either a proper name (for example, "Peter"), an indirect name (such as "son"), or a class (for instance, "You who are Israelites"). But the vocative does not name in the same sense that the nominative case does. Here, it is usually (at least in translation) followed by a comma, and then the following words actually address the individual or group named at the beginning. In the sentence "John, will you go get that for me?" the name "John" represents the vocative case. Since you will not find quotation marks in the Greek New Testament, the vocative case lets you know something is a direct address.

In Greek, the vocative of address can take the article, often (but not always) intended to give a special definiteness to the one being addressed (see Principle 1). In Luke 8:54, Jesus addresses Jairus' unconscious daughter, Ἡ παῖς, ἔγειρε ("Child, arise!"). But it is this specific child whom Jesus addresses, so the article ἡ precedes the noun, παῖς. Moreover, sometimes an author designs direct address to carry special emphasis by including the particle (an interjection) ὦ. One sees this, for example, in Matthew 15:28: τότε ἀποκριθεὶς ὁ Ἰησοῦς εἶπεν αὐτῇ, ὦ γύναι, μεγάλη σου ἡ πίστις, "And answering, Jesus said to her, 'O woman, great is your faith.'" The vocative of direct address is there, γύναι, but the addition of the interjection (ὦ) before it adds considerable force. Since γύναι is an exception, this is a good place to say that the vocative case in the singular often ends with an epsilon (ε), but the plural vocative words are spelled the same as the nominative.

A particularly interesting and provocative example of the vocative is found in Luke 1:3, the verse in which the gospel's author mentions the one who is to receive the work: ἔδοξε κἀμοὶ παρηκολουθηκότι ἄνωθεν πᾶσιν ἀκριβῶς καθεξῆς σοι γράψαι, κράτιστε Θεόφιλε, "it seemed good to me also, having investigated from their source all things accurately in order to write to you, most excellent Theophilus." It is a classic use of the vocative case (Θεόφιλε), with an adjective (κράτιστε), but without an article or the interjection ὦ.

Again, you will encounter many more than these five cases as you work with an analytical lexicon. But these five, we believe, will be of greatest value to you in your Greek exegesis.

Adjectives

Adjectives are invariably the close companions of the nouns, and, as we indicated earlier, everything that we have said about the number, gender, and case of nouns applies equally to adjectives. So close is the companionship between nouns and adjectives, in fact, that when an adjective modifies a noun, it must agree with the noun in all three of those dimensions. As we have said, this helps solve the problem of which adjectives go with which nouns. In Greek, adjectives can appear virtually anywhere around a noun, in front of it, after it, even separated from it.

For example, John 15:1 attributes this statement to Jesus: Ἐγώ εἰμι ἡ ἄμπελος ἡ ἀληθινή, which is literally, "I am the vine, the true" and in better English, "I am the true vine." Ἀληθινή is the adjective, but it follows and is separated from the noun it modifies (ἄμπελος) by the article ἡ. But in all three aspects the adjective matches not only its noun but also its own article. Like ἄμπελος, ἀληθινή is nominative, singular, and neuter or feminine (the two are spelled the same). In both its uses, the article ἡ matches both the noun and the adjective in that it shares the same case, number, and gender with both. In Principle 1 we discussed the translation of a sentence like this from the standpoint of the articles.

The relationship between adjectives and the nouns with which they appear can take two distinct forms and positions:

1. The first is called the *attributive position* of the adjective. In this form, the adjective ascribes a quality to the noun and appears in close conjunction with it. For example, when Luke 18:6 speaks of ὁ κριτὴς τῆς ἀδικίας ("the unjust" or "unrighteous judge"), the adjective ἀδικίας is in the attributive position. It "attributes" something to the judge.

2. The second form of the adjective is called *the predicate position*. In this position, an adjective does not attribute something to the noun, but instead, makes an assertion about the noun. For instance, in Mark 9:50, Jesus is reported to have said, καλὸν τὸ ἅλας, that is,

"salt is good." Notice three things about this example: First, there is no article before καλόν. Second, the adjective can precede the noun as well as follow it, and, third, this construction is the same as if the word "is" stood between the substantive (τὸ ἅλας) and the adjective (καλόν).

There are complexities involved in recognizing the multiple constructions for the attributive and predicate adjectives. For instance, adjectives in the *predicate* position are never preceded by an article. However, adjectives in the *attributive* position may be with or without an article. Moreover, the distinction between these two positions is discernable only when the noun is preceded by an article. That is, the noun is anarthrous, and there is no way of knowing if the adjective is attributive or predicative. (For example, καλὸν ἅλας.) Consequently, you need simply to follow the lead of an interlinear English-Greek text in order to determine which position the adjective occupies.

One thing, however, is vitally important here. As important as the attributive adjective can be in modifying its noun, when an adjective appears in the *predicate* position, its force in modifying the noun is magnified dramatically. An adjective is invariably placed in the predicate position for strong emphasis, and the student of the New Testament text needs to read it that way.

We conclude this discussion of the adjective by reminding you of its use as a noun (that is, its substantive use). This means simply that sometimes an adjective can function as a noun. A good example is the famous saying found in Mark 2:17: οὐκ ἦλθον καλέσαι δικαίους ἀλλὰ ἁμαρτωλούς ("I have come to call not the righteous but sinners"). In this sentence, the two adjectives—"righteous" (δικαίους) and "sinners" (ἁμαρτωλούς)—function as nouns. They mean "righteous persons" and "sinful persons." When an adjective seems to stand alone without a noun to modify, consider the possibility it may be a substantive adjective.

PRINCIPLE 9

Filling in the Pronouns

Pronouns in Greek, as in English, fill in for the nouns. To a certain extent this common wisdom is true: Pronouns appear in order to avoid the sheer repetition of nouns. Instead of saying someone's name every time we want to refer to a person in a sentence, we can first identify that person and thereafter simply speak of her or him with "she" or "he." But in most languages, Greek included, there is a great deal more to the use of pronouns than that. Pronouns have roles to play, both in creating meaning and in making meaning more precise. For one working with the Greek New Testament text, key signals about meaning, emphasis, and nuance are often given by pronouns.

The most basic pronouns are well known. They are the first, second, third person pronouns, singular (I, you, he–she–it) and plural (we, you, they). But this in no way exhausts the key dimensions of the pronoun that you will need to work efficiently with the Greek text. In this section, we will outline the major kinds of pronouns, as well as the most significant elements of each.

Six kinds of pronouns have special uses that can easily be recognized with the help of an interlinear text. A single fundamental principle undergirds the use of the pronoun in virtually all its forms in the Greek New Testament, namely, it is possible in many contexts to write perfectly well, and with considerable clarity, *without* pronouns. Not that one would merely repeat a noun again and again. In Greek most often the verb itself contains, or implies, its own pronoun by the kind of ending it has.

Take for example the verb λελάληκα in John 16:1, from the phrase, Ταῦτα λελάληκα ὑμῖν ("these things I have spoken to you"). The verb is first person singular, "I have spoken." In using the verb by itself, no additional pronoun is necessary to name the speaker and the subject of the sentence. The pronoun ("I") is implied in the verb. In verse 3 of the same chapter, no pronouns appear in the clause καὶ ταῦτα ποιήσουσιν ὅτι οὐκ ἔγνωσαν τὸν πατέρα οὐδὲ ἐμέ, which translates, "and they will do these things because they have not known the Father or me." The verb is ποιήσουσιν, and as an interlinear says, it means "they will do." Again, the subject of the verb ("they") need not be mentioned, for it is contained within the third person, plural form of the verb "they do." This practice is common throughout the Greek New Testament. When a phrase or sentence appears without either a noun or pronoun, one can always read the pronoun as first, second, or third person, singular or plural, within the verb itself.

The reason this practice is important to us is because in many cases when a pronoun actually *does appear* within a phrase or a sentence, it has been deliberately put there by the writer. It is there for some reason, most often to place a keen emphasis on the pronoun itself. With that in mind, we will turn to the seven kinds of pronouns that can actually appear within the text: personal, relative, intensive, reflexive, reciprocal, interrogative, and indefinite.

The Personal Pronoun

The personal pronouns are the ones to which we have already called attention in English, the ones we know best: I, you, he-she-it; we, you (plural), they. With these pronouns, the *principle* that we discussed above applies with particular force. They can be in any verb, but when they actually appear in the text, they "reinforce" their presence in the verb. They are inserted for emphasis, and the student of the text should not miss that. While an interlinear text will most often alert you to the presence of a personal pronoun, the most common ones that are emphasized are ἐγώ (I) and σύ (you). Various forms of these two indicate the first or second person, and various forms indicate the plurals as well. In the Greek New Testament, you will frequently find interesting and important constructions that utilize the personal pronoun.

Look, for instance, at John 1:25:

καὶ ἠρώτησαν αὐτὸν καὶ εἶπαν αὐτῷ,   τί   οὖν
And they asked him and said to him, "Why then

βαπτίζεις   εἰ σὺ οὐκ εἶ ὁ χριστὸς οὐδὲ
you are baptizing, if you not are the Christ   nor

Ἠλίας οὐδὲ ὁ προφήτης;
Elijah   nor the prophet?"

Look closely for the pronouns, both in English and in the Greek. We will return to the opening phrase, "And they asked him and said to him," but at this point look at the question that is asked: "Why are you baptizing?" There is no separate personal pronoun, and the second person singular pronoun, "you," is contained within the word βαπτίζεις, "you are baptizing." Next notice the "if" clause that follows. There the personal pronoun σὺ appears. The emphasis of the question falls on this pronoun. "Why are you baptizing, if *you* are not the Messiah or Elijah or the prophet?" Some translators would suggest that the pronoun might be rendered "you yourself," in order to capture its emphasis in the Greek.

In the next verse, 26, John answers: Ἐγὼ βαπτίζω ἐν ὕδατι, "I baptize (or am baptizing) in water." Exactly the same thing could have been said with only βαπτίζω ἐν ὕδατι, "I am baptizing in water." But the ἐγώ is inserted into the phrase for force and to accent the speaker. Its presence alongside the verb produces an emphatic "I." That will almost always be the case when a personal pronoun appears along with a verb that implies the same personal pronoun.

Now we need to return briefly to the phrase in John 1:25 that we bypassed a moment ago. There we can readily see a form of two pronouns as well: καὶ ἠρώτησαν αὐτὸν καὶ εἶπαν αὐτῷ, "And they asked him and said to him." Think back on the earlier principle concerning nouns. Wherever a noun can appear, a pronoun can take its place, which is the case here. The "hims"—αὐτὸν and αὐτῷ—are objects of the two verbs, "asked" and "said," respectively. The force of these two pronouns is in their status as "objects" of the verbs.

Those objects are specific and emphatic, but the two verbs of the opening clause of verse 25 stand without the emphasis of pronouns: ἠρώτησαν, "they asked," and εἶπαν, "they said." The personal pronoun "they" is implied in these two verbs and not emphasized. Attention is directed away from "they" to σύ ("you"), which appears later in the question they ask him. The emphatic use of the personal pronouns used for and by John the Baptizer contrasts with the more usual form of the pronoun "they" contained in the verbs. This distinction between personal pronouns as subjects of verbs and as objects of verbs is an important one that appears in many texts that one studies. It suggests that the "direction" of the verbal action is of particular importance.

The Relative Pronoun

The relative pronoun is a connecting pronoun. It refers to and modifies a noun that is its antecedent. Most often it connects a qualifying clause with the main clause in which the pronoun's antecedent occurs. The relative pronouns are usually translated "who," "which," and "that." Again, when any one of them appears, it does so for the sake of emphasis, and the clause of which it is a part provides an important qualification. It is one thing to say, for example, "The woman was touched." But "the woman, who was touched," implies something stronger. The first is a simple statement, while the second underlines the relationship, in a sense, between the woman and the touching. The presence of the relative pronoun and its clause indicate that just such an emphasis is expected.

An interlinear will usually indicate clearly the presence of the relative pronoun. The principal ones are ὅς, ὅστις, οἷος, ὁποῖος, and ὅσος. You will come to recognize the variations of each of them. In Colossians 2:10, a familiar use of the relative pronoun appears: καὶ ἐστὲ ἐν αὐτῷ πεπληρωμένοι, ὅς ἐστιν ἡ κεφαλὴ πάσης ἀρχῆς καὶ ἐξουσίας ("And you are having been filled up in him, who is the head of all rule and authority"). The personal pronoun αὐτῷ ("him") appears as the object of the preposition ἐν ("in"). Then comes ὅς, the relative pronoun that connects the main sentence ("and you are being filled up in him") with the subordinate clause that follows ("who is the head"). Ὅς is a connecting and emphatic link. It refers to the pronoun "him," informing us who this one is with whom we are filled.

A different form of the relative clause appears in Acts 16:17, where the slave girl follows Paul and his companions, crying out, οὗτοι οἱ ἄνθρωποι δοῦλοι τοῦ θεοῦ τοῦ ὑψίστου εἰσίν, οἵτινες καταγγέλλουσιν ὑμῖν ὁδὸν σωτηρίας, "These people (are) slaves of the most high God, who announce to you a way of salvation." An interlinear text will identify the relative pronouns οὗτοι ("these") and more importantly, οἵτινες ("who"). However one interprets this interesting text, the force of that pronoun (οἵτινες) should not be overlooked. In this case, it refers to "these people" (that is, Paul and his companions) and tells us something about them and their mission.

To take another example, a number of these pronouns appear in Romans 16, and at the end of verse 12 we find this sentence: ἀσπάσασθε Περσίδα τὴν ἀγαπητήν, ἥτις πολλὰ ἐκοπίασεν ἐν κυρίῳ, which may be translated, "Greet Persis, the beloved, who labored many things in the Lord." An analytical lexicon will indicate that ἥτις is the nominative singular form of the relative pronoun ὅστις. In this case, the relative pronoun's clause (ἥτις πολλὰ ἐκοπίασεν ἐν κυρίῳ) tells us something precious about a woman named Persis (a common name for a slave) that we would otherwise not know. Whenever you encounter such a word as ἥτις, even though an interlinear may name it a relative pronoun, you would do well to look it up in a lexicon just to make sure. There are too many other relative pronouns for us to list them all, but the use of an interlinear and a lexicon will enable you to spot them.

The Intensive Pronoun

Αὐτός is the intensive pronoun with which you will become very familiar in its various forms. Actually, αὐτός is a very versatile word and can appear in many guises as a pronoun, but its intensive use is one of the most important.

Αὐτός can, of course, be simply the third person personal pronoun, meaning "he," "she," "his," "her," and so on.

It can mean "self," as in "I will do it myself," or "you are doing nothing but hurting yourself."

As an intensive pronoun, it means "the same," or "this same (whatever)."

Usually the sentence in which it appears will make clear when αὐτός, or one of its forms, is being used as an intensive pronoun. Even then, however, it is often interesting to try out all three of these possible meanings and let them play on one another.

A few examples will indicate both how αὐτός is used and its importance as an intensive pronoun. In Luke 13:1, for example, we find this striking sentence:

Παρῆσαν   δέ τινες ἐν αὐτῷ τῷ καιρῷ
Were present and some in the same   time

ἀπαγγέλλοντες   αὐτῷ περὶ τῶν Γαλιλαίων ὧν
telling (reporting) to him about the Galileans   of whom

τὸ αἷμα Πιλᾶτος ἔμιξεν μετὰ τῶν θυσιῶν
the blood Pilatos   mixed with the sacrifices

αὐτῶν.
of them.

If you look closely at this verse, you will see αὐτός used in three different ways. Αὐτῷ appears twice and αὐτῶν once. An interlinear text will provide guidance in how it is used in each of these occurrences. Αὐτῷ appears first as an intensive pronoun and calls for an emphatic sense of the "same time." If you look back to the verses of the preceding chapter, this verse takes on new meaning, which is due in no small part to the work of the intensive pronoun. Jesus has just spoken of the necessity of discerning the importance of the time (12:49–56), and even as Jesus was saying these things—not afterward, but at that very time—he was told Pilate had already mingled the blood of Galileans with their sacrifices.

See also this statement in Romans 8:21:

ὅτι   καὶ   αὐτὴ ἡ   κτίσις   ἐλευθερωθήσεται
because and (even) itself the creation will be freed

ἀπὸ τῆς δουλείας τῆς φθορᾶς   εἰς τὴν ἐλευθερίαν
from the slavery   of corruption into the freedom

τῆς   δόξης τῶν   τέκνων τοῦ θεοῦ.
of the glory of the children of God.

Here αὐτή (a feminine variant of αὐτός) plays a significant role in this sentence. It is one thing to say that "the creation will be freed from the slavery of corruption to freedom." To say, "the creation itself will be freed" underlines creation. It suggests something like, "*even the creation* will be freed from the slavery of corruption." Not only humanity, but the whole of creation, needs liberation. Preachers who study this text should not miss the point and should be provoked to consider its implications for the proclamation of its message today.

One other text is instructive; it comes from 1 Thessalonians 4:9:

Περὶ   δὲ τῆς φιλαδελφίας οὐ χρείαν ἔχετε
Concerning now the brotherly love no need   you have

      γράφειν ὑμῖν   αὐτοὶ γὰρ ὑμεῖς
(for me) to write to you, yourselves for   you

θεοδίδακτοί   ἐστε εἰς τὸ ἀγαπᾶν ἀλλήλους,...
taught by God are (for the) to love one another...

This is still another passage that requires us to think carefully through the arrangement of the Greek and English words. The second half of this verse uses αὐτοί as an intensive pronoun. "For you, your very selves, are taught by God that you are supposed to enter into love for one another."

Paul compliments his readers, and the emphasis of the intensive pronoun adds dramatically to the force of that compliment. Having won their favor with this statement, he later goes on to urge them to do even better!

The Reflexive Pronoun

The reflexive pronoun is similar to the intensive. It provides the same kind of accentuation, but turns it in another direction. With the reflexive pronoun, the emphasis falls back onto the person or persons to which reference has been made. It is used as "you yourself," or "I myself," and in that sense, it is similar to the verse we just looked at in 1 Thessalonians 4. The same kind of emphasis can be made with a form of the intensive pronoun *or* with a reflexive pronoun, but the difference is that the reflexive reflects back to the subject of the sentence. Among the regular reflexive pronouns, these four are the most important: ἐμαυτοῦ (of myself), σεαυτοῦ (of yourself), ἑαυτοῦ (of himself or herself), and ἑαυτῶν (of themselves). These, too, will become easily recognizable. You will notice that they are all built on the stem αυτου (a form of the intensive pronoun).

Romans 2:1 is one example of the use of the reflexive pronoun:

Διὸ   ἀναπολόγητος εἶ,   ὦ ἄνθρωπε πᾶς
Wherefore inexcusable   you are O human   everyone

ὁ κρίνων· ἐν   ᾧ   γὰρ   κρίνεις   τὸν ἕτερον,
judging.   In what for you are judging the other

σεαυτὸν κατακρίνεις,   τὰ γὰρ   αὐτὰ
yourself you are condemning,   for the same things

πράσσεις   ὁ   κρίνων.
you practice the one judging.

The similarity between the reflexive and the intensive is clearly visible in this sentence. The intensive αὐτά is an example of how it can mean "the same." (Since αὐτά is neuter, "the same things" is the most likely translation.) The reflexive pronoun, σεαυτόν, accents the identity of those who judge others. The reflexive, then, stresses the actors, and the intensive pronoun in this case underlines what they are doing. In some ways, the two appear to be similar, but each provides a significant and peculiar emphasis in the clause or sentence in which it appears.

A simple example of the use of the reflexive first person singular pronoun is found in Galatians 2:18:

εἰ γὰρ   ἃ   κατέλυσα   ταῦτα   πάλιν οἰκοδομῶ,
For if what I destroyed these things again   I build,

παραβάτην ἐμαυτὸν συνιστάνω.
a transgressor myself   I show(to be).

Paul is trying to defend himself and his understanding of the gospel. He says that he will demonstrate his own sinfulness if he undermines what he had previously taught and then tries to reestablish it. Paul accentuates his own culpability in this by using the reflexive pronoun ἐμαυτόν.

The Reciprocal Pronoun

This type of pronoun suggests interaction, mutuality, and even congeniality. As a pronoun it refers to specific people whom the text identifies; but it refers back to those individuals *together*—not simply as a "they," but as a fully interacting unit. The function that the reciprocal pronoun provides is not to identify who the people as such are, but to stress their interactive nature. The reciprocal pronoun is ἀλλήλων, or some clearly recognizable variant of that, such as its accusative form, ἀλλήλους.

We find it in its most common form in 1 John 4:7: "Beloved, let us love *one another,* because love is of God"—Ἀγαπητοί, ἀγαπῶμεν ἀλλήλους, ὅτι ἡ ἀγάπη ἐκ τοῦ θεοῦ ἐστιν. The reciprocal pronoun ἀλλήλους does two things in this sentence. First, it refers back to all the "beloved," and second, the pronoun expresses the idea of "one another"—the nature of the interaction among the beloved.

This is an important term whenever and wherever it appears. For example, in Romans 12:5, Paul writes, οὕτως οἱ πολλοὶ ἕν σῶμά ἐσμεν ἐν Χριστῷ, τὸ δὲ καθ᾽ εἷς ἀλλήλων μέλη, which may be translated, "So we, who are many, are one body in Christ, and each one members of one another." We are many, but we are a single body in Christ, and each one of us is a member of all the others. The reciprocal, or interactive, pronoun gives this text its primary focus.

One of the more interesting uses of ἀλλήλων is found in Ephesians 5:21–22:

Ὑποτασσόμενοι ἀλλήλοις   ἐν φόβῳ   Χριστοῦ,
Being subject   to one another in (the) fear of Christ,

αἱ γυναῖκες τοῖς ἰδίοις   ἀνδράσιν ὡς τῷ
the wives   to their own husbands as to the

κυρίῳ...
Lord...

This is part of a complex text about both the church and the relationship of wives and husbands. However, the discussion of husbands and wives follows immediately after the short statement in verse 21, and verse 22 begins, "The wives to their own husbands as to the Lord." In a sense, the form of verse 22 even suggests that the relationship between husband and wife is an outgrowth of what verse 21 says. That verse begins with "being subject" (ὑποτασσόμενοι). After the discussion of wives, then, from verses 22 through 24, the subject turns to husbands. But verse 21 provides a preface to both discussions by saying, "being subject to one another"—ἀλλήλοις. The pronoun suggests mutuality and egalitarian interaction. Of course, we are each responsible for interpreting this entire text for ourselves, and yet in our interpretations we must somehow take into account fully the role of the reciprocal pronoun at such a critical point as this.

The Interrogative and Indefinite Pronouns

We treat these important pronouns together here because they are often the same word. However, one major difference between them that is easily overlooked is the accent mark. The basic pronouns in both cases are τις and τι in a variety of forms, most of which are easily recognizable. As interrogative pronouns, τίς and τί almost always have an acute accent. As indefinite pronouns, τὶς and τὶ almost always have a grave accent (as we have shown here), or they will be without any accent mark at all. With the help of an interlinear text, these two uses of the same words need not be confused with each other. But distinguishing them is very important.

Just as their label suggests, τίς and τί are interrogative pronouns. They are the pronouns that set up or imply a question, and most often mean "who," "what," or "why." In Matthew 7:3, for example, τί introduces this question: τί δὲ βλέπεις τὸ κάρφος τὸ ἐν τῷ ὀφθαλμῷ τοῦ ἀδελφοῦ σου, τὴν δὲ ἐν τῷ σῷ ὀφθαλμῷ δοκὸν οὐ κατανοεῖς;...—"And why do you see the chip in the eye of your brother but do not notice the log in your own eye?" Τί signals the question "why?".

In Matthew 20:22, we find the use of the same interrogative pronoun but in a slightly different form: ἀποκριθεὶς δὲ ὁ Ἰησοῦς εἶπεν, οὐκ οἴδατε τί αἰτεῖσθε. δύνασθε πιεῖν τὸ ποτήριον ὃ ἐγὼ μέλλω πίνειν; λέγουσιν αὐτῷ δυνάμεθα. The NRSV translates the verse this way: "But Jesus answered, 'You do not know what you are asking. Are you able to drink the cup that I am about to drink?' They said to him, 'We are able.'" This time, the τί is not the first but the third word in the sentence, yet it still means "what." In this case, τί is in a statement ("You do not know *what* you ask"), but still alerts the reader to the question that follows ("Are you able?").

When τίς or τί is an indefinite pronoun, however, it has a different importance. It specifies something in the text as "indefinite," that is, undetermined. Often the indefinite pronoun seems to be a deliberate addition to a sentence. The indefinite pronouns τὶς and τὶ mean "anyone" or "anything." That is the nature of their "indefiniteness." Sometimes the context will indicate that τὶς or τὶ suggests "a certain person" or "thing" that is unspecified. Other times they suggest a person "who could be anyone" or something that "could be most anything."

You should also know that there are many occasions when τὶς or τὶ appear without any accent at all. When this happens, you may conclude that the words are indefinite pronouns and not interrogative ones, because as interrogative pronouns, τίς and τί are always accented. The reasons for dropping the accent from the indefinite pronouns altogether are technical and need not be our concern here.

As one might expect, the indefinite pronoun is common in the New Testament. We find it, for example, in 1 Corinthians 14:37: Εἴ τις δοκεῖ προφήτης εἶναι ἤ πνευματικός…, "If anyone thinks to be a prophet or a spiritual person." In Romans 14:14, Paul writes, "I know and am persuaded in the Lord Jesus that nothing is unclean in itself, except when one counts anything (τι) to be unclean." With the indefinite pronoun, he accentuates the fact that absolutely anything can be counted unclean by some people.

We find an interesting use of indefinite and interrogative pronouns in Luke 15 and 16. As you know, chapter 15 is composed of a short setting in which the religious leaders complain that Jesus associates with "sinners and tax collectors" (vv. 1–2). Luke follows this introduction with four parables, three of which make up the rest of chapter 15. In 15:4 Jesus begins the first parable with an interrogative pronoun: τίς ἄνθρωπος ἐξ ὑμῶ ἔχων ἑκατὸν πρόβατα ("Which one [or man] of you, having a hundred sheep") and goes on to tell the story of the one lost sheep (vv. 4–7). Then verse 8 begins, Ἤ τίς γυνὴ δραχμὰς ἔχουσα δέκα ("Or what woman having ten silver coins") and continues by telling the story of the lost coin. The first two parables each begin with a question, signaled by the interrogative pronoun τίς, and feature first a man (a shepherd) and then a woman.

Now, however, the so-called parable of the prodigal son (vv. 11–32) begins not with a question, but with an indefinite pronoun: ἄνθρωπος τις εἶχεν δύο υἱούς ("A certain man had two sons"). The first verse of chapter 16 has a similar construction: ἄνθρωπός τις ἦν πλούσιος ὅς εἶχεν οἰκονόμον ("A certain rich man had a steward"). For other examples of the use of this construction to begin a parable, see Luke 10:30 and 13:6.

The last two of the four parables in Luke 15:1—16:9 begin, not with a question, but with reference to a "certain person," who could be any of us. The evangelist skillfully introduces these four stories with use, first, of the interrogative pronoun τίς, and then of the indefinite pronoun τις. Preachers can see that skillful construction and use it to their advantage in sermons.

Now that we have seen how Luke the evangelist "dances" with τις and τίς, we ask how we can learn to "dance with words."

Dancing with Words

Finally, working with a Greek–English interlinear New Testament lets you do something of what scholars have long called "word studies." Of all the dimensions of interacting with the interlinear text, this one is probably the most enjoyable. To be sure, the word studies that preachers do are far less technical and complicated than those produced by scholars. However, with a basic knowledge of Greek, as we have laid out here, you can explore the nuances of words for yourself, often in highly creative and original ways. From such studies you can then develop valuable materials for the sermon. Word studies are a delightful form of verbal dancing. In this concluding principle, we will explore and illustrate some of the fundamentals of Greek word study for the pulpit.

How Do Words Mean?

Words never have single or fixed meanings. They are always products of a particular culture at a particular time. The current meaning of words such as "gay" or "cool" in our culture suggests how the meaning of a word changes and is a product of particular cultural usage at a particular time. Words in any language and for any culture have the meanings they have because people of that culture agree (through how they *use* the words) that this word shall mean this and that word shall mean that. (Have you ever noticed how new English dictionaries have to revise or add meanings because of common usage?) The meanings of the Greek text of our New Testament were hammered out in the Greco-Roman culture, and in that process the meanings of some words in classic Greek changed in the new culture.

However, the meanings of words are also reflections of their use by specific authors as they think creatively. We use words to mean what we want them to mean. Words are most often tools by which we attempt to accomplish something, if only to transmit what we are thinking. The flexibility of language allows anyone to use words in different settings than those in which they are normally used. An old word "jumps" into a different situation to mean something new. Paul did this very thing in 1 Corinthians 15:8. After reciting the list of persons to whom the risen Christ had appeared, Paul says, "Last of all, as to one untimely born, he appeared also to me" (NRSV). The phrase translated "one untimely born" is ὡσπερεὶ τῷ ἐκτρώματι. In its normal setting, ἐκτρώματι meant a premature birth or a miscarriage. But Paul stretches the word and uses it metaphorically to speak of the fact that he came along later, after the period of the resurrection appearances.

The observation about the flexibility of language suggests the question of the "boundaries" of a word's use. Here "boundaries" refers to the sometimes highly creative and original use of the same word in multiple settings and constructions. In interpreting a biblical text, we are occasionally not looking so much for the specific use of a word in this sentence or that context. That is important, of course, as we will see. But we are also interested in what we might call a word's "generic" meaning within Greek.

For example, in English we might use the word "bank" in any of these sentences:

"We are going to the bank downtown to take care of some business."

"We are going to the bank of the river to take care of some business."

"Look at the bank on that race track."

"That's what I said; you can bank on it."

There is no particular ambiguity in these sentences, and yet the key word in all of them is "bank." However, that word means different things in each sentence. There is a bank downtown, a bank of the river, and one on the race track. And somehow we can also use the same word to mean "trust." The word's context in a particular sentence makes its meaning clear.

Let's look closer. We approach the search for meaning of words in any sentence at the levels of our three kinds of study—semantic, grammatical, and contextual. First, at the semantic level, we ask the generic question of a word: *What is there about the word "bank" that permits its use in each sentence, even though each use is so different?* That is, what is the *common ingredient* that lets us move the word from one context to the other, even when the contexts themselves seem strikingly different? What is a term's elastic or "generic" meaning? For the English word "bank," the generic meaning is "something that holds things in." Often, but not always, a Greek word might have such a generic meaning. When Paul employs the word ἔκτρωμα, as we just noted, he appeals to a generic sense of the word, which means something like "coming at the wrong time."

However, at the levels of *grammar and context,* we are interested in the way a word is being used in a given phrase or sentence. What does the word "bank" mean when it is used in this particular sentence? When the notion of "river" is present in an English text, to talk about "bank" means a particular thing. Its use is not only generic—which is important—but also specific. One must, in other words, take careful note of the words that surround a particular term in order to grasp how a word that has many potential uses is employed in a specific text. In the case of Paul's use of ἔκτρωμα, we search for its meaning in terms of two contexts. We are interested in its use in this sentence, which places the word in the context, first, of a final point in an order of words and phrases, and second, in a broader context of the list of resurrection appearances.

The relationship of words and meanings is much more complicated than this. However, if you approach the Greek text with these observations in mind, you will be better equipped to dance with its words in creative and enlightening ways. However, we are also interested in other matters in our search for meaning.

Compound Words

Earlier, in our discussion of prepositions, we looked at the merger of words with prefixed prepositions. The prefix produces a "compound" word, insofar as the word comprises several separable components. Now we focus on compound words created by the combination of other words, not just with prepositions. If you have studied any German, you know that that language allows for the combination of words into new words. Greek allows for the same possibility. Sometimes we can easily recognize compound Greek words, but other times we must look at a long word, guess that it might be compound, and then consult a lexicon. Of course, not all long words are compounds, since some word endings and prefixes can extend the length of a word considerably. But when a word is made by putting other words together, you need to take it apart again and "play with" the possibilities for the merging of the two meanings into something new.

In analyzing compound words, we will sometimes find that one of the components is dominant and determines the meaning of the new word. Other times, we may find that the fusion of two or more words creates an entirely new meaning, which may or may not seem logical in the light of the meanings of the words joined together. This means that we should not begin the work of dissecting compound words with any preconceived notion of what we are going to find.

Here are some examples of compound words that we find in the Greek New Testament and sketches of how one might go about analyzing them.

φιλο- *Words*

Let's begin with some words where we are on familiar ground. There is a series of words that include as their first component some form of φιλο, related to the noun φίλος, which usually means the love most clearly reflected in human friendship. In the Introduction, we saw how this word is used in the gospel of John in the encounter between Jesus and Peter. In each of the following words, φιλο is the first and "governing" component of a new word.

Φιλανθρωπία (Titus 3:4) combines φίλος with ἄνθρωπος—"love of persons." (Note that this is the source of our English word philanthropy.) In a sense, that meaning is already expressed in φίλος alone, so what does an author gain by using a compound of it with ἄνθρωπος? It may be that the compound word *doubles* the emphasis on loving others. In Titus 3:4, the author uses this compound to stress God's love of humans that appeared in Christ.

Ἀφιλάργυρος (Heb. 13:5) is a bit more complicated. It is made from φίλος and ἄργυρος, with the prefix α. Ἄργυρος is the word for "silver" and was used for money. When put together, the compound word itself means something like a "friend of money." However, the prefixed α makes the compound word a negative, "not a friend of money."

ποιέω *Words*

Another common element in compound words in the New Testament is the use of some form of the verb ποιέω ("to do, make, perform") as the word's last component. There are a number of compound words in which this verb maintains its strength and dominates the new meaning created by the combination. Such is the word ἀγαθοποιέω. As we noted earlier, ἀγαθός means "good." So the verb ἀγαθοποιέω emphasizes the *doing* of good. (See Lk. 6:9.) Its opposite is κακοποιέω, since κακός means "wrong," "bad," or "evil."

σύν *Compounds*

Reading the Greek New Testament brings us face-to-face with a good many compound words that begin with the prefix σύν. While we have already looked at compounds that are made with a prepositional prefix, the number of interesting words with σύν is impressive, and they merit examination.

Συγκληρονόμος (for example, 1 Pet. 3:7) is a compound word, one element of which is the prepositional prefix σύγ (from σύν). In many instances, when one looks this word up in an analytical lexicon, the prefix will be shown as broken off from the main word, as σύν plus κληρονόμος. Hence, σύγκληρονόμος may be defined as a "fellow-participant" or "co-heir." You should recognize the meaning of the preposition σύν as "with" or "together with," and you can readily see how this shapes the sense of the word.

But the prefix is only one of the three components of this word, as you might sense. So we should look up the word κληρονόμος without the prefix. It is usually translated "heir" but is sometimes used to refer to the fact that Christians are children of God and hence, heirs. When we find it in an analytical lexicon, we discover that this word is the compound made up of κλῆρος and νέμομαι. An analytical lexicon will tell us that κλῆρος usually means a "lot" or a "die." That is, it is something used in determining chances as in "to cast a lot." It can also mean a "portion" that is shared as a result of casting the lot. (See, for example, Mk. 15:24 and Acts 1:17.)

Νέμομαι is more difficult, however, since it is never used in the New Testament and therefore does not appear in an analytical lexicon. But with a little bit of detective work, one may see the possible connection of νέμομαι with νόμος, which means a law or a rule governing the dispersal of things. Or in a Greek lexicon you may find that νέμομαι could be related to νόμισμα, meaning a form of coinage (for example, Mt. 22:19). In either case, the association is with words that refer to a standard of some sort. Now you can reconstruct the word out of its various pieces, giving each piece its full due, and get a sense of the notion "co-heirs." Together we share a portion of the inheritance that comes by law or some standard.

Συναρμολογέω and συμβιβάζω appear together in Ephesians 4:16 and merit consideration. Ephesians 4:16 comes in the midst of the writer's discussion of the unity of the church in Christ, and verse 16 in the RSV reads, "from whom the whole body, joined and knit together by every joint with which it is supplied." However accurate it might be, the translation "joined and knit together" covers up two remarkable compound words, which are used almost as synonyms. They are συναρμολογούμενον and συμβιβαζόμενον, present passive participles respectively of συναρμολογέω and συμβιβάζω. As intimidating as they may seem, the length of the words signals that they may have multiple parts. Let's examine each of them separately to see why the author might use them both.

Συναρμολογέω (συναρμολογούμενον) is a three-part compound word made up of the prefix σύν, followed by ἁρμόζω and λογέω. You will probably first recognize λογέω as a possible form of λόγος. That means you need to look for the root ἁρμο in an analytical lexicon, and in doing so you will be led to ἁρμόζω. It means "to fit together" or to be bound together as in marriage or some other legal arrangement. You may already know that λόγος means "speaking" or "word" (remember Jn. 1:1).

Now we can piece this compound word together. It means to be "fitting together" in a binding, almost legal fashion. When the prefix is added, we think of "fitting together with" each other. But how do we understand the meaning of λόγος in this unique combination? Perhaps the "togetherness" is made visible and revolves around the processes of "speaking with each other" and even "being spoken about" with each other.

Συμβιβάζω (συμβιβαζόμενον) is simply a verb with σύν attached as a prefix. However, in this case, when σύν is attached to a word that begins with a consonant—as the β in συμβιβάζω—it is spelled σύμ. The main word is βιβάζω, and though it is not found in the New Testament, it means something like to "knit together" or to "unite through a process of seeing the world the same way." Combined with σύν, the verb again means something like "knit together with."

These two extraordinary words mean essentially the same thing, with only slight variations of shades of meaning. How many times is the idea of being "knit" or "tied together" included in these two words? Three times in the first word and twice in the second. This stunning redundancy is the way the writer emphasizes the connectedness of those who are part of the church in Christ. The English translation tries to get that said, but clearly falls short. The only way that you can truly capture the depth of idea and feeling in the passage is to open up the two words with which the idea is expressed in Greek.

Families of Words

Compound words lead us to the consideration of linguistic families. Word "families" are of two kinds. One family is composed of words that share some common *root*. The other kind is made up of words that have some common *meaning*. We will briefly describe the nature of each with at least one example.

Words with common roots are easy to spot. While the relationship among the words in a single family is often very clear and visible, the differences among them are often subtle, but very useful in pinpointing the emphasis of a text.

The διδα- *Family*

Consider first the words that are constructed on the root διδα-. All the words in the New Testament constructed on this root have to do in some way with teaching. A list of them with their general meaning might help you: διδακτικός (skillful in teaching), διδακτός (taught or imparted), διδασκαλία (the act of teaching or that which is taught), διδάσκαλος (teacher), διδάσκω (to teach), διδαχή (teaching as an activity or the content of teaching). These words form a linguistic "family" whose members run throughout the New Testament, and because of their common root we can easily recognize them. The precise meaning of some of them, however, is not quite so easy.

Both διδασκαλία and διδαχή can mean either the act of teaching or the content of what is taught. Now you do not have to be able to discern this difference on your own; simply follow the lead of your interlinear and analytical lexicon. However, this explanation may help you understand in a general way what is going on when these words shift in meaning. In Romans 15:4, for instance, διδασκαλία refers to how the scriptures are written for the purpose of teaching us, but in Mark 7:7, it means the content of what humans have taught. The difference is that in the first passage διδασκαλία implies an action. In the second passage, however, the word is the recipient of the action of a verb (in this case, a participle). The same difference occurs in the uses of διδαχή.

The πιστ- *Family*

This is another example of a family of words in which the members share a common root, and it is one which is of special interest to preachers. The primary members of the πιστ- family and their general meanings are πιστεύω (to believe), πιστικός (genuine or unadulterated), πίστις (faith, trust, or commitment), πιστός (faithful or trustworthy), and πιστόω (to feel confidence or be convinced). When you come upon a word beginning with this root, you know that it has to do with faith and related concepts.

Families of Shared Meaning

Another kind of word family involves *meanings* that cluster together or are related. These families may include some words that are related by common root, but also include some entirely different words that share only a general meaning with the others.

One of the most interesting of these families is that of "preaching," and the many ways in which the New Testament refers to the process of preaching or proclamation. When you encounter one of the words for "preaching," it is important to take care to distinguish which one it is and how it fits into the context in which it appears.

The most common of the words for preaching is κηρύσσω, which means "to announce" or "to make known." It usually refers to the act of preaching, but it is closely aligned with the noun κήρυγμα (translated "announcement" or "proclamation" or even "preaching" by one sent from God). However, in the New Testament κήρυγμα came to indicate *what* was being preached, the content of the Christian message.

First Corinthians 1:21–23 contains both κήρυγμα and κηρύσσω in that order. Paul writes,

> For since, in the wisdom of God, the world did not know God through wisdom, God decided, through the foolishness of our proclamation (κηρύγματος), to save those who believe. (22) For Jews demand signs and Greeks desire wisdom, (23) but we proclaim (κηρύσσομεν) Christ crucified, a stumbling block to Jews and foolishness to Gentiles.

The two words seem almost interchangeable here, and it may be best to leave it at that. However, might there be an emphasis on the content of the preaching in κηρύγματος in verse 21, while in verse 23 κηρύσσομεν points to those who were doing the preaching?

The word εὐαγγέλιον is another member of this family. Even though it sometimes is translated "preaching" or even "proclaiming," this word refers to the idea of "good news" or "gospel," so it is most often about what is proclaimed. In Romans 1:15–16 it occurs first at the end of verse 15, in the clause πρόθυμον καὶ ὑμῖν τοῖς ἐν Ῥώμῃ εὐαγγελίσασθαι. The NRSV translates this clause, "hence my eagerness to proclaim the gospel to you also who are in Rome." An analytical lexicon will tell you that εὐαγγελίσασθαι is the aorist middle infinitive of the verb εὐαγγελίζω, so the sense is both the act of preaching and its content, the good news. However, in verse 16 the same root word appears as a noun and is handled differently: Οὐ γὰρ ἐπαισχύνομαι τὸ εὐαγγέλιον, "For I am not ashamed of the *gospel*."

Καταγγέλλω is another word in the "preaching" family, but it gives the idea a slightly different flavor. As you see, it is a compound verb, comprising αγγέλλω with the prepositional prefix κατά. (Ἀγγέλλω is found only in Jn. 20:18, where it describes Mary's act of sharing the news of Christ's resurrection with the other disciples.) Καταγγέλλω means to proclaim something. However, when we disassemble the word, we see that κατά may give the verb the meaning "to proclaim across"or "to proclaim over differences." We find this word in Romans 1:8: ὅτι ἡ πίστις ὑμῶν καταγγέλλεται ἐν ὅλῳ τῷ κόσμῳ, "because your faith is being announced in the whole world." It is difficult to say how, if at all, the prepositional prefix changes the meaning of the verb itself.

Still another word that carries the idea of preaching or proclamation is νουθετέω. Technically it means to "admonish, warn," or "instruct." Acts 20:31 is a striking example of the use of this verb: διὸ γρηγορεῖτε μνημονεύοντες ὅτι τριετίαν νύκτα καὶ ἡμέραν οὐκ ἐπαυσάμην μετὰ δακρύων νουθετῶν ἕνα ἕκαστον. The verse quotes Paul as saying, "Therefore be alert, remembering that for three years I did not cease night or day *to warn* everyone with tears" (NRSV). It is a fascinating reference to Paul's speaking and pleading. Does it mean to include his preaching?

Another word we might include in this "preaching" family is πείθω, which means "to persuade, convince, appeal to," or "win over." Another meaning it sometimes has is to "depend on, trust," or "obey." Second Corinthians 5:11 is an example of its use: Εἰδότες οὖν τὸν φόβον τοῦ κυρίου ἀνθρώπους πείθομεν ("Knowing, therefore, the fear of the Lord, we try *to persuade* human beings"). Paul probably means it to include preaching, as well as other forms of human interaction.

Finally, there is παρακαλέω. It means literally "to call alongside," but took on additional meanings: "to appeal to, exhort, or encourage"; "to request" or "implore"; and "to comfort" and "encourage." Paul uses it in Romans 12:1: Παρακαλῶ οὖν ὑμᾶς, ἀδελφοί, διὰ τῶν οἰκτιρμῶν τοῦ θεοῦ, "Therefore, I *beseech* you, brothers, through (or by) the compassions of God." When used in reference to Christian preaching, it may sometimes stress the passionate intent of the preacher.

We have certainly not exhausted the words that in various ways imply the idea of preaching. However, we hope you get a sense of how relatedness of meaning forms a kind of linguistic family. Investigating such a family can be very rewarding and a valuable resource for good biblical preaching.

Words in Context

We conclude this discussion with the importance of the literary context in studying an occurrence of a word. One of the recent criticisms of word studies is that they do not take seriously enough the variety of meanings a single word can have depending on its context. For a time, scholarship tended to draw words out of their contexts and make generalizations about them in the abstract. We know now, however, that perhaps the most important factor in determining a word's meaning is the situation in which an author uses it.

Our goal here is to present several examples of determining meaning on the basis of context. But determining the peculiar influence of a context on a word requires knowing how the word is used in other contexts. When you study a passage and locate a key word you would like to investigate, we suggest you do so in the following way:

1. Determine the word's general or usual meaning by use of your interlinear and analytic lexicon, as well as a general lexicon.

2. Ask if and how well each of those general meanings fits in the context in which the word occurs in the passage you are studying.

3. Look up and study as many occurrences of the word in other passages as you can.

4. Return to the passage you are studying and make a judgment about the word's meaning there.

We will try to demonstrate this process with two examples, beginning with a relatively easy word and then a more complicated one.

μεταμορφόω

Suppose we are working on Romans 12:2 for a sermon. The Greek reads, καὶ μὴ συσχηματίζεσθε τῷ αἰῶνι τούτῳ, ἀλλὰ μεταμορφοῦσθε τῇ ἀνακαινώσει τοῦ νοὸς εἰς τὸ δοκιμάζειν ὑμᾶς τὶ τὸ θέλημα τοῦ θεοῦ. This may be translated, "and do not be conformed to this age but be transformed by the renewing of your mind for you to prove what is God's will." Here μεταμορφοῦσθε is a passive imperative, which must mean something like "allow yourself to be transformed." It is the opposite of being "conformed to this age." The verb συσχηματίζεσθε is also an imperative in either passive or middle voice. So it seems to mean "allow yourself to be conformed." Paul appears to have in mind some change God can bring about, but only if a human wills it. Moreover, it looks like the change is an inner shift of character, which is evident from the phrase "by the renewing of your mind" (τῇ ἀνακαινώσει τοῦ νοός).

A Greek lexicon informs us that μεταμορφόω means to "transform" or "change in form," but it can be a change either in physical appearance or in ways not visible to the eye. It is a compound verb, constructed from the preposition μέτα and the noun μορφή, so it means something like "moving beyond a form (to another)." The sense of an inner change of form seems to fit the meaning in our passage here.

However, now we should investigate the other occurrences of the word in the New Testament. Μεταμορφόω is used only four times in the New Testament—twice in accounts of Jesus' transfiguration (Mt. 17:2 and Mk. 9:2) and twice in Paul's epistles (Rom. 12:2 and 2 Cor. 3:18). In the stories of Jesus' transfiguration in Mark and Matthew, the evangelists both tell us in exactly the same words that Jesus μετεμορφώθη ἔμπροσθεν αὐτῶν ("he was transformed before them"). Again the verb is passive, but this time the change of appearance is visible.

The other use of μεταμορφόω is 2 Corinthians 3:18, where Paul writes, "And all of us...are being transformed into the same image from one degree of glory to another; for this comes from the Lord, the Spirit." In this case, the verb is μεταμορφούμεθα, a present passive participle of μεταμορφόω. Clearly, μεταμορφόω can be a transformation either in physical appearance or inner character. We find the use of this verb to mean some spiritual change only in Paul. What the passage from 2 Corinthians suggests is that the change is a process under way in the present, but which comes from God and is not the result of human will.

Returning to Romans 12 with the study of these other passages in mind, we see verse 2 in a slightly different way. Most notable is the imperative use of μεταμορφόω. It is the only time the verb is used in the imperative. Every use of the verb in the New Testament (including this one) is passive, and even Jesus was the passive recipient of transfiguration. So what does it mean to command transformation, Paul? We will not try to answer that question, but we can recognize there is some sense in which human cooperation is needed in a process of change that God (or the Holy Spirit) is directing in our lives. Now there's a basic theme for a sermon!

μένω

The investigation of μεταμορφόω is relatively simple, but a word study of μένω is a challenging project. Nonetheless, we can make even that sort of study of a word in its context manageable.

First, let's suppose that we are preparing a sermon on John 15:1–8 (the assigned gospel lesson for the fifth Sunday of Easter in the Revised Common Lectionary Year B). The frequency of the word μένω alone makes us curious about its meaning in this passage. It occurs seven times in these eight verses. When we isolate these occurrences, we note first that it is always used with the preposition ἐν. Moreover,

1. In five cases μένω appears with ἐν ἐμοι, "in me" (twice in v. 4 and once each in vv. 5, 6, and 7).

2. Once it speaks of μένῃ ἐν τῇ ἀμπέλῳ ("remains on the vine," v. 4).

3. A conditional clause in verse 7 says, "if you remain in me and my words remain in you" (ἐν ὑμῖν μείνῃ).

4. And verse 5 speaks of a mutual or reciprocal "remaining" — ὁ μένων ἐν ἐμοὶ κἀγὼ ἐν αὐτῷ ("the one who remains in me and I in him/her").

It is clear that the concept expressed in μένω is crucial to understanding this passage.

But what does μένω mean? An interlinear will probably translate the verb "remain." However, *The New Analytical Greek Lexicon,* edited by Wesley J. Perschbacher,[1] provides us with no less than nineteen different meanings of the verb along with New Testament references for each. The various meanings are to "continue, dwell, lodge, sojourn, remain, rest, settle, last, endure, be existent, continue unchanged, be permanent, persevere, be constant, be steadfast, abide, be in close and settled union, indwell," and "wait for."

In our passage the sense of remaining seems appropriate, but so does lodging, abiding, indwelling, and even continuing. In this case, the analogy of the relationship of a healthy branch to its vine suggests that the branches must remain attached to the vine and explicitly says that believers too should and must remain "attached" to Jesus. But what does that mean exactly? What might the basic sense of this verb be, if indeed there is a basic sense?

We cannot and need not examine all the passages in the New Testament where μένω is found. Actually, the list of occurrences of the word in a Greek lexicon goes on for two and a half pages! But our analytical lexicon gives us a narrowed selection of passages. From the list we find there, let's choose four that seem to be likely candidates for the word's meaning in John 15:1–8. Certainly we should begin with a passage where the analytical lexicon suggests μένω means "remain." Then we will take a look at three other passages in which the lexicon suggests the word means to "continue," "dwell," or "be in close and settled union."

---

[1] Wesley J. Perschbacher, ed, *The New Analytical Greek Lexicon* (Peabody, Mass.: Hendrickson Publishers, 1990), 270.

The first passage for investigation is John 9:41, which the lexicon claims is an example of the use of μένω to mean "remain." At the end of chapter 9, Jesus meets the blind man whom he had earlier healed, converses with him, and then speaks to some Pharisees who overhear their conversation. The religious leaders take Jesus to mean that they are the blind ones. In the NRSV, Jesus' reply reads, "If you were blind, you would not have sin. But now that you say, 'We see,' your sin *remains.*" The Greek for the last three English words is ἡ ἁμαρτία ὑμῶν μένει. In this case, μένω means the continuation of wrong in the Pharisees' lives because they claim to see even though they are blind. It describes the presence of an inner entity, sin, and its persistence, and in this sense is similar to the way the verb is used in Romans 9:11.

Next, the analytical lexicon directs us to 1 Corinthians 7, where it tells us μένω is used in the sense of "to continue." This is the passage in which Paul counsels the Corinthian Christians to remain in the social situation they were in when they first became Christians. It is not necessary, he says, to change social relationships such as marriage, just because you become a Christian. Verse 20 summarizes his point: "Let each of you *remain* in the condition in which you were called." Here μένω appears in the imperative—μενέτω—and means "do not change." In this case, however, it refers not to an inner matter of character but to a social relationship.

The case is only slightly different when we examine Acts 9:43, where our word is translated as "dwell." The narrator tells us Peter "stayed in Joppa for a time," and "stayed" translates μεῖναι, an aorist active infinitive of μένω. The word is used here in the simple sense of a physical presence, "spatially" remaining in a place. It is apparently used in the same sense in John 1:39.

Finally, we should look at a passage in which μένω has the sense of being in "close and settled union." To do so, we are back in John, which is famous for its extensive use of μένω. In 14:10 Jesus speaks of God's "dwelling" in him: ὁ δὲ πατὴρ ἐν ἐμοὶ μένων ποιεῖ τὰ ἔργα αὐτοῦ ("but the Father who dwells in me does his works"). In this clause, μένω does not necessarily mean "close and settled union." That translation assumes too much that is unsaid. What is clear is that the verb describes the nature of Christ's relationship with God by saying that God dwells or remains or abides in Christ. The relationship is so intimate and close that Jesus can say that he is in (ἐν) the Father (Jn. 14:20). Μένω is one of the terms John uses to explore the mystery of the relationship of God and Christ.

We return to John 15:1–8 armed with some deeper understanding of μένω, as complex as that little word is. What have we learned that alters our understanding of this verb in our passage? First, it is clear that here it is used metaphorically. A branch's relationship with its vine is like our relationship with Christ. The text uses a physical relationship (the branch's connection with the vine) to speak of a "spiritual" relationship of believer and Christ. We have seen that μένω can be used for physical situations (for instance, spatial location) as well as the unseen relationship between Christ and God. Here the two are coupled in the metaphor. Second, μένω may describe Christ's relationship with God, as well as our relationship with Christ. In fact, then, our relationship with Christ is modeled after the divine relationship of God and Christ. Given that fact, does μένω suggest that in being related to Christ, as a branch is related to its vine for its life, we participate in divine interrelatedness itself?

These two short word studies on μεταμορφόω and μένω suggest first that we need to determine the meaning of a word on the basis of its own literary context. Second, however, they also imply that understanding a word in one passage may be aided by understanding how it works in other passages. We dare not assume that a word means the same thing every time it is used anywhere in the New Testament. Still, gaining a broader picture of a word's functions in other passages assists an interpreter in discerning its meaning in one specific context.

In such ways as these, we dance with the words of the text. We understand that words function in many different ways and that sometimes a generic meaning helps us grasp a word's role. We enjoy dancing the analytical steps with compound words and the familial steps with words that share either a single root or a related meaning. But most of all, our dance becomes most lively and enjoyable when we take the role of a detective tracing down clues to the meaning of a particular word in a particular passage. We are now ready to pull together all the principles we have learned and see how they work when applied to a text on which we aspire to preach.

PART 3

USING THE GREEK TEXT IN
SERMON PREPARATION

CHAPTER 1

Through Greek Text to Sermon

Now that we have laid the groundwork and established our ten principles for using the interlinear Greek New Testament, the matters of process and caution are important—"process" or procedure for work in this section, and then the necessary cautions about this work in the next. First, how do you go about studying an interlinear text in a way that moves you through the text into the sermon, ready for preaching? What steps are involved as you learn to do it systematically and expeditiously? Other questions also arise: How much time will it take to do this kind of Greek textual study each week? And how detailed should this work be in order to yield good, reliable results?

The time questions are not easy to answer, of course, since they depend in large part on the length and complexity of the text on which the sermon is based. Short texts of a half dozen verses or less can sometimes be fairly complex, as Pauline or other epistle texts tend to be. Longer texts— a gospel narrative, for example—can be more straightforward and less complicated, requiring you to focus only on a few key points to unravel Greek materials. Often you will not know exactly what is called for in terms of study and detail work until you are actually into an assessment of the text itself. What should be said is that in our judgment, the processes and procedures recommended in this book can be carried out by any preacher on a week-to-week basis in the normal round of sermon preparation.

Our concern is that you develop a rhythm of your own for doing weekly study of the Greek text for the sermon. Most likely no two preachers will work this out in quite the same way. So everything we have said so far and the general procedure that we will outline here are intended to let you do a careful interlinear study of a text in the course of a day at the most, as an initial part of your preparation. As other homileticians often urge, we too recommend that as much as possible you work two to three weeks ahead with your preparation; preliminary work with the Greek text in those weeks ahead will pay enormous dividends in the sermons that you end up preaching. Whether you preach from a lectionary set of texts or not, let your sermon planning be such that you know a couple of weeks in advance what your upcoming sermon texts will be. Then, for an hour or two in each of those preparatory weeks, spend time with the Greek text in at least the initial ways that we will suggest here.

Seven steps make up a good general procedure that can be used week in and week out as one works with the interlinear Greek text for sermon preparation. The two sermons that follow in chapter 3 of this part, one by Robert Kysar and one by Joseph Webb, in various ways have followed these steps of study and preparation.

1. Assessing the Text Visually

First, do an overall assessment of the text itself in its interlinear version. The emphasis here is on "assessment," not on the details of the text. You read the text, but more specifically, you "look at" the text from top to bottom. To begin, read the English text in the outside margins of your interlinear at least twice. Now read the English lines below the Greek lines as you find them in your interlinear version. Think about the relationship between the English translation you have read, whether it is the NIV, the RSV, the NRSV or some other, and the broken English version that you have read through in the interlinear version. Finally, look carefully at the Greek lines of the interlinear. In doing this, you begin to examine the *relationship* between the Greek and the English lines as they appear in the interlinear version.

In this early examination of a passage, you are interested in a number of things: What are you able to actually "observe" about the text? What unusual features do you notice on the surface of the text itself, both in its Greek and its English versions? What, if anything, seems to jump out at you, to demand your attention, whether in English or in Greek? You are not concerned about specifics at this point; you are only assessing, getting a sense of the interlinear formation of words on the page.

As we have tried to indicate in this book, much about the interlinear Greek-English New Testament is visual—you can "see" it; you can "notice" things by looking closely; and the more that you do of this "looking," the more you will understand its value. At this early stage, you are looking for the text's "openings," those places where you will find your initial clues for the more careful study to come. For example, in Kysar's study of the parable of the workers in the vineyard (summarized in chapter 3 of this section), he immediately noticed the importance of the landowner's defense as an opening into the story. Depending on the length and complexity of the text, this step should take you no more than an hour or so. But as you will discover with practice, this will be a very important hour.

Even in this assessment stage, you should begin your note-taking. On cards or half-sheets of paper, write down your observations about the text. When you see something unusual, even in this preliminary examination, write it down. The value of the notes you take about your assessment of the text will grow the farther your sermon moves toward completion.

2. Focus on Unusual Words or Syntax

After you have surveyed the text, you are ready to examine it more closely for what we might call the "features" of the text. To do this, you need to read the Greek text itself, preferably aloud in the privacy of your study. You need, that is, to "speak" the text and in so doing also "hear" it. This is very important. Among other things, this helps you become aware of the transliterated words in the Greek text, that is, those words from which English words have been derived. It also heightens your awareness of how Greek words sound when read one after another. This is our way of detecting Greek alliteration and other "sound-plays" in the text and of becoming more aware of the repetitive patterns of Greek terms. For example, reading the Greek text of Mark 5:25–28, you hear a series of six participles, all of which end with -σα.

Again, work with a note pad so that you can write down any features of the text that seem to stand out, or that you sense might have potential interest or importance. Are any words that you encounter in the reading unusual? Are there words that are particularly difficult to pronounce in Greek, or words that are unusually long or short? As you read the Greek text aloud, notice individual words of the interlinear English translation you are reading. Are there any unusual or unexpected English words used to translate the Greek? For instance, it is in doing this that you would note that the English word "love" appears as translations of two different Greek terms in the Johannine text with which we began this book (21:15–17).

As you read the Greek text aloud, be aware too of the arrangements of the Greek words (such as syntactical constructions) that seem to present difficulty for the translators in lining up English words so that they can make some sense. As we have pointed out, in most interlinear texts the translators may insert small numbers over the English words to assist in "reading" the sentence into English. Watch for these places where such numbers seem to be necessary; you will probably want to come back to them. Often such awkward English word arrangements hold clues to the relationship between Greek and English meaning.

Again, in this second step, this "aural" examination of the text, take notes. Do not try to remember what you find. Your notes in these preliminary stages of study will become crucial to what you end up saying about, and doing with, any given text.

3. List and Look Up All Key Words

You reach the point, then, when it is time to turn to the lexicons. To prepare for this, make a careful list of all of the key words in your text— or as many of them as you can—and look them up. Again, note-taking is essential, but this can all be done fairly quickly after you have practiced it for a while. This involves choices, to be sure, since you cannot include every single word in your list. If you were doing a scholarly paper on the text, that would probably be necessary, but for our purposes of preaching, select what appear to you to be the "key" terms. These are the terms that you most likely have become aware of in the first two stages of your work, your visual and aural examinations of the text.

Two specific cautions. First, *make a list*. Down the left-hand column on a sheet of paper, write the words in Greek, along with the English word that your interlinear has given you for translation. But write the Greek words one under the other, allowing a few lines under each word for the notes that you will take about it.

For example, if you were working with Mark 16:9, your list would look something like this:

Ἀναστάς—rising
πρωΐ—early
πρώτῃ—on the first day
σαββάτου—of the week
ἐφάνη—he appeared
πρῶτον—first
παρ᾽—from
ἧς – whom

ἐκβεβλήκει—he had expelled
ἑπτὰ—seven
δαιμόνια—demons

We are not going to complete the work with this particular list, but this is an operative model for what you should do. The English words listed beside the Greek here are the words that appear in the interlinear text that we are using. You can easily work with a dozen or two of these terms in the preparation of any given sermon. But in just looking at and saying the words in this list (this verse) aloud, you should develop some curiosities that deserve close scrutiny. For example, you might be curious about the word σαββάτου, the word for "appeared," or the word translated here as "he had expelled."

A second caution is to *stick to single words on your list.* At this point, do not write down phrases, particularly phrases that may contain two or even three key words. Instead, break a phrase up if you need to in order to keep each word isolated. After you have looked up each word, then you are free to reassemble the phrases based on what you have found.

Once your list is formed, it is time to look up each word, first in your analytical lexicon and then in any general lexicon you wish to use. You begin with your analytical lexicon since it will provide you with the basic information that you will need to do anything else. That is, you are looking for what we have pointed out as the "parameters" of each word on your list. Each word, that is, must be identified as to its root, what kind of a word it is as it is used in your particular text, and any other basic grammatical information that the word may call for. You will pay attention to whether the word is a verb, what kind of verb it is, or whether the word is a participle or an infinitive. In time you will come to recognize much of this information quickly on your own, for example, whether the word is in the genitive or the accusative case, and so on. These are the word's parameters. For example, you will find that ἀναστάς in Mark 16:9 is the nominative, singular, masculine, aorist, active participle of ἀνίστημι, meaning that Christ's resurrection was a completed event in the past, making possible his appearance to Mary and others. Write down alongside each Greek word on your list all the parameters that you find with it.

But this is only one of the two dimensions you need in looking up the words you have written down. You need the parameters, but you also need the definitions—as complete a set of notes on each word's definitions as you can put together. The basic definition you find in your analytical lexicon will sometimes be all you need, even though you will usually have to move from the word you have looked up to its root in order to find the definition. At other times, you may want to use a more complete, standard lexicon (such as those we discussed in the opening pages of this book), to fill out your definitional notes for various words in your listing. Often a Greek word will have more than one definition, which means that your analytical lexicon's offering might not be the best. For instance, ἀνίστημι is used for a person's standing or rising up, but it is also used in Mark 3:26 for rising up or rebelling against someone. This is an example of how you will probably end up expanding the definition of each of your key words, and often your expansion or clarification of meaning will provide the details from which shades and nuances of new meaning will emerge.

When you are finished with this, you will have a substantial set of materials on a specific text, materials that will serve you well anytime you turn to this text for preaching or teaching. For now, though, these materials form the basis for a rather thorough, but manageable analysis of the text from which you plan to preach.

4. Look for the "Markers" in the Text

Experience tells us, however, that you need to do one other thing as part of your "listing" of the text's words. Whether they are in your list or not, you need to locate what can be called the text's "markers." By this we mean those words, usually small words, that signal a beginning, an ending, or a transition. We have tried to call careful attention to them in our principles concerning conjunctions, particles, and so on. But any number of words can serve these transitional purposes, so it is difficult to specify in advance just what they will be. If you have included them in your listing of text words, isolate them in some way, either by highlighting them or even creating a separate list for them.

For example, in Acts 1:6–8, verse 6's οὖν, translated "then" or "so," marks a beginning. It provides a transition from what has been said in previous verses to what is about to happen. Συνελθόντες is an aorist participle that sets the stage for what is to follow ("After they were gathered together"). In Jesus' words in verse 7, notice that the first word is a negative—οὐχ—stressing what is not the case. Then verse 7 is connected with verse 8 with the conjunction of opposition, ἀλλά. This little word marks off the negative part of Jesus' speech ("it is not for you to know") from the positive ("you will receive power").

The text markers in Mark 5:25 are more complicated. The καὶ γυνὴ ("and a woman") registers the break in the story of Jairus' daughter (5:21–24a) and the introduction of another major character about whom a story is about to be told. The title Θυγάτηρ ("daughter") combined with the command "go" (ὕπαγε) in verse 34 is a marker for the decisive word regarding the woman and the completion of this story. Within the story itself surely the verb ἥψατο ("she touched") seems to signal the climax of the story, even though that should be understood more as an interpretative judgment than a grammatical one. As you work with the Greek text, however, you will learn how important these kinds of judgments are in thinking through textual meaning.

5. Examine the Larger Setting of the Text

We have suggested that there are two levels of meaning—semantic and grammatical—so it is important that we look beyond the trees of individual words in a sentence to see the forest of the larger context in which these words are used. The text that you "mark off" for study must also be understood "as a whole," with its pieces interrelated in complex and other very telling ways. As we have emphasized, we are interested in individual words, but often those words are shaped by the contextual system or structure in which they appear. So we cannot overemphasize the importance of this move to larger grammatical structures.

For now, though, what are we looking for in terms of larger grammatical structures? We are looking for what is going on in the whole paragraph of a text, the whole pericope, the whole chapter, and even the whole document from which this text is drawn. We are looking for whatever matters are important that seem to influence the writer's construction of this entire passage.

Webb's sermon that follows in chapter 3 of this part deals with marriage based on Ephesians 5, which is a text with fairly defined syntactic markers. He contends that certain words or terms in the text have been "lifted out of context" in order to argue a point of view that the overall text does not support. One must isolate the text's beginning and ending in order to get a sense of the emphases and the twists and turns of the text itself. One must think about where the text appears in the overall structure of the Ephesian letter, and one must wonder (however well one can actually answer the question) about the author of the text and the situation within which and for which it was written. All these things impact how the words of the text itself are understood.

Or consider again the story of the healing of the woman with the flow of blood in Mark 5. If you skim the previous chapter, you will note that at 4:35 Jesus crosses to the other side of the Sea of Galilee and in the process stills the storm (4:35–40). That story is the first of four such episodes about Jesus' work in the region of the Decapolis (see 5:1 and 5:20). Jesus first exorcizes the demons in Gerasenes, then Mark relates the story of the healing of Jairus' daughter with the account of the healing of the woman with the flow of blood tucked away within the Jairus story. These four episodes—stilling the storm, healing the Gerasene demoniac, curing the woman's flow, and raising Jairus' daughter—comprise a unit that ends at 6:1, where we are told Jesus "left that place and came to his hometown" (Nazareth). An adequate reading of Mark 5:24b–34 requires that we see the one story in the larger context of Jesus' healings.

However, we then note a unique feature of 5:24b–34. It is a story within a story. Jesus is on his way to Jairus' house when the woman with the flow meets him; his journey continues in verse 35, after he has healed the woman and sent her on her way. Again, this is a structural feature and not a grammatical one, but it is most important for the reading of 5:24b–34. What does it mean for the reading of the inner story when it is encased in the Jairus story? This literary feature of the story within a story invites us to interpret each of the stories in the light of the other. The questions to ask, then, include how the stories are alike and how they are different. For example, the woman is at the extreme opposite end of the social spectrum from Jairus, the prominent leader of a synagogue. She is in effect a social outcast, unclean by virtue of her bleeding. Other comparisons and contrasts are equally important (for example, Jesus calls the woman "daughter" and then cures Jairus' daughter).

We will not carry our analysis of this text further, since our intention at this point is only to alert you to the need to keep the larger aspects of your text in mind at the same time that you are working on the text's specific language. Granted, "opening" the features of a text's larger context for meaning is a complicated process, but we urge you to take it a step at a time and try your best.

We are also suggesting two things, however. First, we are suggesting that as important as it is, your work with Greek words and meanings should not be seen as the end of the process. It is, in fact, only the beginning, since you will need to move from word and grammar study to the larger issues of relationship between context and how words are actually used by the writer of your text. Second, we are suggesting that if you learn and follow these steps in dealing with texts, over time you will become remarkably adept at handling even the most complex problems relating to textual meaning, including background and literary purpose. Moreover, your aptitude with the Greek will assist you whether you are dealing with biblical narratives, epistles, or even more esoteric texts such as the apocalypse.

One thing should not go unsaid. At this stage of the process, particularly in considering the backgrounds of a text about which you will preach, it is time to turn to some reliable commentary or historical materials to fill in both information and other opinions regarding the text. As we emphasized earlier in this book, we urge that this *not be done before you begin your Greek study,* but here is the place to bring those important sources into play. What about the text's literary and historical setting? What about authorship—what do the scholars think? What about the problem or problems being addressed here? These are matters often quite beyond the grammatical work that this book is about; and for these matters, the work of the best scholars, past and present, is clearly indispensable.

In all this background and contextual study, of course, take notes—always take notes. Whether your notes ever find their way into your sermon itself, they will give you an enhanced sense of memory that in itself will deepen the sermon that you end up preparing and delivering.

6. Fashion Your Meaning for the Text

Now you are ready to use all your notes in constructing, or reconstructing, the meaning or meanings of the Greek text that is before you. You must do this carefully, starting with the words that you have researched and examined, moving to phrases and then on to verses, on to sections and, finally, to the larger contextual setting, which we just talked about. If our experience is any guide, then you will find yourself doing the same process in reverse. You may start with the larger context and then work back down to the individual words again. It will all be very much an interactive process as you are filled with a sense of openness about the text that you are studying.

There is no substitute for learning the principles Part 2 discussed, and the better you have learned them, the more quickly and easily you will be able to construct your own meanings for the sentences and the texts before you. There are ways to become proficient at the overall process, but there are no shortcuts. However, this is where all the "detective work" of your textual study comes to fruition.

At this stage, near the end of your work, we recommend you construct an expanded translation of your own. This is not a word-for-word translation as an interlinear provides, but a fully expanded sense of what you think that the text is saying. Put in all the nuances of language and meaning as necessary. Add whatever glosses are needed to say what you mean about the text. Take account of all the words and their arrangements, as well as all the contextual matters that bear on these words and arrangements. Make this the capstone of your study: your own translation, with emphases and nuances where you believe they come. This need not be exhaustive for the entire text, particularly if your text is a long one, but it should be expanded at crucial points where meaning or meanings seem to turn.

For instance, here is an expanded translation that might result from a close study of Acts 1:6–8:

But in response to their question, Jesus said, *"No! Absolutely not!*

You do not need to know the times of seasons
    that God has set by divine authority!
    (That's God's business and none of your business!)

But I will tell you what you do need to know:
    (That is, what *is* your business.)

You will receive a dynamite power
    that will come to you from the Holy Spirit,
and I promise you that (empowered by the Spirit)
    you will be my witnesses all over the known world

    – starting right where you are now in Jerusalem,
        and continuing out to Judea,
           and then to Samaria,
              and finally even as far as the end of the earth
                (the furthest imaginable place)."

It has been spaced out so that its appearance on paper reflects the interpreter's understanding of the content of the verses. This is a practice you may or may not find helpful.

This kind of summarizing all that you have learned about a text is absolutely crucial to the process we propose. Nothing you do will prepare you better for the actual work of creating sermons that will speak from specific texts, and nothing will be more vibrant and alive when you deliver the sermon than those places where your own original study of a text actually shines through.

7. Thinking about a Sermon

Finally, you are ready to make the move from the Greek text toward the preparation of your sermon. Here a lot of decisions have to be made, though with practice you will become adept at making them. First, for example, you will decide between a broad general meaning of the whole and a more specific meaning of some part of the text. In some cases you may want to draw a general conclusion about the meaning of the text as a whole and preach on that wider meaning.

However, most texts will have a significant number of different textual elements, many of which will be worthwhile, if not vital, to the text's unfolding. So in some cases, you will be faced with having to select which element, or small set of related elements, from the text you can actually use in *this particular sermon*. You will probably find that you cannot incorporate them all and *should not* try to include all in your sermon. In fact, in most cases, you will have to leave untouched more elements than you decide to use. What this suggests, however, is that with any given text, the unfolding of the Greek can provide you with a whole series of sermons, either from the text's general meaning or from significant portions of the passage. That being the case, of course, you might return to the same text not just once but a number of times. This is especially advantageous to those of you who preach on the three-year lectionary, which requires that you return every three years to the same set of assigned readings.

There is another important alternative and choice to be made, however. It has to do with whether you will actually prepare and preach this sermon *about* this text, taking specific account of its meaning or meanings, or whether you will merely draw on some element from this text as a part of a larger issue which comprises the sermon itself. That is, the text gives you entry into an extensive issue that reaches beyond the text itself. Either approach to preaching or some combination of the two is legitimate. The first sermon will tend to be more textual while the second will lean toward being a topical sermon. The fact is that you should know how to do both, with a judgment about the nature of the sermon resting on the text and the occasion for preaching.

Invariably, the dominant question confronting the preacher at this stage of sermon preparation has to do with the relationship between the meaning of the text, as the preacher has formulated it, and what the sermon will say. Two directives seem to us to be particularly valuable. The *first* is a keen understanding that *a biblical text never has only one meaning!* No matter how carefully one studies it with Greek tools and principles, you can never exhaust a passage! We have all had to come to terms, in our day at least, with the fact that there is no such thing as a single "true meaning" of any text. We preachers know how our listeners can assign radically different meanings to our sermons, even though they all hear the same words. Language always exceeds any one set of boundaries of meaning. So we are not looking for the *true meaning* of the text. Instead we are looking for a sense of being as true to our understanding of the text as we can be—fully aware that others who study the same text may determine that it means something different than what we have concluded.

What we are doing as preachers who have devoted ourselves carefully to the text, then, is determining to speak about our own "best sense" of what we believe is embodied in the text. This kind of preaching becomes, as it should, our "witness" vis-à-vis this particular text. In this context, we can speak with passion about what we find in the text. Moreover, within the confines of good taste and openness, we are free to contend for our own relationship to the text without claiming that it is the only possible relationship. In the sermons that follow, we take positions about our respective texts—positions that are not shared by everyone who studies these texts. We say, however, "I have studied this text as carefully as I know how, and here is what I have found in it. Here is where I take my stand as far as this text is concerned." But that is not the same as saying that I have found the "final truth" of this text. Yet it is giving our own clear witness about our encounter with this particular text at this particular time.

The *second* thing that is important about working from "the meaning" of a text to the sermon is that the jump between those two things should be made *in the most playful manner* possible. The sermon should be framed with a certain passion, and it should speak of things about which the preacher believes deeply. There is considerable homiletical literature about the use of imagination, but we are concerned with its use at this stage of sermon preparation. Wrestling with a text for preaching should be framed with a playfulness that reflects the vulnerableness of all who speak with passion. In both the preparation and preaching of a sermon, one "plays with" words, explores them, and toys with syntax. We dig into syntax, staying open to new ideas and ways of thinking and whatever we might find, even about texts that we think we know well. One works creatively, pushing the edges, mulling over possibilities—even possibilities that seem to stretch the limits of where things are or ought to be. This process may lead us to drawing diagrams, doodling, or whatever facilitates creativity. Part of this imaginative play is challenging in a friendly way things in the text, in one's own heart or in the milieu of the culture the preacher and congregation share.

There is no way to say exactly what "playing" in sermon preparation really means, and a full discussion of it is beyond the scope of this study. But there is a childlike quality about it, and in many ways it is that childlike digging and speaking that, in the end, should probably characterize the preacher's process of studying and preaching a text. That play is part of the way we set up this complex and endlessly fascinating encounter among ourselves, the congregation (in all its own complexity), and a biblical text. Having said all this, however, there are some very important cautions about the use of the Greek text in preaching that have to be addressed before we are finished with this study of preaching.

CHAPTER 2

Cautions about Greek
in the Sermon

Learning to use the Greek text of the New Testament in sermons involves more than just the technical materials we have discussed in detail in this book. It also entails developing certain sensitivities about the nature of the sermon as well as about the people among whom we preach. In that regard, you need to keep in mind some cautions as you begin your work with an interlinear Greek-English New Testament and as you make the bridge between your Greek exegesis and your preaching. For the most part, these are cautions about the use of Greek within the sermon itself. First, though, an important clarification is necessary.

One homiletics professor used to say to his seminary students in a basic preaching course, "Exegesis is like your underwear; you should wear it, but it shouldn't show." While the motives behind that statement are healthy ones, as we shall see, the aphorism itself needs to be thought about very carefully. Behind the statement is the idea that the sermon cannot be prepared without doing good biblical exegesis, whether that involves work in language or languages, in biblical backgrounds, or in other kinds of historical-linguistic work. In a sense, this is technical work in which the preacher uses all the specialized skills of study and analysis that he or she has learned in seminary. The idea is that the *fruits* of this work will often find their way into the sermon, but that the work itself should not. How one goes about doing technical things should be hidden from congregational view.

This is based on two assumptions. First is the idea that the congregants who share the sermon are interested in what the preacher has learned, but not in how the preacher has learned it. They are not interested in the technical aspects of the preacher's labor. Second is the idea that when preachers get into "technical things" in the pulpit, they are liable to become boastful, whether intentionally or not, about things that they know that the congregants do not. And as everyone knows, such boasting is simply inappropriate, if not downright offensive, in the pulpit.

It is fair to say that in years gone by, for the reasons we have just indicated, the aphorism about not letting your exegesis show was adhered to closely. In fact, it was a homiletical rule. Exegesis was for sermon preparation only. The preacher was not tempted to "show off," and the congregants were interested in what the preacher knew rather than in how the preacher knew it. So, like underwear, Greek exegesis (along with other forms of technical study) served a specific function, but when the sermon was preached, the study was to remain invisible. Or, to shift the metaphor, the exegesis (including Greek study) was to serve as scaffolding for the building of a wall. The wall could not be built without it—in fact, it was the secret to how the wall was built—but when the wall was finished, the scaffolding was to be removed. The wall was what was important, and people could only marvel at the wall's construction.

The aphorism, however, is less telling today than it was in the past. There is still the danger of appearing to "show off" when one discusses more technical matters of Bible study in the pulpit: "I know this, and you do not." Or, "Here is what I know because I am now well-educated, and you are not." Whether this is conveyed indirectly or implicitly, the preacher must be constantly on guard against giving such impressions. In fact, this is probably the overriding caution to be observed when one brings anything about the Greek language into the sermon. And there is still the danger that beginning preachers, whether in seminary or out, can become so mesmerized by their newly discovered understanding of the Bible that they overload their sermons with exegesis.

But—and it is a very important qualification—the "other" concern of the aphorism has changed dramatically in recent years. We can illustrate this change within a larger, non-sermonic framework.

One of the great theater attractions in Southern California for many years has been the month-long run of what is called the "Pageant of the Masters." It is an evening of famous paintings, but each one is life-size and all of the people in the small painting are real people, in full makeup, on stage. The curtain opens and, as in a museum, one is looking at an enormous and virtually exact replica of a recognizable painting. Except that the people in it are real. They are actors and actresses, often children, who are fixed, unmoving, in their places. It is a living art museum, in effect.

What those who have produced the pageant tell us is that for years audiences were satisfied with the staged paintings themselves, one after the other through the evening. For the last several years, however, there has been a strong and growing desire to see how the process itself is done. So now, when one sees the "Pageant of the Masters," the show is different. For about a third of the "paintings," all the house and stage lights are turned on, and the audience watches as the stage props are rolled into place and the complex backdrops are unfurled. Then one by one the made-up "actors" move onto the stage and take their places, many of them strapped or braced into place, since the positions called for by the paintings are often unusual or strained. The audience watches as stagehands prepare each person in proper position. When everything is ready, all the lights are turned out, and then the finished "painting" appears with every detail properly arranged and just as it should be. Even though the audience has watched with unforgettable fascination the preparation of the painting, the gasps when it is finally revealed in completed form indicates how unprepared everyone is for the realism of the finished product.

Such a change has also taken place vis-à-vis the sermon over the past couple of decades. Whereas in years past, the exegesis and sermon preparation process were hidden from view when the sermon was preached, now there is an intense desire to know how the finished product was actually put together, how the exegesis itself was carried out, and how the language was handled so that this particular conclusion was reached by the preacher. Or we not only want to admire the wall but also are very interested in how it was actually built. What this means, in short, is that whereas in the past, the preacher's Greek study and other exegesis were hidden from view, now they form what is often a very important and intriguing component of the sermon itself.

How then should we handle the Greek in a sermon? There is no single way to answer this question, of course. Different preachers will make choices differently, and different sermon situations for different congregations and texts will call for different approaches, even within the work of the same preacher. Common sense, combined with a sensitivity to your congregation, goes a long way toward handling the matter appropriately, so what we have to say may not be necessary in your particular case. Still, we feel an obligation to mention some of the dangers entailed in sharing your knowledge of the Greek text with your listeners. What follows are a few guidelines that might help you in your sermon preparation after you have done a good job of Greek exegesis. We call these guidelines, because we recognize that every congregation is different, and preachers vary immensely in their posture toward their laity. So read these suggestions, weigh them, and then adjust them to you and your situation.

The First Guideline: How Much Is Enough?

What we have said above points to the importance of the preacher's knowing her or his congregation. This is good advice for preaching in general. However, we suggest that, as you develop your skill in reading and interpreting the Greek text, you consider how your congregation might respond to the use of Greek in the pulpit. Will they be delighted to know their pastor has some knowledge of the original language? More than likely they will, since we live in a time when the desire for education, if not educational opportunity itself, is remarkably widespread. Many people wish to learn about the Bible, about its backgrounds, about "what it says," and they go to church knowing (or at least hoping) that there they will be educated about it. Sadly, such a hope does not always materialize between the pulpit and the pew, but it is far more pervasive than most preachers today realize.

For many of us who teach homiletics or preaching, one of the marks of a good sermon is that it has an educational component. People want to learn, and many of us believe that the listeners ought never to leave a sermon without knowing something about the Bible, biblical background, or theology that they did not know when they came in. So while preachers must be careful not to overwhelm congregants with knowledge (particularly technical knowledge), they must also realize that congregants do want to "learn along with" the preacher, as it were.

This is the same sort of issue you will face with regard to theological language. With what kind of vocabulary is your congregation familiar? An experienced pastor of a relatively large suburban church composed of a good number of professional people tells this story. A member of the congregation came to her to discuss her preaching. He complimented her for her fine preaching, but then made a request. He asked her please not to use such technical theological terms. She asked him for an example, and he responded with a word he had heard in last Sunday's sermon: reconciliation! She could hardly believe that reconciliation was strictly a theological word, but she took seriously the fact that as sophisticated as this congregation seemed to be, many congregants were still infants in the faith. Some of us may have to learn the same lesson with regard to how our congregation feels about the use of Greek from the pulpit.

One pastor who had studied some Greek in seminary attended a workshop on preaching the gospel of Luke. He was fascinated by the fact that Luke uses the verb σπλαγχνίζομαι (to feel compassion or pity) only three times—once for Jesus' compassion for the widow at Nain (7:13) and twice in Jesus' parables (10:33 and 15:20). The word fascinated him so much that in his sermon for the workshop, he began with the single Greek word—pronouncing it loudly and emphatically—and then proceeded throughout the whole sermon to use it as a kind of refrain. Actually, it was a rather good sermon, but some of us had to wonder how it would be received in the small rural parish he served. We can only hope that he was sensitive enough not to overwhelm his beloved ones with his newfound knowledge.

Whatever you decide about your congregation and its willingness to hear about the Greek in sermons, be alert to the possibility you might "turn them off" with your knowledge. The preacher who has just discovered the joys of reading the Greek text will exuberantly overflow with insights into the Greek text. Be temperate with your Greek. Go slow. Avoid a lot of detail, especially at first. Introduce your congregation to the Greek with a single and simple point the first time. Listen to the response its use gets; you can probably be assured that your parishioners will talk about it among themselves, if not to you. Feel free to inquire about what they thought, doing so openly and with a full measure of curiosity. Through this, it is possible to cultivate their appetite for the original language, and then in time you can begin to use more and more complicated information about the Greek text. This cultivation will work over time, especially if you do it with a keen sense that this is part of an ongoing educational process—a way to teach about the Bible and a way to enable your congregants to get to know for themselves "what the Bible says."

There are a couple of commonsense and simple ways to avoid smothering your congregation with your new knowledge. First, you may not have to say the Greek word or words in your sermon. Instead, you can simply say "the word that is translated 'such and such' could also be translated 'so and so'." In this way, you can still use your lexical knowledge without seeming to be overbearing.

Second, if you need to introduce a feature of Greek grammar, try to find a way to explain it with an English example, if there is one. For instance, we can explain the subjective and objective genitives with the "love of God" example. Sometimes you can use a deficiency in English to point out a feature of the Greek. For instance, the lack of a plural pronoun for the second person "you." Your parishioners will then understand why you want to make sure they know the author of a text is addressing a community and not just individuals. The Greek middle voice is harder to explain with an English example. The best possibility is to use the reflexive, such as, "I shot myself in the foot." Explain that Greek has an entirely separate form of the verb to express this idea of the speaker being both the actor and the acted upon.

A Second Guideline: Check Your Findings

One danger you will face is making a mistake, misunderstanding a portion of the text, and then misleading your congregation. It is only natural that this might happen. The language is difficult enough and the grammar complicated enough that misreadings are likely. It is easy, for instance, to confuse the preposition εἰς with the numeral εἷς, a difference of only breathing marks and accents. It is equally easy to read πλανᾷ (the root verb is πλανάω, "lead astray" or "deceive") as an indicative when it is subjunctive, since they are both spelled the same. In John 14:1 πιστεύετε can be either indicative or imperative, for again both are spelled the same. All these possibilities plus the more complicated matters of grammar, such as the functions of the participle, make it easy to err. Many errors, however, can be avoided or corrected by checking your analytical lexicon and/or interlinear Greek text on those materials that you plan to use in your sermon.

We say all this not to frighten you into paralysis but to invite you to check and double-check your results, especially if they are crucial to the sermon theme you are developing. You can, first of all, go back and retrace your steps in coming to your interpretation of a passage in order to make sure that you did not make a false move. Then, in some cases, you can check your findings against those of scholarly interpreters, whether they be in the commentaries, theological dictionaries, or Greek introductions and grammars.

We have said very little about the use of commentaries when interpreting the Greek text for preaching. That has been intentional, for we want you to learn to work independently on the Greek text itself. When they take the place of full immersion in the text itself, preachers misuse commentaries. However, there may be times after you have done your own translation of the Greek text and have begun to shape a sermon focus when you might want to consult a commentary. On rare occasions, too, the Greek text may stump you, and you may need some help in understanding it. *We suggest that you use commentaries to learn what others have said about the passage but not necessarily to learn what you should say.* You may want to confirm an idea by using a commentary.You may be puzzled by a peculiar Greek construction on which you may need help. Our point is simple: Don't let the commentaries substitute for your own work with the Greek text.

There are two types of commentaries we think you might want to use.The first is a commentary on the Greek text that might help you find your way through a particularly confusing and complicated Greek passage.

The International Critical Commentary on the Holy Scriptures of the Old and New Testaments is an old series published by T & T Clark (Edinburgh) and edited by S. R. Driver, A. Plummer, and C. A. Briggs, in which nearly every volume is technical and meticulous in its attention to the original languages.This old series is being rewritten now under new editors J. A. Emerton and C. E. B. Cranfield, but is still published by T and T Clark.

The authors of *The Word Biblical Commentary,* ed. David A. Hubbard, Glenn W. Barker, John D. W. Watts, and Ralph P. Martin (Waco, Tex.: Word Books, 1982) tend to be more conservative in their theological orientation, but their devotion to understanding the original language is unquestionable.

The series *Hermeneia—A Critical and Historical Commentary on the Bible,* edited by boards of eminent scholars and published by Fortress Press, is very technical and seldom offers much in the way of contemporary meaning but nearly always provides helpful insight into the original languages. Some of these volumes are translations of important European works.

The New International Commentary on the New Testament, ed. F. F. Bruce (Grand Rapids: Eerdmans) uses Greek in the footnotes when it is needed.

Word studies may also help you in checking your findings, particularly when they are based in large part on the use of certain words. In Principle 10, we warn that word studies have sometimes not paid enough attention to the different contexts in which a word is used. So beware of generalizations. Nonetheless, you may find these works useful:

Theological Dictionary of the New Testament, ed. Gerhard Kittel (Grand Rapids: Eerdmans, 1964–1976), ten volumes. A one-volume digest of the dictionary is also available now from Eerdmans.

Exegetical Dictionary of the New Testament, ed. Horst Balz and Gerhard Schneider (Grand Rapids: Eerdmans, 1990), three volumes.

Theological Lexicon of the New Testament, Ceslas Spicq (Peabody, Mass.: Hendrickson, 1994), three volumes.

Returning to commentaries, the second kind of commentary that may assist you at times are those in which the authors make suggestions regarding the meaning of the passage for today. These ideas may be too general or too vague for actual sermons but may still stimulate your thought. Some of the ones we can recommend to spur your own thought are these:

Interpretation: A Bible Commentary for Teaching and Preaching, ed. James L. Mays, Patrick D. Miller, and Paul J. Achtemeier (Louisville: Westminster John Knox Press) is just what the subtitle suggests. In this series some of the volumes are written by professors of preaching as well as biblical scholars.

The *Sacra Pagina* series, ed. Daniel J. Harrington, S. J. (Collegeville, Minn.: Liturgical Press [Michael Glazier books]) is devoted strictly to the New Testament. In these volumes Roman Catholic scholars interpret the New Testament as the church's book and as speaking to the contemporary church.

The New Interpreter's Bible: A Commentary in Twelve Volumes, Leander E. Keck, senior editor (Nashville: Abingdon Press) includes what are called "Reflections" on each passage in which the author draws some suggestions for contemporary meaning.

The *Good News According to...* series has three volumes written by Eduard Schweizer, each devoted to one of the synoptic gospels. These are older publications of John Knox Press, in which the noted German scholar is very intentional in asking how passages address the contemporary world.

Finally, the volumes of the *Augsburg Commentary on the New Testament,* ed. Roy A. Harrisville, Jack Dean Kingsbury, and Gerhard A. Krodel (Minneapolis: Augsburg Publishing House) are each written with clergy in mind, and the commentators freely propose contemporary meanings.

The Anchor Bible, William Foxwell Albright and David Noel Freedman, general editors (Garden City, N.Y.: Doubleday) is somewhere between the two categories of commentaries we have recommended. It is a very uneven series in which some volumes are contemporary classics and some have been quickly forgotten. The authors often use the transliterated Greek and make reference to the meaning of passages for Christians today.

Here comes the tough question. What if I have double-checked my exegesis, but my findings are different from those of the scholars? Remember, the scholars are not always right, and they are influenced by their theological presuppositions just as you and we are. We cited a number of examples of such scholarly errors in Part 1 of this book. If you are as certain as you can possibly be, and if your findings are important to you, then do not be afraid to take the road less traveled. (Should you choose to do this, however, be sure to take our next guideline seriously.)

In Romans 1:4 Paul may be quoting an early creed when he says Jesus "was declared to be the Son of God with power according to the spirit of holiness by resurrection from the dead." The Greek word translated "was declared to be" is ὁρισθέντος, a genitive, single, aorist passive participle of ὁρίζω. The lexicons generally say that the verb can mean "appoint," "designate," and "declare." It is the same verb used in Acts 17:31. Some scholars, however, have been cautious about its meaning, preferring usually to say that in the case of Romans 1:4 it means something like "was publicly declared to be." Many are hesitant to allow the word to imply that Jesus was made Son of God in his resurrection, for that borders on adoptionistic christology—something the church has declared should be avoided. Yet with this Romans passage and Acts 17:31, as well as some other evidence, there is reason to think that some early Christians may have believed that God appointed Jesus as Messiah sometime in his life or in his resurrection.

Sometimes the text opens possibilities for us that may not set well with our presuppositions. Part of the reason we learn to read the original language as best we can is to get one step closer to the text and hence become more vulnerable to its radical ideas. Preachers who are grounded in Greek exegesis may at times venture to swim against the current. But when we choose to do so, we want to be as faithful to the text as possible, so we check and double-check our findings. However, we are also constrained by another fact.

The Third Guideline: Avoid Literalizing the Text

Moving into the mysteries of the original language sometimes leads us to attend so scrupulously to the Greek text that we begin to assume that we can now credit the New Testament with being word by word the words of God. Greek exegesis entails careful examination of the individual words, even articles and conjunctions, and the arrangements of the words into grammatical constructs. Yet this detailed study does not necessarily mean that we now have access to God's vault of truth.

The Greek text does, indeed, take us one step closer to the original work of the New Testament authors, and that is a valuable step. However, even working with the Greek text, established from a multitude of different ancient manuscripts, still leaves us a long, long way from the first writings (called the "autographs"). Even if we do come closer to the original when we can read it in the Greek, we are still denied access to exactly what the author had in mind when she or he composed the text. Therefore, we can no more claim the absolute authority of the words of the text for the church today than when we were limited to translations.

Actually, just the opposite may prove to be the case. When you read the authors in their original language, you may begin to see their frailties and weaknesses in a way you had not seen them in English translations. Translators sometimes deliberately hide some of the roughness of the Greek and the limitations of the author's style. The gospel of Mark is a good example. This author is addicted to the connective καί to such a degree that its use produces a monotony. The second evangelist is also notorious for some crude expressions, such as speaking of "the stone of a donkey" (μύλος ὀνικός, 9:42) and saying that those who carried the paralytic to Jesus "removed the roof" (ἀπεστέγασαν τὴν στέγην, "the whole roof"?) to get him to Jesus (2:4). Whatever way you may believe about God's revelation coming through such words, the Greek betrays the humanity of the authors of the New Testament.

The Fourth Guideline: Don't Become Dogmatic

We have made abundantly clear that we believe there is no such thing as the "true meaning" of a text. Therefore, we preachers need to be cautious about giving the impression that—by virtue of our knowledge of the original language—we now know exactly what is true and what is false. In our enthusiasm, it is tempting to become a bit dogmatic about some new insight we have just gained from our study. Remember the old saw about the new convert's being the strongest of the believers. And don't forget its corollary: "A little learning is a dangerous thing." Novices in the Greek New Testament are in danger of slipping into the same hole. Greek is not a cure-all for biblical interpretation nor the key that unlocks truth. It is only one more tool to help us.

Let us propose two things to help you avoid a presumptuous and arrogant posture. First, practice a bit of intellectual humility! Keep in mind that you may be wrong; remember that you are only a human interpreter and messenger. Second, entertain the option of inviting the congregation simply to consider the possibility that the text may mean this or that. If you choose this option, while confessing that your view might not be correct, you engage them in a quest for the meaning of the text. The sermon then becomes a contribution to the community's ongoing effort to understand and appropriate scripture.

Mature students of the Greek text believe that their use of the original language is a precious tool in the interpretation of New Testament passages. However, they also know that it does not prevent many of the classical difficulties in interpretation. We are still prone to read the text strictly through our particular lenses of theological persuasion, social class, empowerment, and all the rest. Use the tool, and use it creatively, but don't imagine that truth is at your fingertips now that you know the different types of actions found in Greek verbs.

CHAPTER 3

Sample Sermons with Commentaries

When one takes this study of Greek for preaching seriously, precisely how might a sermon look? What is the actual payoff of reading the Greek, however superficially? In this section we provide you with two sample sermons, each of which would be impossible were it not for some fundamental working knowledge of Greek. These are not necessarily what either of your authors would nominate as among the best sermons ever preached. That is not our purpose. Rather, our purpose is simply to exemplify two of the ways in which sermons arise from the Greek behind the English translations. We will preface each sermon with an introduction that is designed to demonstrate more precisely how the Greek influenced the formulation of the sermon.

"The Bible and Being Married" (Eph. 5:20–33)

Introduction

The following sermon, by Joseph Webb, demonstrates a fairly direct way by which the Greek can be used in making statements about texts. The sermon was originally one of a six-part series on the challenge of being married in contemporary society.

We have already made clear how the reading of the Greek influenced this sermon. At several points in Section 2, we discussed Ephesians 5:20–33. You will recall that in Principle 9, we saw that the pronoun ἀλλήλοις in verse 21 provided a preface to the discussion of the relationship between husbands and wives and suggested that the marriage relationship was one of equality and mutuality. Earlier, in Principle 5 on conjunctions, we stressed the roles of ἵνα and πλήν in reading verse 33. First we argued that in this case ἵνα did not introduce an imperative but stated a wish or desire, and then we noted the radical disjunction between verses 32 and 33 signaled by πλήν. Along with others, these examinations of Ephesians 5:21–33 provided the foundations on which the following sermon was first constructed.

The Sermon

We are not at all sure who wrote the words that you heard read from Ephesians chapter 5. Tradition says Paul the apostle did. Most likely he did not; the language doesn't sound like him. I guess what I would really like to know was whether the person who wrote this was married. Did he—or she, could it be a she?—know anything about marriage…firsthand? I had not paid a lot of attention to this text until I was asked to do so in these sermons. I think—mind you, I *think*—that the writer here was married and was struggling to make new connections to marriage in the light of this still very new Christ religion.

But this text is about marriage. Some say it is about the church—there was that inserted line about marriage as a metaphor for Christ and the church. But this text *is* about marriage, and it makes no pretense not to be. The problem, though, is that this text is often called on to do—and to mean—what it neither does nor means. As a result, here is a marriage text that often—in my judgment—does damage to marriage; and since this is the Bible, it does that damage in the name of Christianity.

A few years back, I served a relatively new church in Southern California that owned no building; our services were held in an elementary school building. So a good deal of what went on in small groups during the week took place in our big, rambling suburban house. On one particular early evening, my wife was ill, and fifteen or so people were due a bit later for a Bible study at our house. We always served refreshments—a dining room table with coffees, teas, cookies, a cake: You know how it works. My wife always took care of preparing the table, which was always extraordinarily beautiful, always done in the same way—as far as I could tell. An artist, she took considerable pride in how it looked; I was proud of it too. I always helped, of course, as much as I could, and as much as she let me (if I may say it that way).

On this particular evening, I suggested that since I had watched her do it for quite some time, I knew quite well how to prepare the table, and that she should go on back to bed and leave everything to me. Just this once. Reluctantly, she agreed to do so. I got out everything and started to put the dining room table together. I put the saucers and cups on the end where I knew she placed them, arranged the pots for coffee and tea on the edge along the kitchen side, lined up the spoons and forks on that other end, and set a stack of good napkins near them. When I finished, the table looked really nice, as it always did for her; and in the middle of the table I added the decorated sheet cake that I had bought. When I finished, nearly at the time for our guests to arrive, I was so proud of how it looked that I went back to the bedroom to ask if she would come and, well, "inspect" what I had done. Again, reluctantly, she agreed to do it.

A few minutes later, when she came around the corner of the living room into the dining room, she—I don't know how else to say this—she exploded. The table, she hollered and stammered, was a mess. How could I have done this?!!

"You have never paid a moment's attention to the way that I do the table, have you?" she asked, though it didn't sound like a question. "Where have you been all the time I have been doing this?"

I shouted back: "Of course I have paid attention, and this is the way it looks when you do it."

"It has nothing to do with how I set the table. It is just awful! You don't care at all what I go through for these people. It just goes to prove that you do not pay any attention to what I do around here." She was ill. She was not feeling well.

"But I do pay attention," I tried to insist.

She was just getting warmed up—illness or no illness.

"Look at that! Look at that!" She was pointing to the table. "That is not the way you stack the saucers; they get all scarred up that way. And you have never noticed, have you, how the cup handles all point in the direction of the window. And the spoons and forks—that is not how they are supposed to be lined up. And you've just *thrown* the napkins into the stack; they are supposed to be slightly swirled. You've never paid any attention, have you? And the cake is never directly in the center of the table!"

I launched into my counter-mode.

"The table looks beautiful, and you know it does," I sputtered. "This is the way you do it. And besides, the people will not be able to tell the difference!" Which I should not have said, of course.

"Oh yes they will," she retorted. "These people are not the barbarians that you are. You midwesterners just do not care how things are done, do you?"

"Yes we do!"

"No you don't." And then, with considerable hurt, she said, "If you had just paid some attention, you might have been able to do it right."

Well, the crack about "you midwesterners" was meant to underscore her origin, not in California, but in Chattanooga, Tennessee, where she had been reared with the special entertaining talents of the south, something—clearly—that I did not possess. What we both realized later that night, when we talked a bit about what had taken place between us, was that we were products of two very different places, that things she had been meticuously taught and that were very, very deeply important to her were—honestly—not that important to me; or at least they did not register as deeply with me as they did with her. And vice versa. And yes, I had paid attention to a lovely table over many weeks, but the details of it all? No, I had not.

I tell you this innocent little story because it is neither very innocent nor very little. It is about the sheer difficulty of being married, of two people from very different upbringings, with all their different ways of doing things and with all of their deep emotional involvements in those specific ways, of these two people trying to get along in what is often a very small space. The explosions—many of them about matters far more serious than how a table is set—can come almost daily, often with pain, anger, resentment, and even violence. Sad but true. Who among us does not know about all this—whether we are married or not?

We Christians like to turn to the Bible for help with these sorts of things. And we always seem to do so hoping that our questions will be answered and our problems solved. Most often, though, neither of those happens. We would like the Bible to show us an ideal marriage—in the Old Testament perhaps. But no, there is no such thing there. When it comes to marriage and family, the Bible is a virtual catalog of dysfunctional behavior. Think about Abraham calling his wife—twice—his sister, about Isaac and Rebecca, and Jacob and his wives—strange marriage behaviors at every turn: deceit, lying, cheating, neglect, angers, hurts. Perhaps that great forebear of Jesus, David, might show us how to make a marriage work—but there the whole process would be comical were it not so tragic.

What if we turn to the New Testament? There are Jesus' words prohibiting divorce—probably a step forward—in a culture in which divorce, at least from a male point of view, seems to have been fairly easy. But where else? And we end up with a text like the one before us here, from Ephesians 5. A few words—a very few words indeed—about one of the most challenging, indeed troubling, of human relationships. This is all, this text. If this is what we have, then what do these words from Ephesians tell us about marriage? What are we to make of them? I raise the question not because I think everything we want or need to know is dealt with here—or that what *is* dealt with is even very clear. No, I raise it because this text is so often used in today's Christian world to affirm something that I don't think the text affirms at all. The text gets skewed—and for religious purposes! Oh, what arises from the skewing provides what for some is a "solution" to the male-female relationship in marriage, and I am putting very large quotations marks around the word "solution." But the solution is not a solution at all. In fact, it violates what for many of us is at the heart of Christianity itself, which is not the continued oppression, under whatever guises, of women, but the freeing of women within the marriage relationship. So, as some preachers like to say it, what does the Bible say about marriage? What, specifically, does this marriage text in Ephesians 5 have to say about marriage? These are useful questions for all of us who are in the church, and who do care about the Bible, but who are worried about marriage in contemporary life.

So I want to tell you some things that I think are in this particular text and what they seem to me to say to both women and men in marriage. I do this realizing, of course, that not all of you here are married; many of you do not contemplate marriage, or you have in mind some alternative to marriage. Regardless of that, views of marriage are in many ways crucial to other aspects of our living together as a community, as a church, respecting one another's views. So, having qualified what I want to say, I ask you to look at this text with me.

In short, it is my view that whoever wrote this text was onto something. The writer was trying desperately and carefully—if not completely successfully—to embody a new sense of what marriage should be, from a Christian perspective, and he, or she, was doing so in a culture in which most of these ideas about marriage were quite foreign. Ironically, these ideas are still not grasped very well, even among many Christian denominations and sects within our own culture.

Usually, the line we hear from this text is the one in verse 23. It says that the husband is the head of the wife, who is subject to him in everything. It says that. Clear enough? It says that, of course, if one does not take any account of what *surrounds* that line, what precedes it and follows it. But many Christians prefer *not* to go beyond that line. So that simple, seemingly unambiguous line provides the working philosophy of Christian marriage. Husband rules; wife obeys. God said it; I believe it; now go do it. And with that, it is believed, the problems that crop up in a marriage are taken care of.

My friends, please slow down with me here. Please look more carefully at what this text says. Yes, it says what I just said. But it does so within a framework that goes back to verse 21, two verses earlier than that line. What sounds very much like a *principle,* a principle that, by its grammar, is meant to then point to the relationship between husbands and wives. The principle is this—and I will quote it as most of our English translations put it. It says: "Be subject to one another," and then it adds, "in the respect of Christ." Some translations say "out of fear" of Christ, but the word is much more accurately translated as "respect" of, or for, Christ. Then, without a break in the Greek sentence, the next line refers to wives: "Wives, to their own husbands as to the Lord." But that idea of wives being subject to the husbands is stated in the full understanding of the principle that this "being subject" is a two-way street. The word that is used after "be subject" is truly "one another," "to one another." Being subject is meant to be reciprocal. You do it for me, and I will do it for you. Wives and husbands are to be subject—to one another. What a remarkable concept! What a difficult concept to actually elaborate in a meaningful way!

Wives, be subject to your own husbands, as you would, or are, to Christ. Got that? Yeah, we got that. Parenthetically, what may be going on here, at least to an extent, is that some, if not many, married women were being attracted to the church, but they were married to men who wanted nothing to do with it all. Some of these women may very well have been looking for a way out of their marriages; or under their newfound freedom in Christ—as they were hearing it preached—they were starting to fidget and even to rebel under the heavy-handed marriages of their day. Don't do that, or be very slow to do that, is what the writer of this text seems to be saying—however clumsily. But what also gets said is *that principle* first: Be subject to one another—wives, you to your husbands. And then—

And then—the writer turns directly to husbands. You, too, must be subject, to your wives. But instead of emphasizing the idea of "be subject to your wives"—that is already in the principle—the writer, in no uncertain terms, directs husbands to *love their wives.* That is the other side of the "be subject to one another" principle! Husbands, love your wives. As Christ loved the church and gave up his life for it! Keep yourselves, husbands, without spot or wrinkle; keep yourselves holy and without blemish. In the context of that day's view of marriage, that was strong language indeed. Husbands, love your wives as you love yourselves. It is a firm, flat-out, no-nonsense way of repeating the principle: Husbands, it is not just that your wives are supposed to be subject to you—that is the first half of the "one another" principle—but you are supposed to be subject to them as well. Call it loving them, call it whatever you want; just don't call it oppressing them or dominating them or lording it over them in any way. The "one another" principle is a reciprocal thing.

Two words in the Greek language are most interesting and informative as they are used in this text. One is pronounced *para-stasa* (παραστήση). It is found in verse 27 in reference to Christ *presenting* the church to himself; "presenting" is the word used to translate *para-stasa*. The word *para-stasa,* however, is a compound word that means to "stand beside"; *stasis* means "*to stand*" and *para* means "*beside.*" The whole idea of *partnership*—of *standing next to each other,* rather than in some kind of above and below relationship—is carried by that word. Marriage as partnership, not as one over the other.

The second term that jumps from the Greek text is that husbands "*ought*" to love their wives. It is the word *ophilo* (ὀφείλω), which is a "debt" word. Somebody actually "owes" someone something. There is a debt to pay here. That is the term used to say that husbands "owe" this to their wives. Who knows what to make of that exactly? But it is strong language.

What cannot be missed in this text is that the writer is much more concerned about husbands than he—or she—is about wives. "Be subject to one another" is the principle—wives to their husbands, of course; but—but—but—husbands subject to their wives as well. Call it love your wives. But you had better get this straight. The obligation of the husband toward the wife is intense, a debt to be taken seriously, a debt that the wife has a right to collect, as it were, and here an effort is being made by this writer to drive that home in no uncertain terms.

There is one final element of the language of this text that I think you should be aware of. It comes toward the end, in verse 33. And it is striking, indeed; it is also fully in harmony, in my judgment, with everything that we find from the principle of "mutual submission" on. Again, the statement is directed clearly to husbands. In our English translations, it reads like this in verse 33: "Let each one of you love his wife as himself"—that has already been emphasized in the "love your wives" section. But then comes a precise and very profound Greek word, even though virtually all our English translations either miss it or do not know what to do with it. It is the Greek word *hina* (ἵνα)—that is how you pronounce it, spelled in English, h-i-n-a. Its meaning is clear and direct. It means "in order that"—"in order that." The way that I read the text, with that word *hina* in it, is that the writer is saying—repeating really—that husbands are to love their wives as themselves—*hina*—"in order that" wives may respect their husbands. That's the rest of the line—that wives "respect" their husbands. But the word *hina* puts it all into an odd, but deeply moving, light. Husbands are to love their wives as themselves "in order that" wives may respect them!

Does that mean what it sounds like it means? I think it means exactly what it sounds like it means. Earlier, I suggested that new Christian women, married to men who wanted nothing to do with Christianity or the church, those women were struggling with their own marriage roles, with the sense of freedom that this new religion seemed to hold out to them and for which, for the most part, they were deeply hungry. Look back, then, at this text. There is the mutuality principle: Be subject to one another, out of respect for Christ, for your new religion, as it were. Wives, be subject to your husbands, and husbands, yes, to your wives. Husbands, your subjection will be shown, explicitly, in the ways in which you treat your wives—with purity and gentleness and, beyond that, by making your wives your partners—full partners "standing alongside you"—within your relationship. And you are to love your wives as yourselves "in order that" they may stay in their own role within your life.

Is there an "out" for wives there? It sure sounds like there is to me. If you are not treated well, with love and partnership, in your marriage, then the idea that you, wives, are to "respect" or even "submit" to your husbands, seems—by this text—*to be nullified*. Wow! I don't know if we want to say that out loud or not. But here it is. This is not a text that crowns the husband king and makes the wife and kids subjects within the king's castle. This is not a text designed to hold women, wives, down; nor is it one that calls for wives to be under the "control" of the husband, whatever his decisions or his whims. This is not even a text that wraps marriage up in some kind of shiny package with a big bow and seeks to preserve it at all costs. This is a tough text that almost "reminds" wives that they have certain responsibilities in marriage, but that then lowers the boom on husbands. Your obligation, husbands, is to be subject to your wives—yes, let's use that word—subject to your wives by loving them and loving them and loving them and seeing that they are full, equal partners with you, both in your home and outside it. That is what this text seems to me to come down to.

We men may not be at all sure how we feel about this—at least I for one am kind of taken aback. But the text pulls no punches—or so it seems to me. In fact, the view of marriage that emerges from this text calls men, husbands, to account—and that probably is as it should be, both in those ancient cultures and still in our cultures today.

One of the things that preachers do—some quite often—is perform weddings. We marry people. A preacher has a lot of decisions to make about marrying people who come to him or her, since to join two people in marriage—whether in a church sanctuary or not—is to imply a certain blessing, not only upon that marriage but upon the two people who are being married. Some preachers say, "I will marry these kinds of people, but not those. Divorced people, no, I won't marry them." Some take that stand. Not too many these days, but some. Or "They are too young," or "Their backgrounds are such that I cannot 'sanction' who they are by participating in their marriage." Preachers think about those things.

For myself, a long time ago I vowed that I would seldom be inclined, whatever the circumstances, to refuse to marry two people who came to me. As a result, I have taken part in a lot of different kinds of weddings. Truth be told, I enjoy a lot of different kinds of weddings. With weddings, wherever they are held, there are wedding rehearsals; and I go through the rehearsals, in a general way, so that bride and groom, attendants, family members, ushers, whoever, know where to stand and how to get there and get away from there. What I always tell the bride and groom, however—either during some initial counseling or talking or at the rehearsal—is that at a certain point early in the ceremony, I get to say some things. I don't read them from a book, and I never think of it as a sermon, or use that word for it, but I get to say some things that are on my mind— no more than ten or twelve minutes worth. But they should be prepared to listen to me as best they can.

A few years ago, I was approached by a young women whom I knew, asking if I would perform the wedding for her and her boyfriend, soon fiance. She told me a little about him, how she met him, and so on, and then I met with them both a few times. I was suspicious of him from the start. He was tough—tender around her, but tough. I talked a bit with his family and found out that he had a violent streak, one that frightened me. I asked her about it—she knew about that, she said, but he had promised that his outbursts were a thing of the past. Yes, I tried to talk her out of the marriage, but that was clearly not to be. If I wanted out, she would let me out of it. I decided I didn't want out of it. In another session, we all three talked about it, and he said everything right. But I remained worried. Still, I was going to perform the ceremony.

When the day of the wedding came, I made a decision that I had been pondering. It was a joyous occasion, of course, with ten decked-out attendants and a church full of people. I don't think I could even be seen from the congregation. But after the normal wedding preliminaries, it was my turn to talk for a few minutes. I said what was on my heart—to the shock of everyone in the place. I said how difficult a normal marriage in our day could be—differences of opinions, emotional insensitivities, and so on—but then I said that violence in the home is the number one killer of women who marry violent men. I said that I was worried for this young woman, since when male anger flares, it can sometimes have disastrous consequences. And he had a temper; he had acknowledged as much himself. Since I was participating in this marriage, I was going to keep an eye on how this marriage went in the future. Then I spoke the man's name—"and will you promise, really promise, here before all of us, and before God, that you will not strike her or injure her or hurt her physically in any way?" I said, "We are not at the marriage vows yet, but will you make her this vow before we get to those other vows?"

He was shaking, and tears had formed in her eyes, and she looked at him intently, wanting to hear what he would say. He spoke softly, but the microphone I was wearing picked up his word clearly: "Yes," he said, "I will promise that."

We went on through the service, everything else as normal. No one said anything about what I had done. Except within two weeks I received two notes in the mail. One was from that young bride, who wanted me to know that in the short time they had been married, on three different occasions he had grown very angry, but in each case, she said, he seemed to remember what he had said that day, and had pulled himself together. That note didn't surprise me, but the second one did. It came from the man's mother. She just wanted to thank me for understanding her son so well. "I pray every day," she wrote, "that he will not forget what you made him say." And then she added, "You were right. I am so glad that you understood him."

To this day I do not know if I did the right thing. Nor do I know how things are going with them. What I know is that men are still the main problem in marriage—not the women. Not all the time, I know. But almost all the time. When you visit the shelters, you know. It is clear that as a church, we need to be saying new things, liberating things, protective things, about women in marriage. We need this text. A lot of people *do* care "what the Bible says." And often what it says is not what we think it says, or what we have been taught that it says. This text, as far as I can tell, is a clear affirmation of what marriage could be. And for us all—particularly us men—to hear that affirmation could be an important part of renewed Christian living!

"Envious Eyes" (Matt. 20:1–16)

Introduction

Preaching Jesus' parables is fraught with dangers as well as grand opportunities, and the following sermon by Robert Kysar confronts both with its close dependence on the gospel text. The trouble is that many of the parables we find in the gospels are puzzling and seem designed to force us to question what we think we know. Matthew's parable of the workers in the vineyard is one of those troubling parables. It is a masterfully constructed story that surprises us with its conclusion. To preach this parable demands that we allow it to trouble us and then facilitate its troubling the congregation much as Jesus did for his listeners.

A number of features of this parable are worth pointing out before turning to the Greek of the story. The first is that Jesus begins the story with the words, "For the kingdom of God is like (ὁμοία)," leading us to suppose that there is some way in which the story illumines God's rule in the world. The second observation is that "for" (γάρ) in the introductory statement connects the story with the saying that immediately precedes it: "But many who are first will be last, and the last will be first" (19:30—see Principle 5). That same saying appears again as the epilogue to the story (20:16), and the story itself is about some who were first becoming last. Verse 16 begins with οὕτως and connects the story with the saying occurring both in 20:16 and 19:30. The word is actually an adverb, but here its function is to summarize the parable just as it is in 13:40.

The narrative is told with a recurring use of aorist participles and verbs (see Principles 2 and 3), as verses 3 and 6 suggest. The aorist tense appears throughout the story, but its conclusion switches abruptly to the future in verse 16 with the verb ἔσονται. The completed action in the past points us to the future. The conjunction καί is used as a simple connector for narrative purposes—that is, to move the plot along (see Principle 5). Altogether, the word is used at least sixteen times—a perfect example of its use as a simple connector.

The Greek text especially stimulated this sermon by means of two things in the landowner's defense of his action in verses 14 and 15. The first is accurately translated "what belongs to you" (v. 14) and "what belongs to me" (v. 15). But the Greek is succinctly and powerfully expressed: τὸ σὸν and τοῖς ἐμοῖς. Notice that the articles in both cases stand for "things" or "possessions" (see Principle 1). The first is neuter singular, and the second neuter plural. The idea of who owns what becomes one of the themes incorporated in the sermon.

The second contribution of the Greek text to the formation of the sermon is verse 15b, ἢ ὁ ὀφθαλμός σου πονηρός ἐστιν ὅτι ἐγὼ ἀγαθός εἰμι; the English translations, "Or are you envious because I am generous?" (NRSV) and "Or do you begrudge my generosity?" (RSV) both conceal some nuances of meaning that may be important in this parable, namely, that it is the eye that is envious and that ἀγαθός means good, as well as generous. (The Greek word, ὀφθαλμός, provides us our word ophthalmologist.) This became the central idea of the sermon. It is worth noting that Principle 8 and the use of adjectives illumined this passage. The word ἀγαθός is in the predicate position and makes a statement about the noun, which is ἐγώ. In this case, the predicate position emphasizes the word's use with the subject of the sentence, and the line between noun and adjective is blurred.

The use of the particles ἤ...ἤ in verse 15 is also interesting. (Note, however, that the first ἤ is not found in some of the early manuscripts of this passage.) It is what we call a "disjunctive" particle in Principle 6, because it sets two things in opposition. In this case, the opposition is between two reasons the grumbling workers are upset. The owner challenges them with these two options, though neither is positive.

Finally, the most creative use of the Greek entailed what we have called "Dancing with Words" (Principle 10). First, even though it did not get into the sermon, I could not resist playing with the word ἑταῖρε (v. 13), translated "friend," and had to look up its uses elsewhere in Matthew. In 11:16 it is used of the playmates in a little parable, then of Judas in 26:50, and finally of someone whom the speaker does not know (22:12). While it is cordial in tone, this word does not have the force of friendship love (as, for instance, in φιλία). A beautiful example of a compound word is found in verse 13—συνεφώνησας, an aorist indicative of συμφωνέω. It comprises our favorite suffix, συν, and φωνέω, which in its form as a noun (φωνή) can mean a declaration. Hence, the compound word means to declare together.

A note about the introductory story of the sermon. I had used this personal and true story in a sermon some years ago and only later read Barbara Brown Taylor's sermon "Beginning at the End," in which she tells her own version of a similar story. In case you wonder, I did not "steal" it from Taylor, though I am complimented that our minds conceived similar stories in connection with this passage![1]

---

[1] See Thomas G. Long and Cornelius Plantinga, Jr., eds., *A Chorus of Witnesses: Model Sermons for Today's Preacher* (Grand Rapids: William B. Eerdmans, 1994), 15.

The Sermon

We arrived early—almost the first ones there. We had intentionally come early so that we could get the best seats. At last we were going to see and hear our favorite musical group in concert. But there were no reserved seats for the concert. So we came early to be sure that we were among the first to enter the hall.

And now we were positioned very well: right in front of one of several doors to the concert hall. Others began to come now, each finding a place toward the rear of the lines that had formed at the doors into the hall. We must admit we felt rather smug. Those poor souls back there in the line. They would end up at the rear of the hall, while we would surely be in the first half dozen rows. Pitiful persons!

The time for the concert approached, and finally the doors were opened for admission. *But not the door in front of which we stood!* It remained locked! The other doors to the left and the right were open, and people were pouring in. Just to be sure, I tried the door near us. But no, it was locked tight. We had no choice but to find our way to the back of one of the other lines moving through an open door. Well, we finally made it. But what seats! A pillar right in front of us, so we had to bend to the left to see the stage. And even then, the stage looked like a tiny postage stamp way down there.

I had two choices that night. I could have been glad for those latecomers who had ended up with better seats than ours. I could have taken pleasure in their good fortune. But instead, I moped about in anger. I felt cheated. *It just wasn't fair!* We had been among the first to arrive at the hall. Why, then, did we end up among the last to enter the hall? I had two choices that night. But I could only be angry and envious of the others.

It was a shock for us to end up last when we thought we would be first. But what a much greater shock those workers must have felt. Especially those who had come early into the vineyard and worked the whole day in the hot sun. How shocked and angry they were! Other workers who had come later and who put in only a couple of hours received the same pay as the early comers received. The very same amount for those who worked eight hours and those who worked only two hours! That would make anyone angry. If such a thing occurred today, the labor unions would most certainly have something to say about this terrible injustice.

Jesus' parable is puzzling and disturbing. The landowner at first seems a very just and good guy. He carefully makes contracts with all those he hires. And then he keeps going back to the village square to hire still more workers. And he promises each group he will pay them justly. It gets later and later in the day, and he continues to hire additional workers—not once but four times. Why? We are never told why he went back to hire others. We are not told whether or not the work was too much for the present number of workers to handle, so that others had to be hired. However, we may get the impression that this landowner is a very generous and kind man who did not want to see anyone go unemployed for the day.

This impression of the landowner makes the conclusion of the story that much harder to take. He seems a very just fellow. But when it comes time to pay his workers, he chooses to pay first those who came to work last. And can you believe it? He pays them a full day's wages! That naturally makes those who had worked harder suppose that they would get paid even more than a full day's wage. But when the employer comes to the others, he doesn't pay them more. When he comes to those who had worked all day, he pays them exactly the same as those who put in only a couple of hours. *A full day's wage for all the workers—the first and the last.*

Perhaps some of you are like me and tend to share the indignation of the first workers. I'm right there with them grumbling about the pay. It is unjust! So I am listening carefully when the landowner finally defends himself in the closing verses of the story. He says two things. First, he claims that it is his privilege to do what he wishes with what is his. *It's his money!* If he wishes to pay the latecomers as much as the early arrivers, he may do so. We might agree with him—at least reluctantly. But it still seems unfair to the first workers.

The landowner says he can do as he wishes with what is his. "Am I not allowed to do what I choose with what belongs to me?" Whose money is it anyway? Those words may cut deep! Especially if we think this story has something to do with us and our Christian lives. Whose money is it anyway?

Sometimes we may think we have some kind of monopoly on God's grace and love. Particularly when some newcomers enter our church. We may ask, "Are they really worthy of God's grace? Should they be allowed to take communion? We don't want those kind among us unless they change their ways!" But Jesus makes us ask, "Whose love and grace is it anyway?" Not ours! We are but poor servants who share it with others. The church would do well to consider this point, especially now when—once again—there are those whom some would like to lock out of the church. *It's God's grace, not ours.*

But the landowner in Jesus' story has something else to say. The *New Revised Standard Version* translates his words this way: "Or are you envious because I am generous?" That translation hides some interesting shades of meaning in the landowner's words. The Greek actually reads like this: "Is your eye envious (or evil) because I am good?"

Is your eye envious? Is your eye evil? That's a strange expression, and we see why the translators have left out the word "eye." But the question suggests an important idea. In the Bible, the eye often expresses the attitude of the person. So its use here makes us ask, is it all in the way we look at things? Does it depend on our eyes, and how we perceive something? One perspective produces envy. But another perspective might produce joy for the others.

You can bet that my eye was envious that night at the concert. From my perspective, I was angry that the latecomers got better seats than we did. Another perspective might have rejoiced for those who had the better seats for whatever reason. Had I looked at the situation from the perspective of those latecomers, I might have seen what happened in a different light.

What's our perspective? When we look at events in our lives and in our world, what's our perspective? We can choose to be envious, angry, indignant. We can choose to scream, sulk around, and jump up and down, crying "foul" and demanding justice. Or we can choose to see it from the perspective of the others who have been given a gift they had not earned.

The situation comedy "Frasier" offers us a good example of the envious eye. Niles and Frasier are brothers—both cultured and learned psychiatrists. But they are entrapped in an old jealousy—a jealousy such as only siblings can experience. When either of them gains something good, when either of them is successful, or when either of them gets something he has not earned, the other throws a temper tantrum, a fit of envy. Two grown men acting like they are still children. We laugh at their childishness. Often it is simply hilarious! The trouble is that their behavior makes some of us nervous. Their rivalry often holds up a mirror before us. And we see ourselves in these two brothers. We see our own envious eyes in their jealousy. We see our own unwillingness to rejoice in another's success in the actions of the jealous brother.

However, the landowner asks, "Is your eye envious because *I am good?*" There is nothing wrong with the translation "because I am generous." The word fits the situation very well. But it hides the fact that the landowner's eccentric generosity arises from his basic goodness. It is his goodness that motivates him to pay all the workers a full day's wage. It is goodness expressed concretely in the form of generosity.

"Is your eye envious because I am good?" Are we envious when God is gracious to another who doesn't deserve it? Are we jealous when some are embraced by God's love, even when they are unworthy? To use biblical language, are we envious of those who experience God's righteousness?

God's grace and God's justice are beyond our comprehension. We know God is good; God is generous. God is filled with grace, grace that forgives again and again. But we believe, too, that God is just. Jesus' parable of the workers in the vineyard forces us to remember this: Our comprehension of justice and grace is not necessarily God's. When we think that we have gotten God figured out, this parable upsets our confidence. Just when we think we know how far God's love stretches, this parable proves us wrong. It is not for us to tell God who can be held in the arms of divine love and who cannot. Nor is it for us to tell God what is just and what is unjust. The workers thought they could tell their boss he was wrong. They thought that they had some claim to the owner's money. In fact, we go on and on trying to grasp God's ways.

Job did the same thing. Remember? He thought he knew how God should run the universe. Finally, God answers Job out of the whirlwind. And all Job could do was to put his finger to his lips and admit that he was a human, not God.

There is one thing we do know for sure. God's gracious love has embraced us. Whether we are the first or the last makes no difference. We know God claims us as part of the divine family and makes us brothers and sisters together. That's what we know! We know that God's justice has stretched *a long way* to bring us into the divine dominion in this world. We know that love overcame justice when God accepted us as we are. And since we know the embrace of God's grace, we have a different perspective. Different eyes. Our eyes are no longer envious, but gracious— generous like God's eye.

"Is your eye envious because I am good?" "The last will be first, and the first will be last."

Conclusion

These two sermons illustrate two ways by which Greek exegesis can provide the foundation of a sermon. We hope that you see some of the possibilities inherent in an ability to read and understand a Greek text for preaching. Such an ability is not a magic wand that will take the work out of the task of preaching. Quite the opposite. It probably makes for even more work. However, some skill with the Greek opens new possibilities for preaching almost any New Testament text.

We leave you with one final bit of advice. The creative use of the results of Greek exegesis demands a certain self-confidence and independence of thought. Of course, one could say this of preaching in general, regardless of whether the preacher uses the Greek text or a translation. However, developing a sermon from your own reading of the Greek takes a particular kind of bold self-assurance. Self-assurance may not be something you yet possess, at least in your capacity to read and understand the Greek text. However, we believe that practicing the principles you have learned in the course of this study will nurture self-confidence. The more you experience that wonderful "ah, ah" insight as a result of reading the Greek, the more assurance you will have in constructing sermons out of those insights.

So, we conclude with what Paul encouraged his sisters and brothers in Christ to do: περισσοτέρως τολμᾶν ἀφόβως τὸν λόγον λαλεῖν ("dare to speak the word with greater boldness and without fear" [Phil. 1:14, NRSV]).